After the Republic

After the Republic

1845-1849

This book is based on real persons and true stories.

Joe L. Blevins

Copyright © 2008 by Joe L. Blevins.

Library of Congress Control Number: 2008904673
ISBN: Hardcover   978-1-4363-4375-6
               Softcover   978-1-4363-4374-9

All rights reserved. No part of this book may be reproduced or transmitted in any form or by any means, electronic or mechanical, including photocopying, recording, or by any information storage and retrieval system, without permission in writing from the copyright owner.

This book was printed in the United States of America.

To order additional copies of this book, contact:
Xlibris Corporation
1-888-795-4274
www.Xlibris.com
Orders@Xlibris.com
48288

CONTENTS

Chapter One: The Lonesome Dove, And The Bad Bear..............15

Chapter Two: Sam Houston And Governor Henderson's Kiowa Council....................34

Chapter Three: The Tejanos And The Battle Of Buena Vista..........66

Chapter Four: The Return Home From War....................87

Chapter Five: William Goyens: A Freed Slave Like Andrew..........98

Chapter Six: The Good And Bad Neighbors........................110

Chapter Seven: The Quilt Raffle And The Cakewalk....................122

Chapter Eight: The Chupracabra....................131

Chapter Nine: Deaf Smith And The Caddo's Canoe....................154

Chapter Ten: The Mexican Deserters And The Sick Stragglers....................163

Chapter Eleven: The Falling Star....................170

Chapter Twelve: The Kiowa, Comanche, And Kick-a-poo Capture Horses For The Army....................181

Chapter Thirteen: William Wallace: Texas Ranger, Contrary, And Missionary....................193

Chapter Fourteen: The Meeting At The Caddo's Bent Tree....................204

Chapter Fifteen: The Peace Treaty And The Gold Rush....................215

Bonus Features:

Glossary Of Unfamiliar Texan Terms....................235

Why Should We Remember Our History?....................256

The Peters' Colony In Texas....................258

The Caddo Nation In Texas....................266

Medicine Men And Good Medicine....................269

Acknowledgements....................273

TABLE OF ILLUSTRATIONS

The Map of the Red River Settlements: 1846. Plate A 13
The Caddo's canoe. Plate B 18
The Lonesome Dove Church. Plate C 29
Josiah and Sam Bird get baptized. Plate D 30
The Kiowa Council meets General Sam and
    Governor Henderson. Plate E 35
Kiowa Chief Spotted Tail (Hawk) saves the lost boy. Plate F 52
Andrew's Texas land certificate. Plate G 53
Santa Anna disguised as a peasant farmer. Plate H 86
Fossils from the Flood: an Ammonite, and a sea urchin. Plate I .. 92
William Goyens: a freed slave, like Andrew. Plate J 101
The Ancient Alligator. Plate K 107
Young Bull and the giant Catfish. Plate L 114
The Quilt raffle and a Cakewalk. Plate M 121
The Chupracabra. Plate N 130
Deaf Smith and the Caddo's Canoe. Plate O 157
The Texas Rangers. Plate P 162
A sky stone on a travois. Plate Q 169
The Sam Houston knife. Plate R 185
The Cayuga steamship. Plate S 191
William Wallace: Texas Ranger, Contrary, Missionary. Plate T .. 192
The Caddo's Bent Tree. Plate U 203
Mesquite beans and prickly pear fruits. Plate V 214
The Little Tejano guitarist. Plate W 221
Sarah's Shaw Dance. Plate X 222
The Kiowa village. Plate Y 234

To Philip and Pauline Bryant, my uncle and aunt.
Our family stories inspired me to write this book.

PREFACE

After the Republic begins, as Texas becomes the 28th State to the Federal States. An uneasy peace between the Kiowa and Comanche nations are helped by Andrew's friendship and horse-trading between the tribes and the army at the old Bird's Fort, and the building of the new Fort Worth. The new Governor James Pickney Henderson brings General Sam Houston to offer gifts to important tribe members to reinforce the principals of the Great Council. (The tribes felt threatened by the change in leadership: as when General Houston stopped being president of Texas, and Mirabeau Lamar took over the reigns of power. Things changed drastically in the Texan republic as President Mirabeau Lamar used the army to attack the Comanche at San Antonio at the Council House, and the Cherokee in the Piney Woods of East Texas. As president of Texas, he went opposite of Houston's policies. Now, as a state, John Tyler is the Federal president. ("What next?!" Many tribes asked. This led to threats of internal strife with those tribes that had signed treaties, and felt that they had been betrayed.) Many new settlers come as Peters' Colonists to help hold the land from any new attacks from Mexico.

The Federal President John Tyler encourages continued new settlements with the Peters' Colonists. The settlers form new counties from the Red River County with Collin McKinney keeping a good balance between all involved in the negotiations. Mexico continues the threat of war with the Federal States since they have annexed Texas as a state against their wishes. The saber rattling continues with the battle for the control of Northern Mexico and the full-fledged war with Mexico continues for over the next two years. Internal strife would be a terrible cancer on Texas and the Federal States. Peace between the tribes is even more precious as Texas cannot risk a battle on two fronts. Texas joining with the Federal States gives them the military and financial support that Texas has sorely suffered from as an independent republic for close to a decade. (Texan money has a value greatly discounted for so long. It was not set to the gold, or silver standard, but to the "horse standard." Horses held a high value with so many needed for the Mexican War, and so many new settlers arriving to the new state.) See how tempers flair between the Federal troops and Santa Anna's forces hoping to reclaim the land of Texas and their loosening grip of the land in California. Texas tries to interrupt Mexico's Santa Fe trade to pay war debts, keeping the Mexican government deprived of money for their war effort. The end of the war comes with the recapture of Santa Anna at Buena Vista. The Tejanos in San Antonio lose their influence in government, and many Mexicans loyal to the Texan cause are branded "traitors" or "sympathizers" by newcomers that want to oust them from government. Mexico becomes inflamed again with the 1849 Gold Rush in California, and the acquisition of New Mexico. This added continually to the pull between Mexico and the Federal States as the wounds between them were trying to be healed. The Texas Rangers, a group of citizen-soldiers helped maintain the peace on the frontier, and between the settlements. These men supplemented the efforts of the army, and they acted in a bold manner to suppress trouble at its source. **Bold highlighted words are found in the glossary for the reader to have better understanding since this book is written in a 19th century perspective.** Some word usage here is different from today's meaning. There are additional bonus features that help give some of the background details and information relating to the story. Read the second of the trilogy beginning with *The Texas Republic*, and now the story continues . . . Enjoy the journey through history. May you discover things that are new and exciting to learn about our great historic past.

Joe L. Blevins *After the Republic.* 1846-1849.

ABOUT THE AUTHOR

Joe L. Blevins is a character actor, artist, musician, and scriptwriter. Joe has a great love of Texan, and American history. He also loves to study natural history: the study of fossils, and artifacts. Blevins started drawing at the age of five, when a lady at church gave him a paint set, and drawing paper. For over forty years Joe drew the animals in the fields, and the faces of historical figures from old photographs, and descriptions in historical archives. Joe drew the faces of the Indians he knew of to help document them, and let the reader see them as real people, with problems, and concerns. Joe's family came to Texas in 1843 as Peters' Colonists to the north Texas area, between the Elm Fork, and West Fork of the Trinity River. Joe's family moved to a place called the "Cross Timbers," at Dove Creek. This was the historical "Lonesome Dove Settlement." * This was the first settlement in north Texas. (*This is NOT to be confused with the fictional story, and book by a similar name, where another author "borrowed" the name: "without permission".) Joe asked permission to use the name from the church that owned the rights to it, in reference to a real historical location that relates to a true story. A true story has more merit than any fictional accounts that are without fact, or merit. Many people are ignorant of real history, and accept fictional stories as factual information! This story is based on real characters, and true historical facts. This is what Joe writes about here. His concern is to tell these stories before they are lost, and forgotten. It is his obligation, and duty to his family, to tell this story. It was given to him as a terrible burden, and a great responsibility to pass it along to be told properly: as it should be. The people that came before us need to be remembered well as they set the standard for our society. To do less is disrespectful and a terrible injustice to them.

Joe's family (the Blevins' and the Torian's) is some of the founding members of the Lonesome Dove church in 1845. The settlements in those days had the church as their center. Their faith, and concerns evolved around the church, and its members. Joe's early life was filled with many stories of the pioneer days. Joe is a Christian, and he loves to read the Bible. There are references to the Bible with many of the stories written here. (Andrew, the storyteller was a freed slave that came to Texas. He learned to read, and write by copying letters from an old Bible he had found.) Sam Houston made a peace treaty with the local tribes in the Grapevine area, at Grapevine Springs in 1843. Because of an Indian war started in 1840 by President Mirabeau Lamar, settlements had ceased into Texas. Houston's persistence in getting a lasting peace helped settlements to continue into Texas. Joe heard these stories from his paternal grandfather, Lesley Green Blevins, a justice of the peace in Tarrant County in the 1950's. He would take Joe and his brothers out to show them the places where Houston, and the Indians camped, close to Grapevine Lake; and to the old family's Torian log cabin. The family visited the Lonesome Dove church, where many of his family is buried. These things stirred Joe's imagination to know more. Joe would write down the stories to memorize them for later in his life. Joe, as a youth, worked for a widow that had lost her husband, and needed help. As he worked for her, he learned some of her family's history. She had been related to a Cherokee woman, and a freed slave that came from Louisiana to Texas. This story was intriguing, as the stories were full of many great events worth learning. Joe worked for other families, including his paternal great aunts, his grandmother, uncle, and aunt who told them of their family stories. These people prided themselves in knowing their family history very well. All of them knew how much Joe loves history. They would share stories when it was time to rest after work was done. They shared this with Joe, as he loved to write and draw. Even though these people were from different cultures, there were similar threads that linked their stories together. This started the basis of these books, and the series that follows. As Joe grew older he saved the stories away for a future time to put them together in a way that pays respect to those that blazed the frontier. This story gives us the unique view of the pioneer days through the eyes of Nineteenth century pioneers. There are many details of frontier life: the hardships, and the celebration of daily life.

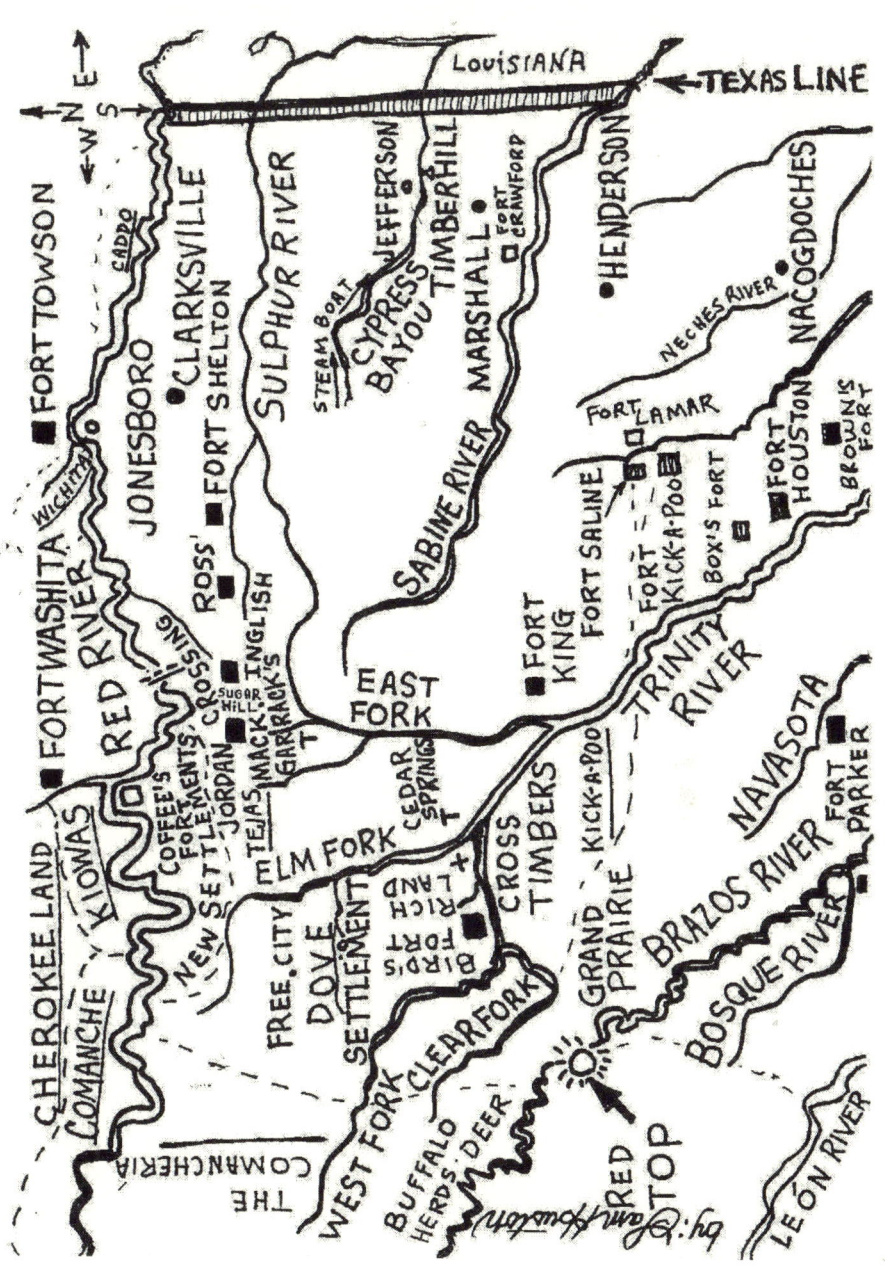

Map of the Red River settlements.

CHAPTER ONE

The Lonesome Dove, and the Bad Bear.

March 24,1846. A **Blue Northern** has come in and snow has covered the ground. It rained and froze the trees with close to a foot of ice. We woke up during the night the past few nights to hear the trees break from the burden of the ice covering them. We woke to more than a foot of snow and rain that froze the ground, and the river solid! This was supposed to be springtime? Four days past **Winter Count**. This cold kept the animals hungry for more hay than we might have if the cold continues for long. The winter supply of dry firewood was getting to the last cord, so we only burned the fire during the night and we danced around the hearth during the day to keep warm while the women cooked the meals. The sandstone hearth was a busy place and we wanted not to be in the way of the women making progress cooking. We went to the smoke house to see that a large bear had torn away the door keeping the meat from being the dinner of others! Coyotes have gone in and did harm as far as dragging away a good part of our last hunt that was to cost us a week's feed. I took Red Bird what was left for he was the one that had killed it. We bundled up the wife and children and took them to Red Bird's homestead for safety. That terrible bear will be back since he had enjoyed some easy pickings at our expense. The women and children stayed at Red Bird's with Ke-Ke. Red Bird and I went to look at the bear's tracks and the harm that he had done to our smoke house. The women tried to feed us a last good meal and we refused it for it was used to feed our family first. Our empty bellies would set us to be determined that the next meat in our smoke house would be from that bear! Red Bird agreed. He said we were going to get that bear if it was the last thing we did. It may be so. We prayed. But the Lord made me stubborn, and for good reason, I believe. We set a trap using some of the broken tree limbs from the ice storm. We were all so hungry today, but our determination and a clear afternoon made for some good progress. We built a box trap that had a heavy stone on top that would make the box heavy. The notched "4" shaped trigger was cedar and the box was strong enough to keep the bear contained while we were able to kill it for meat. We looked for night to come and hoped for a cloudy night to keep the heat close to the earth. It was a clear night and the stars were bright. We could not build a fire for it would scare away the bear. Close to daylight was the coldest part of the night. Red Bird built a fire since we had both lost the feeling in our arms and legs. That is when the bear took to our trap which was baited by some meat that was marred by its meddling. The bear crawled under the propped up end of the trap. Red Bird pulled the rope that kept the trigger of the box trap secure. The weighted log box came down over that bear. It struggled and fought to get out. It was a danger to us, but we were too scared and hungry to let our fear of it to make us fail. We put wooden stakes and stones around the box trap and we let our metal tipped spears end our fear of this bear. This was one of many. This was an evil one to steal from us when he could hunt like everyone else. This is true of people and bears. Red Bird killed the bear. He said that this meat would make us strong against our enemies. We skinned the bear and divided it up well before more snow came. We met our wives whom were watching and waiting for us. Our boys were happy to see us return. The women were tending to the cooking pots and they had the boys gather the last of the dry wood for a good meal of bear bacon. We waited patiently and cleaned ourselves up to get ready for our feast since we had not eaten anything for days. Say-te-Qua had made some great corn cakes and the boys had managed to save us 8 apiece. We ate slowly so we would not bloat up our stomachs. The bear bacon smelled great and we rejoiced over our victory over the selfish bear that stole the food out of our family's mouths. We gave thanks and we made our prayers for spring to come back so we could hunt again to provide for our family. This night we read from the Bible and sang songs that we knew to give thanks to God. Tonight, we read: ROMANS, Chapter 3, Verse 23: "For all have sinned."

March 30. The melting snow and ice has made the West Fork flood terribly. While we were outside following the deer tracks we found a Caddo's canoe! It was empty of persons, but it has many goods inside and it had a large pipe bag and one oar. Someone would be looking for this for it is more than a hollowed out cottonwood tree. Red Bird and Sam Bird came by to say that they saw a canoe float by their place. I had the report that I had tied a rope around my waist and to a secure tree on shore. I waded out and used a long **switch** to try to get the canoe close enough to the shore to retrieve it. We took our boots off to keep them from being spoiled as we walked out to get it. The boys are a big help as my back is not so good with the weather changing so drastically this week. We managed to get the canoe on the boggy shore and we pushed it up into some popular trees. We covered it with limbs broken from the ice to hide it from nosey persons. After all that we were tired. I bragged on the boys for being such a good help to us. We headed home for a well-deserved meal as trying to navigate through that clay and black land gumbo was very tiring. We hung our boots on the wooden pegs of the porch. Say-te-Qua and Ke-Ke offered us a pitcher of water to drink and what was left was to remove the mud on our feet. We went inside to a great meal of bear bacon, beans, and cornbread. We told the women of our busy morning and they wished to see the canoe. I brought in the Caddo's pipe bag to show them and they were very interested in it and what all it contained. There are iron rocks, and Arkansas knife stones, and flint from many places. We took a few pieces of iron rock and flint from the canoe to use as a fire starter kit. There was plenty of it in the canoe, and this would be our small reward from the Caddo's. We will tell the commander of Bird's Fort at the next trade day to make sure this valuable canoe will get back to its owners. We all slept on the floor until the next morning. The rooster's crow woke us early to do the many chores that we are behind on. There is always so much to do and so little time to do everything.

April 1. The cold weather has finally stopped and the past few days we have been trying to catch up on our chores. Red Bird had tanned out the hide of Mr. Bear and it was so large! I am now scared to think how dangerous that was. He took the bear claws off and made a necklace for himself with the right paws, and the left ones for me. I will keep this as a reminder when I get too brave or fool hardy for my own good. We are finishing off the last of the bear bacon and we told the boys to keep away from bears unless you have no other choice but to find them as we did. Sam Bird put the bear's hide over himself and chased Phoebe and Josiah around in front of the cabin. Red Bird smiled at their play together. He told them, "keep your distance from Mr. Bear! He has a long memory of who hunts him. What he likes best are those that are not paying attention to their business!" The children stop their play and pay strict attention to his words. Chief Red Sun comes and the women offer him the smoked bear meat. He smiles and gladly accepts it. We offer for him to stay tonight and catch up on the latest news. He asks Red Bird to tell the story of the "bad bear" and how we put an end to his stealing from our smoke house. We enjoy a fair day together and rejoice that spring has finally arrived for good. Tonight we read: SECOND JOHN, Verse 8. "Full Reward."

The Caddo's canoe.

April 3rd. We meet at Fort Buckner and the city of Mack Kinney to have a big meeting to talk with Collin Mack Kinney. The Red River County is being made into smaller counties of Dallas, Hunt, Grayson, and Collin. Polly Mack Garrack had all the women together at their trading post. Collin Mack Kinney had all us men talking about the days of the Republic, and our future as a member in the Federal States. Red Bird and I had many questions for Mister Mack Kinney. Some of the newcomers asked us what were we doing here? Being that I was a freedman and Red Bird was a Cherokee. Collin Mack Kinney said, "This freedman fought at San Jacinto, and he is here by that merit. Lamar's 1840 law against freed slaves does not apply to him!" He then addressed Red Bird: he said, "this great Cherokee helped General Houston make a Great Council that brought peaceful existence between you settlers and the many tribes that lived here. The Indian attacks in this area during Christmas 1842, or the next year of Dr. Calder and the Muncey family were not his doing! He was responsible for only helping mend the trouble of those times!" He was a quiet man that spoke great when he opened his mouth. It is understandable how he helped write the Texas constitution and was considered one of the great signers of those words. At times he and General Sam would be at odds with each other from what I heard, but a good debate is always interesting to hear. People cheered and patted us on the back until we were well sore from it. We were relieved that there were men of good faith and courage who appreciated us doing our duty. Everywhere we went today we were reminded of it. We were relieved that we were men of good character, for your good name follows you everywhere as well as a bad one. The boys are being chased around by some sweet young ladies whom have set their sights on them. We gave them a silver dollar, and told them to meet us back by mid-afternoon when were set to head back home. Our wives were most enjoying the company of others that shared their concerns. We met in the late afternoon at the trading post and we headed home. There were good friends and music, and excitement for we are making progress as our society grows from what it was just a few years ago. It is good to know that we had made a great contribution to what we have: just by doing what we should do as responsible men should.

Tonight, we read: GENESIS, Chapter 13: "Character is valuing people over possessions."

It is Friday, April 19, 1846. We are meeting with the Peters' colonists that have settled at Dove Creek. We have seen many healthy dove, and deer at the bend of the creek. It was time to settle in. We can hunt with the other men tomorrow. We met many new faces. The population has gone from 12 people, to over 60 people in less than a year! The Cross Timbers has really become the center of things since the Great Council, and the Red Bird Treaty. We talked to the deacons of the church they have here. They did meet at different homes to have church. They just about froze during that Blue Northern that blew in at Christmas last year. They put up homes, and lean-tos in the freezing rain that was coming down. Today, I want to lend them a hand to help them build on their church that they have framed out good. They have built a small room to have services in, but with the way this place is growing, they better plan on building it much larger! We dug post holes to plant proper cedar beams into the ground. It has been so wet that the ground was like digging through the sandstone layers back home. It was tough, and slow going. We took turns digging the earth to leave us some strength to hunt tomorrow. People will be coming Saturday to get ready for Sunday's services. The services will be held out doors. There will be the need to feed those that come here from many miles away. We shall hunt some deer like the settlers do. It will be different than hunting with the Kick-a-Poo. We hear the coo of doves high in the trees around us.

    Pastor Judge Hodges came around to talk with us. He introduced himself, and shook my hand. I apologized for being so sweaty from working. He said that he appreciated our help. He told me how a dove landed on his shoulder while he was preaching outdoors during the fair weather this past February. The name **Lonesome Dove*** fits this place. The church has plans to build, and branch out to establish other churches in the near settlements. The new Pastor, Judge Hodges has big dreams. I believe that he will be able to do what he says, with God's help. Tonight we will sleep well from digging so many postholes. We will go hunt at dawn, if we are able. We pray for this place to prosper like our small settlement has done. Everyone was very nice to us to make us feel welcome.

Tonight we read: HEBREWS, Chapter 12, Verse 28. "Wherefore we receiving a kingdom which cannot be moved, let us have grace, whereby we may serve God acceptably with reverence and Godly fear: for our God is a consuming fire."

April 20. We went out hunting. We got 2 healthy deer to feed the friends that we have met here. Others have brought many fish to feed us today. There are plenty of catfish, and croppies to eat. The deer will be cooked today, and served tomorrow since it is the Sabbath. More people have come here and settled in to camp with us. We will have a fish fry this evening. The venison stew is being cooked well. I love to hear the singing, and hear about where all the people come from. I sing out loud, and a coyote cries out. My wife gets tickled at me, and the singing stops briefly to scare off that hungry coyote that has smelled our supper cooking. We met the deacons James Gibson, and John Hallford. They asked us to move our wagon to a better place where the remudas can be watched. They fear meeting Indians looking to take our horses. I told them we have seen there are plenty of wild horses that the Indians can have. We told them of our experiences with Chief Bowles, and Chief Mush of the Cherokee. Chief Peta of the Nacona Comanches. We told them of the giant To-ha-sa of the Kiowa's. He was taller than General Sam, and almost twice as thick in his trunk, arms, and legs. They stood with their mouths open. We told them to not shoot at strange Indians. We told him of the local Kiowa Chief named Spotted Tail who had went out in a terrible storm to find the lost settler's 3 year-old son. In spite of what they heard the majority of Indians were good people of character, for there are good and bad in all races. We showed how to make the trade signs, and what was fair in trading with them. We told them also that if an Indian offers a gift it is bad fortune to turn it down, or disrespect the terms of the trade. Even if it seems to be a trivial thing to be traded for, take it seriously! That is where trouble can start, I told them. Being ignorant of proper trade practices can be hazardous to your health. This is where those settlers that were slain were getting into trouble. They listened carefully, and asked me many good questions. I did my best to answer them. Being wise and acting properly can lead to a longer life. This is a great group of people! We had a good visit together as brothers and sisters in Christ. God made us different on the outside, but on the inside we have a spirit and a heart that God cares about. We have a great future ahead of us in the Red River settlements.

Tonight we read: HEBREWS, Chapter 13, verses 1,2,3. "Let Brotherly love continue. Be not forgetful to entertain strangers: for some have entertained angels. Remember those that are in bonds, as bound with them; and them which suffer adversity, as being yourselves also in the Body."

April 20. We attend the services held outside of **Lonesome Dove Church**. It is fair today. The church will be larger with the walls framed out better. Say-te-Qua was treated well by the ladies of the church. It is a friendly congregation. They are friendly to Blacks, and to Indians, which was a pleasant surprise. It was a good visit. The preacher spoke well. It is good to meet our new neighbors. Two cabins have been built, and the framework of the church is taking shape. Our settlements are growing stronger by our faith, and determination. We will leave in the morning, at sunrise. There is a brushfire west of us. Someone is getting the fields ready to plant some new wheat and corn. The wind is from the south and a good breeze blows tonight.

Today, the pastor read from MATTHEW, Chapter 25, "Least of them, (unto me.")

April 21. It is San Jacinto Day. Last night I dreamed of the events of that day. This has happened many times. *I did not tell Say-te-Qua because now that she is a Christian she no longer interprets dreams.* She did not sleep well because of my tossing, and turning all night. She did not complain. She made me some coffee, and some for herself. I got the teams hitched up, and all my tools put away. We got ready to leave out when I hear some bird whistles. It is Red Bird, and Ke-Ke. They ride up with the boys in tow. They said that about sundown yesterday, our settlement burned from a grass fire started to burn off some field stubble! The wind changed, and blew the other direction burning our cabin, our school and little church house! The big corral was all that was left. Deacon Brown, and Belle got out in time. **Samson** was unset at seeing his home burn. People had time to run off the cattle, and horses to save them. We can go out and round them up this week. We have been getting some good use of our carpentry skills lately. We have started out and have built from scratch before. We will not let this set us back! Some good men of the church said that next month some of them plan to go to our settlement to help us out! We appreciate the good help of good neighbors! We can cut some scrub trees to make some comfortable lean-tos, in case it rains. We can go to Bird's Fort to get some old army tents that they put out for sale, on trade day at the fort. We will pray for God's guidance to show us the right way to do things. We make it home safe, it was better that we knew about the destruction a head of time. It made it easier to bear the sight of it. The bottom 4 rows of logs were left of our cabin. Our barn was found only to be some timbers stuck in postholes. The hard wood timbers were still good, but the rest was gone, along with a loft full of hay. It was bad, but the main thing is that no one lost their lives due to this wildfire. Red Bird brought out 2 shovels. We make the ruin look the best we can. Say-te-Qua comes up and sobs. She said, *"Our home looks like the ruins of the Alamo mission!"* She said nothing more. The well looks lonesome with out the shade of the cabin. We worked looking through the ashes. We rejoice over the things that have survived the fire. Some of the things are fixable. The hardwood furniture is still good. I can sand off the burned places, to reapply varnish there. It was good that the most important items were with us in our wagon. Seeing Red Bird, and Ke-Ke bring the family safe was what the biggest relief to us! There is much to do, and little time to write.

Tonight, we read: the THIRD EPISTLE OF JOHN, "Well beloved brother Gaius."

April 28, 1846. We make plans to go to Bird's Fort. It looked threatening rain once we got 5 miles out. It was good that the West Fork Crossing is so wide. The bend in the Trinity River is what saved Bird's Fort from burning like our settlement did. We crossed at the shallows of Walker Branch to save 50 cents on using the raft crossing. The wife held out her hand for the 50 cents, to buy with. That was fine that she is so sharp with money. She is a good wife that has my best interest at heart. She will be able to buy, and barter for cloth to make clothes for the children. I could use another shirt, and some lumber from the sawmill to make a dry roof for some lean-tos. I need 2 kegs of nails. We arrived at the fort in time for the sky to open up and it poured down!

We just stood out in the rain and enjoyed seeing it pour down. It makes the stress of the fire seem less that it will be harder for the brush to burn with some steady rain coming down. We plan to spend the night because it is easier to start out fresh in the morning to leave out. Major Patterson met us to show his new rank. He is the Officer of the Day. He said that the army would come to help us put up barns to protect our livestock. I am glad that trading horses has led to such a good friend! I told him that members of the **Dove Settlement** were coming to help us the third Saturday of next month. He said that he would plan to meet the same week. It gives him a chance to see members of the Dove Settlement, and make them aware of events held at the fort to help them build their settlement strong. I go to the trading post. It is full of people standing around to get out of the rain. The owner of the store asked people to buy, or leave out. He worries that too many people standing around might get to taking things. I plan to buy as long as my barter holds out. I brought 2 fine buffalo robes from Red Sun's people. There is enough to buy what we need. We were able to get 2 cross cut saws, and 2 new double axes. We will not be here next month since the army will be coming to help us. We were able to find a good place to rest out of the tempest that was brewing. A dry place at Major Patterson's dog-trot cabin. He gave us some army tents that they had just replaced. We put them down as a pallet in the floor to sleep on. The rain continues here so we may have to wait a day until Walker Branch goes down. Major Patterson said he would send a surveyor to help us layout our settlement. We got some paper to rough out the plans of our homesteads. We talked about what we wanted to improve on since we were building our cabin over. We decided to get some rest to leave out of here as soon as the river goes down.

Tonight, we read: NAHUM, Chapter 1, "The Burden of Nineveh."

April 29. We leave about noon. It still looked rainy, but we must get back home. We end up having to take the raft crossing. It was worth the 50 cents to see the boys carry on. It made going back home a little easier to see the boys happy. Say-te-Qua was quiet all the way back home. When we arrive back home, we see that Red Bird has done a lot to make it look ready to rebuild. Deacon, and Belle came by. We talked about the **Lonesome Dove Church**, and all the wonderful people that we met. It was plain to see that Belle was up set over our church, and school burning down. I told her that I was glad to see them. Say-te-Qua was in the mood to visit. She gave Belle some sewing things that she has bartered for. Belle appreciated the gifts. She hugged Say-te-Qua, and she cried. Then Say-te-Qua really cried for the first time over the loss of the settlement. Belle said that she missed having her piano to play. We all will miss her playing, but she still has her wonderful voice to sing for God's Glory. I would not be so blessed to sing like that! I told them that we plan to attend the Lonesome Dove Church. Deacon Brown said that it will take over a year to save enough money to buy materials from Jefferson to rebuild our church, and school. Deacon said that he was pleased to hear about the army coming to help us build homes, and barns. We went on to tell of recent events of our new neighbors: We were just amazed to see so many new faces here. We saw that the people of the Dove Settlement were coming to help US out! Then Deacon Brown was over whelmed with joy. He had a tough time seeing his home burn down. It is the center of our settlement, so the fire destroyed more than just buildings. "We still have our lives," I told them. Deacon said, "We thank God for that!" We thank God daily for all his wisdom, and strength.

Tonight, we read: NAHAM, Chapter 3, "God's wrath is slow to anger."

May 20, 1846—the army comes here early. The fair weather was to our advantage. They brought out some oxen to plow our fields for us! They brought plenty of good wheat seeds to plant for us! We will be free to help build where we can. Major Patterson brought plenty of able hands to build this place up! In a day it looks more like someone lives here. Major Patterson gave us a copy of the plans for the settlements along the Red River. We figure in to the way of things. There are 2 barns put up today, and 2 more set for tomorrow. The army camps on the edge of our land, close to Red Bird's. Red Bird's lean-to was nice, but he will enjoy a new cabin better.

Tonight, we read: MICAH, Chapter 4, Verse 3. "And he shall judge among many people, and rebuke strong nations afar off; and they shall beat their swords into plowshares, and their spears into pruning hooks: nation shall not lift up a sword against nation, neither shall they learn war anymore."

May 27. People from the Lonesome Dove Church came here. Major Patterson met with the Pastor Judge Hodges. He told them of the plans for the Red River Settlements. They rolled out the map to show the new plans for growth. Englishman W.S. Peters was bringing 120 more families in the next year! Pastor Hodges said that they just white washed the interior of new building of their Lonesome Dove Baptist Church. They finished out the larger sanctuary, which has rough wooden slats for pews to sit on. They have put up quite a lot of building around here. I feel that now we have a better settlement than before! It would not have seemed that way just a short while ago. God has taken away, and built it back better! Red Bird said that in the Great Council the tribes said that, "the settlers would have their homes stacked like firewood!" He was not too happy with the news of any new settlers coming. He said, "the Indians are right, the settlers are crazy!" I told him that it was just a matter of time before people saw that things are booming in Texas." There was talk of continued war with Mexico. We prayed for it to not be so.
Tonight, we read: HEBREWS, Chapter 11. "Faith in God."

May 31, 1846—the army, and the Dove settlers have left this morning. This place looks very smart from all the work that has been done. Our cabin, our barn, and our windmill are restored. Red Bird has a better outlook on things since his cabin was raised 2 days ago. His barn was finished yesterday. We went out and rounded up our cattle to put them in the barn. We found 3 pinto horses with no brand marked on them. The cows, and horses took to their new stalls since they were full of fresh hay. Red Bird said that things are much better the past few days. He was trying to say that he was wrong about what he said about the new settlers a week ago. Some changes take a while getting use to. "Most of the changes are for the better," I told him.

Tonight, we read: GENESIS, Chapter 31, Verses 2 to 12. "Jacob's Despair."

June 6. It comes a heavy rain. The earth is very thirsty. It needed a good drink of water. The black land has cracks in it 2 feet deep. It will take a while to mend the earth. The rainfall comes down all night into the early morning hours. I walked to the barn to milk the cows, and feed the horses some oats. The boys show up to see what I am doing. I think it is time to show the boys how to milk a cow. They get the cow some good hay to eat so she is more agreeable. They rub their hands together like I do. I get a milking stool, and a clean bucket. I told them to always use a good, clean bucket; or the milk will be spoiled, or spilled. The chickens were up in the rafters fussing at us to feed them. I left the boys to let them milk the cows by themselves. I watched them while I fed the chickens their corn feed. I heard the boys carrying on, so I looked down to see both of the boys squirt milk at each other from the cow's udders. They are funny, but I try not to laugh in order for them to know not to be wasteful of things that we are blessed with. The rain stops directly, so I have the boys take the chickens out doors to scratch for the bugs that the rain scares up. Red Bird, and Ke-Ke ride up to get Sam Bird back home. Phoebe has enjoyed her days with Ke-Ke. Ke-Ke has taught her some songs to sing. Phoebe was singing up a storm. The boys started teasing her that she sounds like a saw cutting through a log. She started crying from the teasing. She came over to me because she is still daddy's baby when things go wrong. I put my arms around her, and scolded the boys for making her upset. I told her that the boys were jealous because they sing bad like I do. Phoebe said, "Mother told me that your singing offends the coyotes' hunting!" I laugh realizing that my gifts are limited to building, and making plans. The boys made friends with her, and they were playing outside like nothing had happened between them. We are blessed to have our family, and homes restored. We owe it all to God. We would have nothing, with no hope, without Jesus. All else is done in vain, and with great vanity and despair.

Tonight, we read: MARK, Chapter 5, Verse 6, "Spiritual Thirst."

June 18. Our wheat is coming up. This is the first day that I caught sight of it above ground. Red Bird's wheat was out a week ago. The taller it can grow, the better it can stand the summer's heat. We turned the windmill into the wind and opened the dampers. It took less than an hour to fill the trenches with water. We took the children out to show them about farming. We showed them the wheat plant, and what were weeds to be pulled up. We gave each of them a tote sack, and some encouragement. We gave each of them a **switch** to use to check the tall weeds with. The snakes are bad this year. I told them not to stick your hand in tall grass, or clefts of rocks, for snakes may be abiding there. I showed them how to use a stick to see what in the brush where you can't see well. They each took their turn to show me that understood the lesson to teach them how to be safe. I let them set a few rows a head of me, but to not leave our plain sight. I told them to stay together, at least 5 feet apart. They were to pull what looks like a **tare** or a weed, and stick it in a sack. They did well for the longest. The children were finding rocks in the turned up earth. They played a game to see who could find the most unusual item in the dirt.

They continued to pull weeds when Sam Bird finds a metal arrow point made from a piece of a barrel hoop. Josiah was set to find one over pulling weeds. I told him to pull weeds and he will find a hidden treasure like Sam Bird. Not all treasures would be the same. Some would be different than others. They were happy with that and we made progress on our wheat fields. Josiah finds a flat, round rock that looks like a coiled up snake. Sam Bird marveled over Josiah's treasure. They pledged to make a trade when time presented itself. I smiled at how well things are going. The boys bartered between themselves. They have learned a lot from going between the booths being a pest at trade day. They are some little farmers. They pulled up very little wheat crop, and mostly dallas grass, and rye grass. We showed Phoebe what we were doing. She asked was all that in the sacks something to eat? I said, "No. These are weeds. It goes into the burn pile. If weeds was something to eat, we would never go hungry!" Phoebe smiles. Before sundown we finish the wheat fields. We got us, and the children cleaned up from working. We ate a good beef stew that the women have made. After supper we have the boys show all their treasures to us. We set at the table and marveled at what they found. Sam Bird's iron arrow point got traded proper for Josiah's white stone shaped like a coiled up snake. Phoebe found a little piece of pottery. I looked at it and showed it to Red Bird. He said, "It is from the Wichita that lived here when our grandfathers were young." Red Bird says, "We are stewards of the land. The Great Spirit has given us this bountiful land. We are to protect it, and cherish all the life that lives upon it. White, Red, Brown or Black, it doesn't matter, for the Great Spirit makes no difference between us. He loves us all. Men should learn a lesson from that, but some have yet to see the Truth." We asked Ke-Ke, and Red Bird to lodge here since it is so late. Before we went to sleep I read to them from the Bible. They are interested in knowing more about the Bible.

Tonight, we read: EXODUS, Chapter 36, Verses 5 to 7; and SECOND KINGS, Chapter 12, Verses 9, and 11, "Earthly Treasures." Also we studied MATTHEW, Chapter 6, Verses 19 to 21, and FIRST TIMOTHY, Chapter 6, Verses 17 to 19, "Heavenly Treasures."

June 21. We go to the Dove settlement in the Cross Timbers. "This is the old Rain Dance Day," Say-te-Qua told me. *"We do not dance the Rain Dance today because we worship Jesus, not the Rain Bird Spirit!"* She knows that, but it is hard to change to different ways of thinking after living with the tribes' traditions for so long. She has made progress in learning to speak where people here can understand her better. She has made good clothes for us to look nice for the church meeting. She is a wonderful wife, and a great helper to me. She is the mother of my children.

We hear that General Sam, and Governor James P. Henderson were coming here next month to look at the new settlements. They make plans for more settlers to come from Kentucky, and Missouri to settle along the Red River. Soldiers have mapped all along the Red River from Clarksville, to Camp Carlos. Pastor Judge Hodges showed us the new church building. It looked like a lot of work went into it. It was worthy to be a school, and a House of God. Pastor Hodges showed me the long rows of split logs for pews. The men sit on the right side, and the women and children sit on the left side. The pulpit was made of split cedar that was carved and stained. This is the longest day of the year, so we have daylight past nine in the evening. We have plenty of time to build an outdoor covered terrace for our outdoor services. We moved the wooden pews from the church to the covered terrace. After moving a good many pews from the church, I was ready to get under the over hang of the roof. It is warmer than usual for this time of year, so some shade was important. The deacons helped us get finished by six, just in time for the ladies to serve us a wonderful supper they cooked. There was no shortage of good cooking here! Some people started the singing, and Say-te-Qua was enjoying the music. "It reminds me of some of the prayers that the Cherokee sing together," she said. I want to know the words of the songs better. I was able to buy two hymnals for a dollar donation: one hymnal goes to the church for visitors, and one I get so we can learn the words of songs better. The women brought us fresh water from Dove Creek to drink. We did not stop working until we got the work done. The children were enjoying a shady spot to play.

The Lonesome Dove Church

Josiah and Sam Bird get baptized.

We now have a new place to worship God, the **Lonesome Dove Baptist Church***! We joined tonight, as a church family. There will be a baptism at Dove Branch this evening for our sons, Sam Bird, and Josiah! Phoebe wanted to join, but the pastor wanted to talk with her more to answer all her questions first. Pastor Hodges did not want her to feel pressured to join until she was ready. He will talk with her more. So will I when she has more questions to ask. We saw the boys baptized. We also asked Pastor Judge Hodges to have us a Christian marriage! The Cherokees married us first; now we are married under the authority of the church since we are both Christians! Say-te-Qua is asked to take a Christian name from a list of names the pastor wrote down on some paper. She chose the name **Sarah**, so the people of the church will call her name "Sarah," from now on the pastor said. "Sarah" sounds like the name that her father once called her "SA-RE," the Cherokee word for "persimmon." She stood and she was introduced with her Christian name to the congregation. We were happy with the events of the day. We are truly blessed. We will have a great church service, tomorrow. We talked about

President Polk's declaration of war on Mexico last month. They are kicking a red ant bed and we feel that we are being staked to it. Tonight, we read: LUKE, Chapter 5, Simon Peter, James, and John become "Fishers of Men, for Jesus Christ."

June 22. We have a great service this day. It rained early this morning cooling the morning air. It was a relief from the heat of yesterday. We enjoyed the services into the evening. We then broke out the wagons, and gear to leave out before sunset. The moon will be full so there will be plenty of light to travel by. I tell the children to stay close to the wagon since there are so many horses about. We get home before midnight. We travel following Grapevine Springs Road south. Mars, and Jupiter are the bright evening stars. We have the children watch the stars move across the sky. In no time the children were fast asleep from the creaking of the wagon wheels traveling along. I am ready to sleep, but there is more to do when I get home.

Today, we studied: HEBREWS, Chapter 13, Verse 5, "God will not forsake you."

June 24, 1846. We go out hunting for some fresh meat. We meet Red Sun at the bend of the Clear Fork of the Trinity River. The buffalo have come here to graze on the tall buffalo grass that grows as tall as a man. They have worn down a trail to follow. We make plans as we have Young Bull, Red Sun's oldest son goes to scout-out the buffalo herd by climbing up a tall tree. We later get word of the great buffalo herds that cover the plains for many miles north east of us. We make plans to hunt as many as we need for our smoke house. We find a herd, and we push them toward the West Fork into a deep ravine where we can select the buffalo that we want. We have a buffalo kill of 15. Plenty for us, and the Kick-a-Poo. We barely dent the great herd so they will prosper better.

The women butcher the buffalo by cutting it open from the backbone, from the neck to the tail. We have to eat the buffalo hearts together while they are fresh. I ate parts of 3 hearts, so that was all the raw buffalo that I wanted to eat for a while! Green tree limbs are cut for **travois** to move the butchered buffalo to our hunting camp. We poured salt on the meat to help cure it out. We covered it with a canvas to keep the hot sun off it. The Kick-a-Poo have a great feast planned for tonight. We eat well. Later we have a pipe ceremony to end the great hunt we have together. There is a great dance to celebrate the good hunt of the buffalo. A full belly is good reason to celebrate. We plan to meet in the fall to hunt here again. We traded gifts of tobacco, and some leather pouches that Say-te-Qua has made for us. We enjoy our time together. We part company on good terms. We agree to meet soon to trade horses before trade day at the fort. I told him that General Sam, and Governor Henderson are coming to Bird's Fort the next trade day. He smiles big and he tells others. He said that he would like to see General Houston, and the new Chief (Governor) Henderson. I told him that I would talk with him and ask him if he would meet with Red Sun, and his tribe at the next full moon, where the Clear Fork meets the West Fork. We get back home and get set to put the meat packed in salt in new wooden barrels. We put the sugar cure together, and added water, almost to the top of the barrel. It will set to cure for two weeks, and then we shall fire up the smoke house good with some mesquite, and pecan wood to season out the meat good. Red Bird has several good buffalo to put in the smokehouse. He liked the idea of curing out he meat good before smoking it in the smokehouse. We talked about our plans to talk with General Sam, and Governor Henderson. The Kick-a-Poo are losing more of their land to homesteading. Their road is broken into 2 pieces by settlements, so they cannot charge 2 tolls to cross their road that crosses their hunting grounds. General Sam will know what to do.

Tonight, we read: Tonight, we read: ROMANS, Chapter 14, Verse 6, "Unity."

July 8, 1846. We went out and picked some good pecan wood, and mesquite wood that the storms have broken off the trees. We filled up the wagon in no time. We showed the boys how we have swept out smoke house, and how we hang the meat out to cure. We opened the barrels, and hung the meat a few feet apart to let it cure out good. We took the barrels outside to have strong smelling fat, and water removed. We open the vent in the roof so smoke can escape. We closed the door, and we let the boys help start the fire for the smoke house to get going. They take the flint, and steel and strike it together like we showed them. The pecan wood starts up good, and then we add mesquite wood to make white smoke that goes up to the sky. The fire burns bright until it makes great glowing coals. It is good to sit, and watch the fire together. We watch the white smoke until it disappears in the sky. The crescent moon is framed by the evening stars Jupiter, and Mars, the Farmers' Almanac says. We will be patient for a week while the smoke house goes strong. It will be well worth the time and effort.

Tonight, we read: PSALM. Chapter 23, Verse 1, "God gives freedom from want."

July 15, 1846. Our smoke house opened up so we have Red Bird, and Ke-Ke to enjoy the treat of some fresh smoked buffalo meat. It was worth the wait! All week long I could smell that meat curing out, and it was hard not to sneak in and sample some. We have a feast and we enjoy each other's company. We give thanks for the good hunt, and the meat turning out good. The boys ate like grown men by their big appetite. They have shown themselves to be some little men the way they trade things. We went out and looked at the wheat. "It is knee high to a horses' eyes," Josiah said. They are learning to be wise farmers. They make me smile as I watch them growing up learning to be farmers.

Today, we read: MARK, Chapter 14, Verse 32; and JOHN, Chapter 18, Verse 2, "The Garden of Gethsemane."

CHAPTER TWO

Sam Houston and Governor Henderson's Kiowa council.

July 22, 1846. We go to Bird's Fort to see **General Sam**, and Governor James Henderson. There is a big crowd here to see our leaders tell us of the new settlements along the Red River on the old Wichita hunting grounds. General Sam speaks of the growth of North Texas, and the promise of good crops in spite of the drought threat. Governor James Henderson spoke of the new settlers coming in the next weeks to settle in before winter sets in. General Houston published a map that was passed out to all the heads of the homesteads. The settlements will be north of the Elm Fork, where the Red River floods regularly. "It is some fine farm land from what the survey reports says," the Governor added. "The settlers are coming from Missouri and Kentucky. Many have family members already in Texas, that have set up camps to get ready for them coming." General Sam is to be a Texas' senator to **Washington City**. He said, "Sam Junior is three. Margaret had a baby boy they call "Houston"." He is excited to be a father again. Having a family makes working a pleasure to provide for them. The results are worth the effort. Governor Henderson praised the Dove Settlement for growing so well this year. He got a letter about them, telling how they struggled the first months; and how they have grown strong enough to help the Rich Land Hills Settlement after the wildfire destroyed it. "This is what makes our settlements strong: people that can build something out of this wilderness. People that can rebuild after much destruction, like you have done." He promised, "the army will be a friend to the settlements, not like it was just 6 years ago when Lamar made the Indians go to war!" That was a huge mistake that has cost many innocent lives. That and the new war with Mexico will make things tough on us here in the new settlements.

We talked to General Sam, and Governor Henderson. It was encouraging to hear them speak of the future growth of the Red River Settlements. He said that our trade dollar is no longer discounted since we are now a state. "We can get good prices with out fear of the bottom dropping out of the market. We can get good prices for our crops like we did when we had General Houston as our president. The farmers' co-operative has saved individual farmers from ruin when the drought, and fires have devastated the Rich Land Settlement." (Governor James Henderson said.) He praised the settlers for pitching in, and helping each other build cabins, and barns. He praised the Dove Settlement, and the Lonesome Dove Church. He pledged friendly relations with the Red River Tribes that have held their lands in the **Red Bird Treaty**. Friendly Indians will be treated well. The settlers are to be fair in dealing with them. The army will only defend the settlements from harm from any outsiders. Tonight we will meet Red Sun, and the Kick-a-Poo at the meeting place: where the West Fork meets the Clear Fork. We rest for a few hours, and Governor Henderson's aid comes to get us to go to make a council with Red Sun. The moon is full enough to give us good light to see the trail. We go to Red Sun's camp to find that many braves have gathered together to great the governor, and General Sam. We did not expect to see so many Indians gathered together. Some Kiowa of Spotted Tail's tribe is here joining in a friendly buffalo hunt together. They have a council around the fire. The Pipe Ceremony was held. Gifts of blankets, and tobacco are exchanged. Chief To-ha-sa was not here because he was ailing with a broken leg. He sent his representatives in his place, with a gift of 4 fine horses for Governor Henderson, and General Sam. General Sam tells Governor Henderson that they must offer up a gift in return for To-ha-sa. Governor Henderson offers up a sword made for him as a suitable gift. (It is much like the handsome sword that General Sam gave Chief Bowles as a gift, years ago.) General Houston said that such a gift would be well received by the Kiowa's. General Houston gives Chief Red Sun 1 of the 2 Bowie Knives that he owns that were made for Commander James Bowie. Red Sun sees Commander Bowie's name etched on the handle. General Houston tells Red Sun that the marks on the handle are Commander James Bowie's name. "They are powerful signs! They will make you fierce against your enemies, and strong with your allies. You will stay strong in the Hunt!" Red Sun is most proud of the gift. The Kick-a-Poo passed the knife around, and wondered about it. Next was a feast of cooked buffalo. There was plenty of good food, and celebration. A full belly was good reason to celebrate. The council with the Kiowa, and Kick-a-Poo was a success! It all ends with a great dance to give thanks for the great buffalo hunt. The dancing lasts into the night until the moon sets. There are also prayers offered up for the continued peace to hold strong between the tribes and the

The Kiowa Council.

settlements. We are welcome guests. We are given the nicest lodges reserved for honored guests. We read the signs painted on the outside of the lodge. It has the sun signs painted there, showing unity. It was plenty big enough for us all to sleep in. We talked some and settled in to rest. General Sam read the Bible to us. He is quite a scholar when it comes to books, the Bible included. He turned to read, and he did not have to look at the words. He knew them by heart! He was a good friend and we had missed talking with him. He is always a great mentor and we treasure his wisdom.

Tonight, General Sam Houston read: GENESIS, Chapter 12, "Abraham's Covenant with God."

July 28. It comes a good rain toward sundown. The wheat fields perked up from the cool air of the evening. I was set to irrigate tomorrow on the chance that it would not rain. So there is room in the cistern for some cool, clear water. I got a **hand jack** in place where we can get water in the house with out having to haul it from the **branch. Sarah** wondered at it all. She never thought her home would have the luxury of fresh water with out having to haul it in buckets. We filled up all the gourds, and filled the water jar full. It is great that the drought is broken! We rejoice over the rain coming down. It has made the terrible yellow grasshoppers leave for the Red River where no crops are planted. It continued to rain all evening, into the night. About 2 in the morning it was thundering, and lightning, so we took refuge in the corncrib under the floor. We took some biscuits, and honey left over from supper to keep the children happy. My stomach growled as bad as the lightning, so I had a few biscuits to settle in, to get some sleep. The storm continued until dawn. At sunrise we awoke to find that part of our roof blew off, and there was plenty of water inside the cabin. I took the children outside to check on the cattle in the barn. It was fine, so we went out to tend to the animals. The door on the hayloft was almost blown off in the storm. I was able to set it back in place with a few well-placed nails. I got the boys to help me carry the lumber to fix the roof of the cabin. I showed them how to place the wooden shingles, and how to nail them down with out making them split. I let them place and nail the shingles like I showed them. They had the job finished in no time. Phoebe was helping Sarah clean up the inside of the cabin proper. By the evening things were squared away. Sarah took a string of onions, and a buffalo brisket and she made a great stew. She made some fresh bread. She has been quite the bread maker since she has met with the ladies of the **Lonesome Dove Church***. We will help each other build up our settlements into something great. Something to give our children, and their children!

Tonight, we read: EPHESIANS, Chapter 6, "Stand against Satan."

August 12, 1846. We set to have the wheat harvest. We go to Red Bird's farm to thresh the wheat. I bring an old wagon wheel to drag behind the oxen. The wind picked up and made it pleasant. We get the best part of the fields done today. The rest we do tomorrow evening. We got the old canvas tent laid out for a threshing floor. We laid the bundles that we cut out to be threshed. We had the boys to thresh some, but not too long. They have a bit more growing to do before they can labor as long as we do. The women bring us water, and a fine meal. We were so tired we could not raise our arms to eat. We managed to eat some food, and get the wheat put away where it would be protected from the elements. We put out plenty of hay so that the cattle would not be tempted to eat the wheat crop since it smells fresh cut, and tempting. We close up all the doors and windows to secure the place for the night. We place the tools, and clothes out for our work tomorrow. We have a lot to do to get ready today. The boys helped me get chores, and things from the barn that needed to be done since trade day falls early this month, and the church meeting day fall on the same week. We make the best to work even under the full moon, for we feel that being "moonstruck" is old fishwives' tales. We take stock in the truth, and fables are for the sake of little children. We got to sleep about midnight. The morning comes soon enough.

Tonight, we read: DEUTERONMY, Chapter 6, Verses 5, and 6. "The Great Commandment, and a responsibility of parents to teach their children the Word of God."

August 15. We were set to go to trade day this morning. We heard what we thought was rain on the **window lights**. It was a plague of the bad, yellow grasshoppers coming to eat what we have not harvested from the fields. It was raining down insects, bad as any cloudburst! We closed up the windows, and built up the fire in the chimney to make the big smoke to scare off the bad grasshoppers. We put the children in the corncrib so they did not have to listen to me bad mouth the grasshoppers. We will have to wait a day, or until it rains to make the *plague of Egypt* to leave. Toward sundown it clouded up from the heat of the day. We hear the sound of thunder kicking up, so we know that the grasshoppers will have to find a *dry* place to live. Thank God for small miracles! We looked out the peek hole to see what was happening: the grasshoppers were leaving in the great clouds that they came. Many of them drowned from the heavy rain. We will set the chickens and geese upon them to rid the rest of them. They will do away with all signs of them in no time. The river crossing was going down. We can now plan to go to trade day on our way to the monthly church service. We will be rushed, but we can make it in time for services.

We went to trade our wheat for some solid silver money. The sawmill gave us a premium price for our crop. We gave them a fourth of the crop for milling, and the **grist** left over for feed. It was good to see hard work come to some reward. We have plenty of needs for our want list at the trading post. We hear that Mexico is doing battle along the Rio Grande like we did for independence. **Texas is now the 28th state to the Federal States.** We knew that Mexico feels honor bound to pick a new fight with us since we have stopped their chance of taking us back as their possession. We pledged our support to defend our homes to the death of the last of us. We plan to back that up if necessary! We not let any person, or **varmints** take what we have worked hard for. Not with out a fight. Colonel Patterson said he knew why the Cherokees called me **"Puma."** We made plans to trade with the Kick-a-Poo, on the next full moon, September 13th. We shook hands, and parted company on good terms. We traveled down Grapevine Springs Road. We met others going to Lonesome Dove Church. It was good to travel in the company of good friends. Red Bird, and Ke-Ke came with us. They were received well by the travelers since he was helpful in making peace possible with General Houston. Some people wanted an arrow that was made by Red Bird as a gift. I told them," Now you must have a gift in return." He offers a sack of seed corn. They exchange gifts, and we talk as we ride along together in a group traveling to the church meeting. The route there has been blazed by others, to help show the trail from the **Midway Camp** to the Dove settlement. Signs made from short planks are painted with the sign of the cross for those who do not read well. The arrows point the way. We plan to teach adults to read as soon as we get enough people to teach their letters, as well as their numbers. Counting cattle is good, but reading is even a greater joy. The whole world will open up to those that read. We talked of the grasshopper plague. We talked of the renewed war. We will defend our homes against anyone who seeks to harm us. We talked of protecting the settlements if the army is called away to fight Mexico. Our **stand** is in the Red River settlements, in case of trouble. We have to stay here to protect the settlements. Most of the men here are too young to fight *more than diaper rash!* We will teach them to fight, and to serve our settlement, and our state. We will teach them to be good stewards of the land. We settle in for an evening of communion with our church family. All our problems, and worries go away for a while, while we enjoy the visit together.

Tonight, we read: DANIEL, Chapter 3, "Shadrack, Meshach, and Abed-nego, in the Fiery Furnace." We will study this for is where tomorrow's sermon that is to be preached from.

August 17. We make it back home. The past few days have been busier than any time of harvest that I can remember. There is the need to put the chickens in their own roost since they keep the barn fouled with their roost. I got some lumber out, and we got the boys help build a new coup. They were set to play, but we said that work comes first, then play if there is time. They protested some but I let it slide since boys should have some spirit to match their backbone. We got the coup marked out with stakes. We dug the postholes, taking turns to let the other rest.

We used a live cedar, cutting off most of the limbs. I showed the boys how to cut around the base of the tree to keep it from coming back. We measured the space between the post, and we built the panels to fit between them. "We measure twice, and cut once. This is how you save on what lumber you have," I told them. We built the walls solid to stand up to the terrible wind. The panels all fit well, so we nailed each one to the posts to make it strong. The roof was steep enough to let the rain, and wind run off. We sawed a good door facing east to secure when we have to keep the chickens penned up. We made the planks for the birds to walk up to their house. We put down more posts around the pen to build a fence. The farmers' co-operative has encouraged us to use this new chicken wire that keep the chickens in, and the **varmints** out. The neighbor, Peterson has a goat that always gets in the chickens way, to eat up their food. He is a goat, not a **yard bird**! I took the goat back to his home. When I got home the boys have moved the chickens to their new coup. They also have cleaned out the old roost, making the barn nicer to walk through. I have some candy put back for days like today. I gave the boys the hard candy. I told them that the candy would taste better when we go fishing tomorrow. They are excited about going fishing. I tell them to go out to cut some tree limbs, and some reeds for fishing poles. They went out for a while, and Josiah came back all pale looking in the face. Sam Bird has cut his hand badly with a sharp, fresh cut reed. It was bleeding something fierce until I put pressure on it like **Doctor Anson Jones** showed us at **San Jacinto**. **Sarah** came out to get us to come have supper. She saw Sam Bird's left palm wrapped with a bloody rag, so she was upset. I got a bucket, and some **coal oil**. I put his hand in the bucket to let it soak for an hour. It burned something fierce, but I held his arm in the bucket so that he would not get blood poisoning. Sarah got her fine needles, and a piece of good thread. She put 10 stitches in his hand. It looked much better once we got it cleaned up, and bandaged. Sam Bird held up better than Josiah. Sam Bird was the person that was hurt. Josiah hated to see Sam Bird hurt so badly, he said. Sam Bird was joking, and in a good mood. He said that his hand looks like a **La Crosse** ball. In no time the boys were using some string to finish out their fishing poles. Sam Bird took one of Josiah's fishing poles. He mounted the iron arrow point that he found, on the big end of the stick to make a fish spear. He wrapped it with rawhide, and sinew. Josiah liked the iron point mounted as a spear, so they practiced throwing the spear into the sand pile, where the chickens scratch. They practiced for the longest. We found an old gourd and grabbed a handful of grasshoppers that had lit in the hayloft. We are ready to catch some good fish by tomorrow!

Tonight, we read: FIRST CORINTHIANS, Chapter 15, Verse 24. "The Order of God's Kingdom."

August 19. Yesterday we went down to Walker Branch to catch us some fish! Even Phoebe caught some fish. Josiah caught 10 by hook, and 4 by his fish spear. Sam Bird made a trotline between 2 logs in the water. He caught 8 channel catfish, 2 sand bass, and 4 croppies. There were some powerful snakes about. I walked under the trees with a fishing pole to check for "shoulder drapers," the terrible water moccasins that frequent the trees. I doctored their pant legs with Sulphur to keep the chiggers, and mosquitoes away. We put our gourd full of grasshoppers to some good use, once we were squared away. We got home about sundown. The women have been preparing the fire to cook the catch. The fire pit is dug, and the mesquite coals are burning bright. The green canes are laid over the coals. The fish is gutted, and laid over the fire. The women put onions, and wild garlic's with the fish. They laid more green reeds over the top. They covered it with a wet canvas, and some dirt. It cooked, and crackled for the longest. In no time it was done. Red Bird had been out hunting for 2 days, and all he has was 2 swamp rabbits for his trouble. He shot at a deer and missed. He said, "it will grow bigger for next time we hunt there." Red Bird has a spirit that sees the bright side of things. He will live to be old, and wise by his ways. We gave thanks for the great feast. The women's cooking makes our fishing pay off. Red Bird likes the catfish baked. I fried a few in corn meal like we used to do. He really liked that. I fried some corn bread. He likes them **johnnycakes**! Now we are too full to move. We all sit around until we start falling asleep. We brought out the sleeping pallets, and lodged together as a family. It was wonderful to get some days fishing with the family. The boys, and even our little girl, proved themselves some little fishermen!

Tonight, we read: FIRST CORINTHIANS, Chapter 6, Verse 3. "The Judgment of the Angels."

August 30. We go to Bird's fort to get the rest of our wheat flour. We got good barter for it to buy all the coats, and blankets that we need. We got two new coal oil lamps, and some black ink to write with. We have enough flour, and sugar to last since **Sugar Hill** sent 2 wagons extra. They needed our flour in trade. Since the war was going on flour had been in short supply. Also the sugar my sweet tooth needed. We all prospered enough to have what we need, and some to trade, if need be. We all got a new shirt, and pants. I found a good deal on some cotton material. **Sarah** picked a fair amount of material to make more clothes with. She said that we need new **dew cloths** in our cabin. She wants things to look nice for when company comes. She is the thoughtful wife, my best friend. We got the wagon loaded up when Colonel Patterson stops us to ask about Red Sun, and the horse-trading day. I told him that I would go up on the high hill and build a bonfire. He knows to come the next day, or so, bringing many horses to trade. I told him, "You can depend on us to help build your army's remudas. Their tribe is friendly when treated fairly. If you know horses, you have a lot in common." He enjoyed good news and it put his mind at ease to have some dependable horses in his remuda. I promised him good relations with any tribes that we can manage to make peace with. That included the Comanche, and any of their bands that we could trade with to regain their trust in us again, as **Chief Peta** had done.

We get home by late afternoon to tend to our cattle. Home is always a good place to be. We were welcomed home like we were kings. We had a visitor waiting for us when we arrived back. Company is always welcome, as it gives us reason to celebrate the day.

September 2nd. This has been a busy day with too much to do. As always we manage to make some progress on this rich prairie land. We fixed the roof and managed to put a dozen fence posts up. We then sat by the well to rest. We had a man with a broken wagon wheel asking us to help him. We could not get much done this evening. So we offered him and his wife to rest here until in the morning and then we could do much. It was too late and trying to fix a wheel too close to dark was just asking for trouble. I can't let someone travel in the dark and I would not be much of a good neighbor if I did not help. They were like many of us looking for a place to farm. We had the boys tend to their horses and we made them comfortable and let them rest from traveling. He got out the ***fiddle*** to play after we ate supper. I think that they fell asleep as soon as they put their head down, as traveling far will do. We will go to Simon's to see if he has a spare wheel as we used our old wheel to drag to help thresh the wheat. It was a good day for us all.

September 4th. Today we go to Simon's home to see about helping the travelers fix their wheel. He was getting the plows fixed and the horses shod. They were in a good need of a ***farrier*** with more skill than us. Simon was busy at the **blacksmith**'s shed. We came up as he was busy having his boys unload some iron and some coal. Our boys went to help them, as that is what I want them to know about being a good neighbor. Any chore is not so terrible with more hands to help it get done more quickly and simply. Simon stopped and he had some spare wagon wheels. We helped put the wagon up on a stump to take the wheel off. In about an hour we had them ready to go to the fort. We wished them well. Simon got the coals going well to make some horseshoes. He was showing his sons and our boys how it was done. He had that iron good and hot over that anvil and he had that hammer busy. He had each or the boys make a horseshoe with his careful coaching over how to safely shape and hammer the iron well. They took the pliers and dipped the hot horseshoes into the water barrel to cool them off. The boys delighted in their work. Simon told them that he would take time to teach them if they would come by to help him when he was too busy to do it all. I gave Sam Bird the *rasp* to file down the rough hooves of the horses. Sam Bird loves horses as much as he loves breathing the air. He was delighted to tend to the horses. He brushed them down good also until their coats shined. Josiah was busy with Simon's boys making some new reigns, and tack for a bridle that Simon had made last week. There was always plenty to do and more to learn. The boys had scraps of leather left over from making the reigns. They made a slingshot like little king David made. It was time to eat and the boys were steady practicing let some stones fly. It was most dangerous until they learned to control letting the stones fly toward a target. The trick was to let it fall between two sticks put in the ground. They gave each other a wide berth to make sure no one would be hurt during practice. We sat by the well and ate and watched the boys improve their aim. Red Bird marveled at their new weapon made from the simple strip of reign leather. We called the boys to eat the fine meal of pinto beans and cornbread. I wish I had their energy to go and go as they do! It was getting to be the warm part of the day and we took an hour's *siesta.* We slept with one eye open so we would be guilty of not keeping a good watch as Santa Anna had done. We woke to find the chickens all around us to get the crumbs that we forgot. They had slim pickings with us around! We will make this work part of our monthly chores. We will learn the *blacksmith* skill along with the boys so we can help Simon when there is too much to get done and farming is between plantings. We went back home and told the women of our day at Simon's. Josiah and Sam Bird showed them their new slingshots. They watched out the window to see them show off their new skills. The women were alarmed at first, but then they had to remember not to be such a mother hen to their growing babies. It is better to let them grow up and learn of the world. It has been a great day for us all. We are close as a wonderful family should be. We Praise God daily for our many blessings!

Tonight we read: FIRST SAMUEL, Chapter 17. "David and Goliath."

September 5th. We went to trade day at Bird's Fort. This area has grown so much that the fort can't contain enough room for them all. There is talk of moving to a larger site and building brand new fort to attract more people to come here. It seems that this is the stopping off point since any farther west is part of the **Comancheria.** The family was all packed up and we had several nanny and billy goats to sell. We had a good population of them since last spring. We met the regular friends at the booths and we had to set up early since there was so many here to trade. A new fort might not be so terrible after all. We squeezed in to trade and we did a great barter for our goats. Cotton cloth was abundant and the German ladies made some great cheese. There was hot bread to go with it, and some good friends to talk with. There was news of more **saber rattling** by Mexico along the Rio Grande in an area called Del Norte. There was talk of a call for volunteers for the army by Major Ripley Arnold. I told the boys that they were too young and that they should be concerned about being boys, and to let the adults worry and pray over such things. The boys asked if Red Bird and I were leaving to fight when the time comes? Red Bird said that we would be here to protect our homes and farms. We fought for the republic and that was our time of battle. We are farmers now. Our new battle is to make our home safe by protecting where we live. We went back to the business of trading for what we needed. We picked up some coal for Simon who was still too busy to get away. Some little girls were chasing our boys around and their mothers smiled as they saw that their children were growing up. Ke-Ke said that she was to be expecting a baby. Red Bird was happy that our boys would have a brother or sister to keep them company. Some rain set in about the time we packed up so we headed home before the Trinity River become difficult to cross. We managed to get back home safely. Tonight we read: PSALMS 51. "King David's confession of sin."

September 7th. We were to meet for church at a new settler's home. We had new harrow to break some land. The boys had a chance to try their skills at breaking the new land. They managed to stay on the platform of the **harrow** and keep the horses from running off. The pastor preached as we worked out in the fields. He stood at the side to keep out of the choking dust. We had an unusual service, but the cool break in the middle of summer was a good event that came at a good time. This has been a strange year for weather, even for Texas! Their field had been broken and we had the sod turned up well. We all donated some seed corn. Pastor Hodges made a good service and we helped one of our neighbors start their homestead up well. They will have to plow again in a month to keep the weeds from coming back with a vengeance. We all visited and enjoyed the church service and good company of our new neighbors the Torian's. They gave us a copy of the Red Lander to read about the most recent events. General Zachary Taylor was hurt in battle, so Governor Henderson has resigned in the middle of May to lead the troops in the Rio Grande war. The Lieutenant Governor Horton has taken the reins. They said that he was taller than General Sam by an inch! We were smiling that we have the smartest and tallest heads of state than anyone else. Commander Henderson has been experiencing some of the difficulties that we saw in our battles. Our General Taylor has victories of Palo Alto and Resaca de La Palma May 8 and 9 where the Mexicans were pushed over the Rio Grande boundary to keep them in check. Now there is talk of the Federal States taking Oregon territory and the California's. We all talked about the news and took turns reading the worn newspaper. We were excited about the war making some real progress towards being settled. We hope that it would all be decided soon.

There was talk of President Polk offering the Mexican government 10 million dollars to settle the war and sell the land that was claimed by Mexico and the Federal States. (It was much as Napoleon has done with the Louisiana Purchase in early 1804.) It made sense to us. Santa Anna has returned to power in Mexico after his exile in Cuba. Senator Houston and Colonel Benton have asked for more men and arms from the Federal Congress. They have asked us to plant as much wheat and corn that we can to feed the army. Also we are to catch as many wild horses we can for the army's needs. We have much to do over the next months. It is time to sleep and rest up so we can make our plans for the future. There is much to think about and we pray for the wisdom to do what is right in the sight of the Lord.

September 8th. We go out to capture some horses. We took the boys since they are old enough to help. They climbed up a tall tree and they saw a good herd by their dust. We went west and found a good place to make a **corral**. We found a stand of trees and wove broken tree limbs to make a tough fence to keep the horses pinned in. We covered it with brush and tree cuttings to hide it well. The boys chased down some colts and tied them inside the *corral*. The mares came to find their babies. By the evening we had 10 mares, 6 colts and 4 stallions. We are able to attract a good many horses today. We will bring them food for a few days to get them used to being handled. We picked up 3 more mares and there was a good chance to make about 100 dollars in trade for them since so many horses have been lost in the fighting. These will make good horses for the army fighting north of us. The boys were getting the good experience of living out in the woods. We let them build the fires and hunt the game while we tended to the horses. We stayed up and watched the starry sky. We made a smudge fire from cedar to keep the mosquitoes away. Red Bird said that we should get at least 5 more horses before we head for the fort for trade. We kept a good watch to make sure that our horses would be safe from theft.

September 12th. We go to bring back 29 horses for our trouble. They are a handsome bunch for any **remuda**. We had the boys ride ahead to let the quartermaster have the papers ready. They are most happy to trade for them and we go to get some goods that are badly needed. We got some cloth and things that the women asked for. There were some surprises for them also and they deserved something for their worry while we were gone. We go back home to make a good homecoming welcome and a hot meal that was cooked by a real cook. It was good to be gone and better to be back to see the sweet wife and sister-in-law. Phoebe was so sweet and she cried because she missed us. She had made a basket that she was proud of and she crawled up beside me for some good hugs and the tales of what we had done. She was learning her letters and she could count to 20 forwards and backwards. I was impressed with her. After we ate we passed out on the floor and slept until the morning. We are happy to be back home with the family.

September 14th. We went out and looked at the crops. The little rain that we had last night made them perk up. It will be at least 6 weeks until harvest time. The corn was tall enough to make good and it passed the times of the terrible heat. The wheat was closer to being threshed than the year before so the long days of sun have made us ahead on our harvest. We went out and picked up firewood. There was a good stand of mulberries that I wanted to check out. This would make some good firewood for the smokehouse to season some good meat. The big buffalo hunt would be soon and we wanted to be a part of that event. The Kiowa and Comanche would be hunting west of here about the time that it is to harvest the good wheat. Chief Spotted Tail has said that we are considered good and dependable allies. The Kiowa and Comanche would keep faithful to their word to be peaceful towards us. We went out to get the wood and the weather was good and warm. We got the wagons full of wood and the boys got to try out the new double axes. Red Bird made some travois to carry other firewood that would be for the kitchen use. He showed the boys how to cut the green wood for those *travois.* They were sharp and kept they minds to the tasks at hand. They will have their reward the next time we go to the fort by buying them some things they want. The women made us some 5-dozen fine tamales. We built a small fire to cook them. We boiled some water and it was time to eat. We had a few more hours to work and an empty belly was not going to help anything. About time to eat some Comanches showed up. We shared with them after we made the friendly signs. Chief **Peta** came along with his son who looked to be about 8 years old. His name was **Quanah.** He rode a horse in true Comanche style. He showed off his riding skills for us while we cooked some bacon to make sure that there was enough for us, and the guests to eat. He rode at full gallop and picked up another boy like he would if there was someone wounded in battle. He was a fine boy. He rode on the horse making a jump on his back and he was gone! He stood up and balanced himself while the horse was at a good trot. The boys needed a break and they took **Quanah** down to the *branch* for some water to cool off. We then had a good council with the warriors.

Red Bird got out the pipe bag and some good tobacco. We had passed the pipe around. We then ate some tamales together. We talked and laughed for a few hours. The boys kept us entertained the whole time showing off. We then got our invitation to go hunting the buffalo in a week. This comes before the harvest as we hoped that it would. We were to meet at the Brazos crossing. We gave Quanah a good pony that we had captured and he was most pleased. His father smiled and brought us some nice flints that they had for trade. We had made solid plans for a friendly hunt together. We parted company and went home to tell the women of our good fortune meeting the Comanche on friendly terms. It was a relief to maintain our good character and reputation has stayed intact. We were tired from a full day, so we stayed at Red Bird's lodge. We were glad to be back with a roof over our head. It is good to be back home!

Tonight, we read: MARK, Chapter 12, Verse 24. "Priorities."

September 16th, 1846. We met with the Comanches at the Brazos crossing like we planned. It was a good morning to go on a hunt. We formed some good teams to do the scouting. This gave the boys the chance to do their part. They went with the young braves and looked for buffalo signs. We let them go and get prepared for a full day. The hunters got all their gear together and laid it out for the medicine men to bless for a good hunt. We got up and did the Buffalo Dance. We said the proper prayers for a safe and prosperous hunt. Before the day got too late the boys and the other braves came back with word of the buffalo herds. We got the ponies lined up and the young braves handed us our weapons. We had our army rifles and loads of ammunition. We also had bows, lances, and arrows a plenty incase we run short of something to hunt with. The buffalo were run into the ravines and we shot the best ones. The Comanche made some good kills. But those arrows took several tries to make a good kill. We were asked to kill the buffalo that were merely wounded and most dangerous. Sam Bird fell from his horse and Josiah made a beeline to get his brother safely, just like Quanah had done earlier. I was most proud of that, more than anything else. Red Bird said that a **feather ceremony** was in order for the brave sons when the full moon came next. We should encourage our boys and not just give them criticism. The women were busy skinning the fine buffalo down the backbones. They offered up buffalo hearts, and livers, a most worthy praise for the hunter. We also got 15 buffalo robes for trade and for winter use. The meat was divided up good and put safely on the travois. The food was being cooked for us hungry hunters. The evening was coming on and we were dancing up a storm to celebrate a good hunt. The fires were going strong and the buffalo cooking smelled so good to us. We kept dancing until we thought that we would fall down from being tired. The food was now ready and it was so good to be able to eat some fresh meat. We had a good celebration and a feast fit for kings. We celebrated life together and we gave thanks for a good hunt and our good allies. Some called these Comanches their enemies, and we called on them as brothers and friends! They were concerned because of the army crossing their lands to fight in the **Rio Norte** against the Mexicans. I had my share of fighting and I just wanted to farm and live in peace for a change. It seems that the Comanche, while fierce warriors, are much like-minded as we are. They just want to protect their lands from outsiders taking over. I think that they were voicing their concerns so that we would pass it on to other settlers that we met. That was fair to expect that. We always thought ourselves to be fair with whom ever that we deal with. We will tell the others to keep a wide berth from anything west of Bird's Fort. We felt like General Sam's ambassadors during the **Great Council.** They valued us as friends and as neighbors that they could trust. That was great and we felt honored to be so well considered. Before we were to leave out there was a dispute between two bands of Comanche. They asked us to be impartial judges of what was right and fair. We were in a hurry, but this show of trust and fairness in us would not be disrespected to them. We said, "we would be a judge fair to them." Two women were arguing over a strange buffalo hide that looked to be **pied**, much like some milk cows I have seen. They said that the meat was special as was the hide. To me buffalo meat was good, all of it. "The only bad buffalo meat was no buffalo meat!" I told Chief Peta this, and he told the others what I said in the Comanche tongue. They rallied together in two lines facing each other in the middle of the ravine where all the buffalo were killed. There were arrows in the ground from the hunt and the smell of blood was strong there. The men and women gathered together and the women fought it out until one was knocked down and did not get up. It was most frightful to see women fight as fierce as men do! I wanted to interfere but Red Bird held me back. Then the men from the opposing groups chose to fight with sticks as it is frowned upon to use a pointed weapon on a fellow Comanche. They were **counting coup** on each other until the debate was settled and all the Comanche that wanted to get their chance to fight and get their anger out. I had seen enough of that and I thought it most strange to see them fight over a single buffalo. I went to the butchered buffalo that was in question and I pulled out an arrow that had broken off midway down on the buffalo's flank. It was marked well. I gave it to Chief Peta. He recognized the marking and awarded it to the owner of the arrow. That settled that and I had enough for a day and wished to be going home. We thanked the Comanche and headed for home leaving on good terms. We held up our gifts of flint and we pointed to the travois filled with fine buffalo. We sang a victory song that the Comanche were singing and we left for home. It seemed a long trip over the flat prairie. We crossed the Trinity crossing later than planned. We still had a responsibility to maintain good relationships to all our neighbors. Some will be difficult to deal with, as they won't want to talk with us.

We took some fine buffalo for our smoke house. We put some in a barrel to cure out. The other we put in the smokehouse to start cooking it. We had a good brisket for the women to cook. They praised us well for being good hunters. They hugged and kissed us and they danced around for they had experienced some hungry days in the past that they well remembered. So a celebration was in order. I got my boots off and the boys put away the horses and the ***tack***. I sat down next to Red Bird and fell asleep. They woke us to a great feast worthy of a chief.

Tonight we read: PROVERBS, Chapter 16, "Preparations of the heart."

September 21st. It is time to harvest the wheat. We went out to cut it and stack the sheaves. My back was ready to hurt for a few days. It is well worth it. I knew that this day was coming and I looked forward to a great time of harvest. Simon and his family came to help. We got everything ready for the time in the afternoon when the wind would pick up. It did and we had everything ready to get the job done. We laid out a number of tents flat to use for a threshing floor. We threw the wheat up into the air and the wind did the rest. We picked up the tent's corners to pour the wheat kernels into the wagons. It went well and we worked steady taking turns at tossing the wheat. We had so many helpers and we worked until about 11 in the evening when the wind died down and we were most tired. We figured one more day at the most and we would be finished. We had a late night feast since we had been too busy to eat while the wind was so good to us. We went out and put some of the wheat straw out for our animals to eat. Some of it was good for that and most of it will be for broom making which makes for some extra money later on. Tonight we go to bed knowing that we will again be up early to start it all over again. I wanted to read tonight but my eyes were so tired that I felt that it was not useful to.

September 24th. We had finished our wheat harvest yesterday. It looked like rain so we decided that we would rest today after the regular chores were done. There will be plenty to do tomorrow at the gristmill. We put out the hay and there was rain setting in. My bones do not lie. They know when the rain is coming! It thundered terrible and scared the chickens. We got them into their house, and get them bedded down. There will be no eggs tomorrow as scared as they are. The boys enjoyed being indoors today. We have a checkerboard that we got as a gift. They tried it out and they had some good games and challenges. The boys asked about the story of Chief Spotted Tail. It was a good rainy day, so stories were in order. I told them that it was a day like today. A settler's son went out of his house to wander in the woods. He was only three years old. His parents were alarmed and looked knowing that he would be hard to find in the dark and the approaching storm. Chief Spotted Tail was called knowing what a fine tracker that he is. He said, "If this was my son I would want him found safe, and alive." He knew that once the rain started that the boy's tracks would be lost and there would be no finding him. Spotted Tail went out looking for a trail and found one. He saw a broken limb and a bent twig. He then saw a footprint in the dirt that was smaller than a man's, or child's mark. He followed his senses and went along Honey Creek. He found the boy crying, sitting on a log in the middle of the creek. If it had continued to rain then the river would have flooded the log, and the boy would die from exposure to the elements and from the wild animals that live in the woods. Spotted Tail brought back the settler's son to Fort Buckner where the parents were anxious to hear of their son. Chief Spotted Tail was now a hero in the eyes of the settlers whom considered the Kiowa enemies in the past. Now this has changed and people realized that it was wrong to judge others without the benefit of getting to know them. The same is true of the Comanches. They have been our allies as much as the others that we met with good will and an open heart to learn of them as people such as ourselves looking to make a home for their families and tribes as we have tried to do. The boys enjoyed the story and they continued their checker game. They beat me in four games so I knew that they were sharp as metal in their thinking. We laughed and we had a wonderful day together. We will go to the gristmill tomorrow if the river crossing is down enough to cross safely. Tonight I read to my boys and I know that they learned some important lessons. We read from Proverbs looking to give them some more sound advice.

Kiowa Chief Spotted Tail

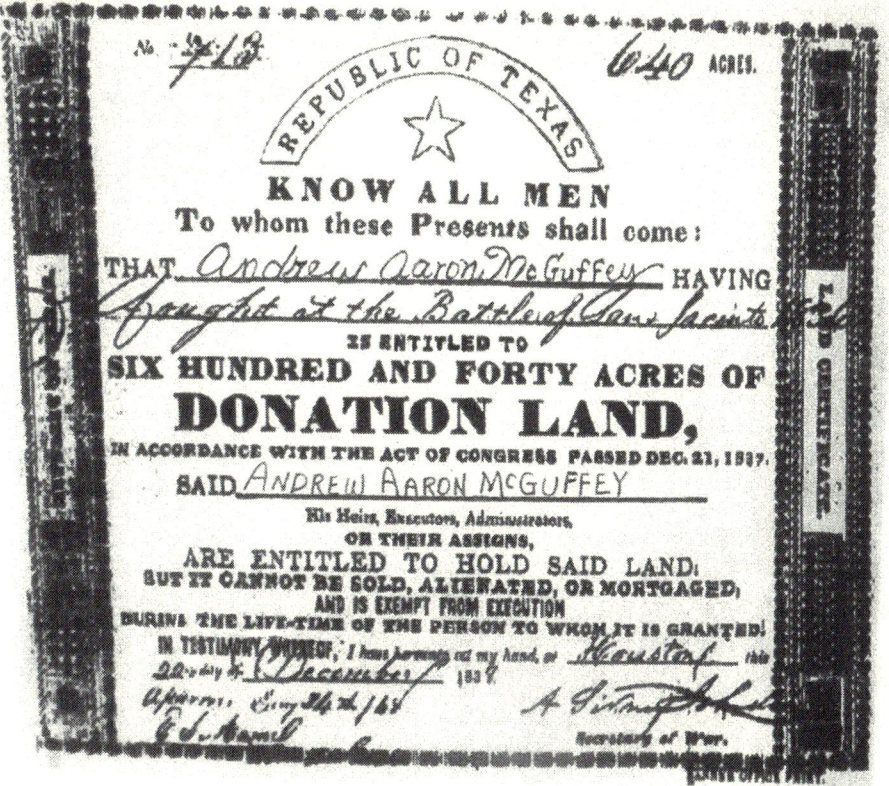

Andrew's Land Certificate

September 28th, 1846. We took the boys out for their first **feather ceremony.** Both our sons were worthy of some merit from their bravery and skill during the recent buffalo hunt. Red Sun also had some young braves due for a ceremony, so we combined the two groups so that they will grow up to know and respect each other. We met by the clear fork of the Trinity and Red Sun was there with the Kick-a-Poo elders to judge the feather ceremony. We told the women that we would be gone at least a week to do all the things need to help teach our sons to be resourceful and live off the land and how to better read animal signs. Red Sun and his oldest son, Young Bull came to where we had pitched some tents. He brought some horses as prizes for the young warriors. He also brought some special ceremonial eagle feathers for the young braves. The boys were given a gourd full of water, an ear of corn, and a sharp knife. We took them to a canyon where we could watch them from a distance without interfering in their education. The elders showed them the skills that they would need. They spent a good part of a day showing how to make good arrows, how to string a bow in a hurry, and how to make a good fire that burns hot but not too bright. I learned a few things myself as I watched them go through their education. Towards sunset the elders took away the young braves' arrows and bows. We just left them in the canyon to fend for themselves. We watched eagerly to see how they would do. It was hard not to interfere to help them, but that would not be helping them learn to do that. Standing back watching them fail would be a terrible thing.

We watched the moon rise over the canyon. We saw the boys taking brush and making a **lean-to** shelter and they had delegated to helping each other gather wood and start a decent fire. They worked well together even thought they did not speak the same language they knew how to make the proper signs that they both understand well. They had been good students and went to great lengths to work together to make their trials a success. The elders hid a safe distance away to keep a good watch on them the elders kept Red Sun informed and what they expected from all of the **braves.** The first day went well and we will see how fast the time goes this week.

September 29th. Today it rained terrible and we had to move our vantage point elsewhere. A pouring rain had washed out their efforts at a dry lodge and a fire. They looked pretty miserable and we wanted to help them, but we are not allowed to. Young Bull helped relocate them and he made a hillside a better camp. He also found some dry kindling and some wood suitable for a fire. The boys all grouped in together to make a lodge that they could all share. They carefully fashioned it during a break in the storms. They learned to work together well and make use of what they could find. We were most proud of the boys and we watched them hunt for rabbits. They went out and made some snares to catch a number of rabbits that the rain had scared up out of their hiding places. About sunset the rain continued strong and we had to take refuge in our own shelters from the thunder and lightning that was so fierce. We wondered how they were and what they were talking about. We hoped that they were all getting along well. It looked to be so and they would have to endure a few more days away from home and the comfortable lodge that they call home. The storm continued and we made a cave a place of refuge as our tents had blown away when the wind changed. So we weren't the only ones looking for some shelter. I am glad that Red Sun knew this area well for this cave would have been difficult to find during a storm. Red Bird was anxious to speak to the boys and see how they were doing. We had to leave them alone and let them learn how to fend for themselves. So far they were doing as good as we could expect them to. I hope that the women are well. Simon said that he would check on them while we were gone. That was something of a relief to know that our good neighbor was looking in on things since Deacon Brown was now gone to **Free City** to live.

September 30th. It turned fair today so we could get out and tramp around in the mud to look at things. The boys' shelter had held up well and they managed to stay dry for the most part. They were holding up their end of the training so far, and we were most proud. The elders reported to us their progress. We got word that they had scouted a buffalo herd so we went to see how well they scouted them out. Josiah and Sam Bird had made some slingshots like king David and they were showing the others how to use them. They were most resourceful and the Kick-a-Poo had never seen such weapons used that way. They looked most astonished to see the force of a rock thrown from the slings. The boys shared their experience and hope to teach them something that they knew well. One of the Kick-A-Poo braves was flaking a red flint he found to make a spear to use on a buffalo to kill it. I would go hungry and starve before I could do that very well. He was quite skillful at flaking that rock that he had put in the fire to season it to flake well. The others had used their knives whittling a piece of cedar for a shaft for the lance that would not break easily. They all worked together and took turn whittling the stick to save their energy for the hunt. The spear was finished in no time and they had a weapon made that would be the pride of any good hunter. The boys took one of their vests and made more slingshots to use against the coyotes, and to hunt with. The elders asked about the slingshots and I told Red Bird to made the signs as I told the story of "Chief David of the Far Away tribe." They liked that story and they marveled at the boys taking turns practicing their aim. There were most impressed. They got out the peace pipes to celebrate our sons working well as brothers from the same tribe. We had rabbit tonight cooked over the fire and it was most tasty. Tomorrow we will have the boys follow and track the buffalo herd. We will give them back their bows and arrows to hunt with. They will also get a new pony each to own and take care of. They had definitely earned them from their careful planning and sacrifice to help each other. The elders were telling us of their next tests and plans for the days after the buffalo hunt. We were very tired and the cave will continue to serve us well these next few days. I felt quite old and tired watching our boys grow up. Most of all I was proud of them working together in spite of their differences. Our children will grow up knowing their friends from their foes. The coyotes were carrying on something fierce. We built the fire brighter and hoped that the young braves would do the same. We watched them bring out more wood to build up a bigger fire and they had their camp guarded well from the ***coyotes*** and their thieving ways. They passed all the tests, and they were using the slingshots by flinging rocks at any coyote that got too near. We took turns keeping watch on them and they were keeping busy. I have to sleep for a while for my watch is coming later before midnight to when the morning comes. The ground is hard but my back will appreciate a solid and comfortable place to sleep tonight. We read First Samuel, Chapter 16: "David and Goliath."

October 1. We see the dust of distant buffalo coming our way. It is the young braves turn to try out their hunting skills. They are good and hungry so their skills will be sharp and their aim will be good. We will keep watch and help only if there is need for us to. The boys had sent out the best tracker to find the signs. The elders made the boys get into groups. Some were hunters and some of the smaller boys were directed in how to start a quick fire to help direct the buffalo into where they could be divided and hunted safely by cutting down on their numbers out of one spot. The fires began and it was time to see the boys mount their horses and get to drive the buffalo to where the other boys were waiting. Once the boys on horseback past them, the boys flung rocks and arrows at the buffalo dropping some in their tracks. Others ran past into a ravine where fires were lit to keep them from turning back where some boys were butchering the buffalo to eat their hearts and livers. They were sharp and good in their aim. They made us proud! We made our way into the hunting party once they had made their hunt complete. We had our share of hearts and livers that were brought to us. The elders smiled at the boys' progress. One got out a drum and gave it to Red Bird to play. The elders sang hunting and victory songs. They burned sage in a fire to bless the hunt. Boy, they danced up a storm and make it a real celebration! The elders showed them how to deal with the butchering and brought the travois to put the meat on to bring it back to camp. The boys had made some the night before so it was less of a burden to do after the hunt to make a few more to bring home a plentiful hunt. We will make a big feast tonight and a ***feather ceremony*** when the morning comes. There was no one seriously hurt and it was a very positive outing for all our growing boys and fine sons.

October 2. The feather ceremony for our boys went well. All 16 boys got their first eagle feather that they are most proud of. The elders were happy that all passed the test and earned their merit feather. The boys had become friends and learned that they are allies even though they are from different tribes. The elders awarded the feathers to the boys by putting the feather in their hair, or tying it with a string of leather to a favorite weapon to hold proud in battle and in the hunt. Our boys were most proud to see the eagle feather awarded to them. The boys also had a good number of chigger bites from running through the tall buffalo and johnson grass. We took them to the salt spring and made them take their clothes in it also to kill the bad itch. They had over 100 bites each and they were most miserable. We will make them do the same in the morning to make them heal completely. Josiah got a bit sick from the terrible itch and too many bites. He will do better after he rests. He has also had a great deal of excitement this past week and getting him back to his own home will always help him to heal. I had not seen the **chiggers** so bad this late in the year, but then it is warmer than usual this year for fall weather. Red Sun came and some of his tribe had the same problem as our sons. We also had some of the same problems ourselves so we did not mind taking the time to set in the salty spring water. So we made a better day of it sharing our camp again. The boys were counting their chigger bites and saying how they looked like the stars in the night sky. We will put more Sulphur on them next time they get out in the tall grass. I don't think that we will have to remind them in the future. We had some buffalo steaks and we enjoyed sleeping under the night sky. Hopefully the chiggers will leave us alone so close to the salt spring. We flaked out a big chunk of salt from the hill to take home to the wife to cook and cure with. All in all it has been a good week for us all. Ben Bird does the sign talking for the others to understand as I tell a story.

Tonight I read out loud for the elders: SECOND KINGS, Chapter 5. "Naaman, the Leper."

October 3rd, 1846. We got back home to find that Ke-Ke had her baby! It was a fine and healthy girl. **Red Bird** was just as happy that it was a healthy baby. It did not matter if it was a boy or girl. He was dancing around beating the drum and celebrating. He then held the baby and smiled. Ke-Ke gave the baby a name, "Jacy" a Cherokee name that means "little Moon." The boys were excited to have a new member of the family, and Phoebe was the biggest helper of all. Sarah told me that Phoebe was helpful during the actual delivery of the baby and that she will become a good midwife in the future. We had all the good news that we could hold, and the baby coming was the icing on the cake. Sarah held the baby and that was no shortage of someone holding her. "It is always good to have a new member to the tribe," I told

Red Bird. We had much to celebrate and we thanked the good Lord for all his blessings to us these past days. We are blessed to have a great family and good health to enjoy it all. That is what true riches are!

Tonight we read the Bible to give thanks for our blessings, large and small. We read PSALM 89, "Acclaim."

October 12. We went out and gathered mesquite beans. We had a warm day to go out with the whole family. It was fair and sunny. We stretched the tent out and tied it between 2 trees like a lean-to for shelter in case we need to rest during our harvest. Phoebe had made some baskets, and so had Sarah from some split cane reeds. Phoebe had cut her hand with the sharp reeds, so she had her hand wrapped with a piece of rawhide. She was able to hold Jacy in the shade while the rest of us picked the wonderful beans. Like a good Indian, she did not cry out when she was hurt. The baby slept and we filled up both wagons in a few hours. We saw the smoke signs in the sky, which meant that the Kiowa were close by camping. Red Bird built a small fire to send smoke signals back to show that we were friendly allies. They sent friendly signals back to us. We took a siesta and made good time getting back home before dark to do our regular chores. It was good to get so much done since we were out past the Clear Fork of the river, close to **Red Top mesa.** We put the goods in the corncrib to keep it nice and fresh until we could take some of it to the gristmill for some sweet flour at the next trade day. We all got a good day's work in and we will reap the rich rewards to eat well this winter season.

October 24, 1846. We had planned to go to the fort for trade day. We found a man that was wounded along the road. He looked to be a Texas Ranger. We patched him up and stopped his bleeding. He looked to be very weak from blood loss; still we hurried to get him there. By the time we got to the fort, he had passed away! We went to the Officer of the Day, Captain Patterson, who got the records down on what had happened. He had some letters, and orders in his saddlebags to be looked at. We handed it all over to the commanding officer. He was satisfied that we did all that we could for the man. I felt bad for him because I know what it feels like to be wounded and feel all alone. The doctor at the fort said that he had a ***saber*** wound, and that is what killed him more than the bullet wounds he had suffered. Still it was not a good feeling that someone had done him harm when he was doing his duty. It was a soldier that had done this! But from whose side?! We did not know. It could not be blamed on an Indian this time. I was glad that the boys were at home with the women to protect them. The commander of the fort sent some men to take our mesquite beans to the gristmill and he did not charge us for anything. He even bought us a meal and lodging if we wanted it. We thanked them, but we could not eat, or rest until we got back home to see if the family was safe. He said that next time we were at the fort that we would get a good meal and the best lodging overnight. We were just glad to help as much as we could. We wished it were more that we could have done for another soldier and ranger that had served and put himself in harm's way as we had done. Getting the flour taken to the mill was reward enough we told the new commander. We parted company on good terms and left for home in a hurry once we crossed the West Fork's river crossing. We were relieved that the family was fine and safe. We will wait until the morning to tell them the details of what happened on the trip. They deserved to have a good night's sleep, and that was no sense in making them upset without due cause tonight. We will put ourselves on guard these next few weeks and talk with our Indian allies soon to see if they had heard of any Mexican soldiers that were deserters in our area. It would be better that we found them than if they found them. They still have contempt for the Mexican soldiers after Chief Coyote was executed, and not killed in battle, which was an honorable way to die. We will use common sense and keep our eyes open. Captain Patterson told us that the horses we have brought have been great mounts for the army. Unfortunately they are the biggest casualties of battle because they are used as a shield on the open prairies where there are few trees and rocks to hide behind. We are asked to bring horses as often as we can catch them. Five at a time are welcomed, as they are needed in service as soon as possible. We do not have any crops to plant, and the Comanche welcome us as allies, so we will go out and scout some horses up this next week. The boys will be cautioned as to what their responsibilities are as braves, and our grown sons will have to protect our homes. Captain Patterson said that the people of California have been having their own revolt against Mexico's rule over them! For 4 months they have been holding their own against Mexican rule! The **Federal's** navy has assisted the **Californio's** hope for independence. Also, this new commander Stephen Kearney, who fancies himself quite a soldier, much like General Sam. Kearney has interrupted the **Santa Fe trade**! Anyone bold enough to take control of the Santa Fe trade is crazy! This Kearney then marched his men to California and took a fort at **La Mesa**! So he is so bold. So crazy that it will keep Santa Anna awake at night. Maybe he will have a battle on many fronts and not have time to give us any new problems. We packed up and headed back. We brought much news home and then we could not sleep for having so much on our minds. We woke the boys and told the family of the recent events. We stayed up well until past midnight making plans for this next week. It has been a long day and morning chores will be here before we know it.

October 29th. Red Bird came to me and he told me that he had found a bee tree. I had finished the chores and the boys hurried to do their part. We all went and found the big hollow sycamore tree. It was a big one. We figured that we could use our army rifle and break off a big hollow limb without too much of a risk. Well, we tried, but to no avail. Red Bird waited until sun down, and since it was still and not too windy he climbed up and pulled out a huge honeycomb. We had a rope and a big bucket and he kept filling it up until it was full. He got stung, but he did not care. It was well worth it according to the smile on his face while he was eating a piece of honeycomb. He told the boys to get some mud to put on his bee stings. They did and he told the boys to put mud on the stings to draw the poison out. He felt poorly for a bit but then he drank some water and ate some sweet honeycomb. Then he was raring to go back to the lodge to show the women how brave he was. He had a big smile on his face and he enjoyed getting a pat on the back. I had a loose turkey feather and I put it in his hat like it was a brief feather ceremony held in his honor. He laughed and told Ke-Ke how crazy I am. I am not the one climbing up a bee tree full of angry bees. I would not criticize my brother for being brave in the face of danger, no mater what the size of it. The women got the big **gourds** and filled them up with honey to protect it from dirt. They put the wooden stoppers in place and they had 45 large gourds full! Red Bird split them between us so we could have something sweet to eat when we wanted it. This has become the land of milk and honey. A place called Texas. A place called home. There is no other place for us to be as it is our heaven on earth.

October 31st. Simon's boys came by with a whole wagonload of their pumpkins. The women were most proud because they love to roast them on the fire to make pumpkin bread. They had plans for most of them. The boys were using their whittling knives to carve out the seeds that they enjoy to eat. I showed them how we've made the pumpkins into jack-o'-lanterns. They liked that. Even Phoebe made one. We had fun and we thought that this would be a nice night for fun and tell ghost stories. We have pumpkin seeds and bread. The honey that Red Bird has found was wonderful. It made the stings from those bees all worthwhile. Simon and his wife came by to get the boys because it had been past dark and they had not returned. Red Bird gave them five gourds full of honey as a gift for the wagonload of pumpkins. They liked that so we made it into a party since it was past dark. The boys showed off their jack-o'-lanterns with some short candles that the women had saved incase the coal oil for the oil lamps went short. They did not mind. We darkened the room and watched the flickering jack-o'-lanterns on the hearth, and told ghost stories. The women popped corn and we had a good time telling the scary stories. We stayed up until midnight, and then Simon and the boys left for home. Sometimes it makes the difficult times better to have a reason to have some fun. We celebrate life when we can. Life is too short not to.

November 4th, 1846. The fair weather has turned and the sky has turned dark. The season has changed to the fall weather. It turned cold and rainy. It was the day for the chicken house to be repaired. We set to gather the eggs and put new hay in their roost. The boys moved the chickens to the barn. They shoveled out the chicken house, and swept it up neat and clean. The roof of their house did not leak because the boys had kept the roof repaired like I had asked them to. I came to inspect their work and they had done a fine job. They know that they can't play until all their work is finished. I was most pleased with their progress and how it looked much nicer than it did. I sent the boys to the barn to fetch the chickens and take then back since the storm had broke for a little while. Sam Bird came back and told me that someone was sleeping in our hayloft. It was an Indian boy, probably a Kiowa, he said. I went to check on the visitor. I went to the hayloft and Josiah was sign talking to him and was making the friendly signs. **Sarah** came to tell us the meal was ready and she smiled when she saw that we had a visitor. She went and got a blanket for the boy because his clothes were soaked from the rain. The boy looked starved and tired, so we made him know that he was among allies and friends. He made the trade signs and we said in the sign talking that we wanted his friendship in trade for our help. He smiled and nodded approval. We brought the boy inside by the fire and we had no trouble getting food down him. Sam Bird said that the boy's name was **Tu-Ukumah, or Black Horse.** He was a son of a chief from a distant Kiowa band. He had fell behind when they were moving to their winter camp with the Comanche close to **Red Top**. The storm had forced him to find shelter somewhere and our barn was the best place to rest. Josiah got a pair of his breeches, and a shirt for the boy to wear. He was beside himself for all the gifts and kindness he was getting. We had made a new friend and we had continued with the promise of the **Great Council** to make peace among those that would be peaceable allies. The boy lie down and fell asleep by the fire and there was nothing better to do but let him rest. We will let him stay as long as he wants, and until he feels stronger. He was a stout, brave boy, and he has been stressed out being left behind.

November 23, 1846. The Kiowa come here looking for their lost son. We welcome them with the friendly signs, and ropes of braided tobacco. Out comes **Black Horse** to greet them. He looked well fed and they were most pleased to see him in good order. They got out the pipes and we had a council in the area before our barn and woods. Red Bird came up and did the sign talking to make sure we answered all their questions. The boy spoke nonstop and made his feelings known that we were well considered allies. The Kiowa seemed most pleased and they asked to camp here a few days. We happily agreed. They liked our barn and thought it to be our council house since it was so large and dry. We allowed them to stay there and they were most happy to have a dry place to stay indoors in case it rained. This is a good time to make a council as we have done so with the Comanche. We will prove ourselves to be worthy of their trust. They have ours.

Tonight I read out loud for the benefit of our guests. Red Bird did the hand signs to tell them what it all meant. Tonight I read: PSALM 119: 103. "How sweet are your words to my taste, sweeter than honey to my mouth."

They enjoyed that as Sarah was just serving them some warm pumpkin bread that she had made with some fine honey. It made it ring true that much more true to them. The Kiowa planned to have a big feast to celebrate the safety of the chief's son, Black Horse. They insisted to go hunting wild turkeys tomorrow and have us as honored guests. We will happily do this as new allies, and the return of a lost son is good reason to celebrate.

November 24, 1846. We have fasted for a day, as it is custom to do before a hunt. They get their best turkey callers and some long arrows ready for the hunt. They have baited the ground with corn to attract some of the wily birds to the brush where they have set up to hunt. They make the scratchy sounding calls and the birds came to us. They were very smart and a few got wise to us and they flew away. The bird callers did the trick so they fooled some tasty birds. The archers took them down, and they caught a hen by stunning it by using a blunt tipped arrow. They tied it with a rawhide thong to a nice stout branch. Then the tom turkeys could not resist their calls now. The archers took their pick of some nice ones. There will be many accepting our dinner invitation. I learned that a turkey was wise for a bird, and that they would be difficult to catch if you were not wise yourself. I am always amazed at how people living so close to nature can understand more that what most educated people think that they know. I got a chance to use the bow, and I also held an arrow in my teeth. It was a matter of being quick and sure of my aim. I knew that they would judge me badly if I missed a simple shot. Fortunately my aim was good and I did not embarrass myself. A young brave went along and stuck a turkey feather in my hat. The hunters that had hit the mark wore the handsome turkey feathers. We came back to camp and people stood and nodded their approval as we walked by with a nice bunch of turkeys from the hunt. The elders sang a good hunting song, and the drums started strong. They built the fire much bigger and we told stories from today and from great hunts from past days. They are a most handsome people and I am glad that we are allies. This is the start of a great friendship between us. We thank the good Lord for them, as we have learned that our allies have kept us alive through many difficulties here.

November 25th. Today the Kiowa made a great feast of boiled corn, squash, some Mexican tomatoes. 4 turkeys roasted over a fire for hours. The turkeys smelled great as their women cooked them up good. Sarah and Ke-Ke made some fine cornbread, and it all was good to everyone here. We then had a dance that lasted until after midnight when the moon set behind the far hills. We had quite a celebration and passed the pipes around for good measure to make our friendship complete. The Kiowa gave us a **lance** to hang over the fireplace in our lodge to show their protection and friendship. It was a beauty from tip to end. We had a great time and there was quite a bonfire that they had built using the broken limbs that were along the trail. We had new friends so we can live here safely west of Bird's Fort in the land that belongs to the Comanche and Kiowa. This is our home too. We are thankful for all our blessings and our good allies. We went and hung the friendship lance over the fireplace to show our acceptance of their friendship. We had a pipe ceremony and danced outside our lodge until we fell down from being tired. The Kiowa picked us up and placed us in a safe place among their councils. A friend helps a friend when they fall down to pick them up. This is the start of a great friendship as we are now recognized as good allies.

We woke up later and went to our own lodge and we let the Kiowa continue the celebration until the time before dawn came. We woke early to make our chores finished as we had much to do. We went to the hen house and brought their chief several baskets of fresh eggs. He smiled and ate them raw and passed them among themselves. They were most pleased. We had a dozen pumpkins left and we gave them to our guests. We gave five gourds of honey to them and they were most pleased to have our friendship. They pledged their protection and to pass the word among their tribe, and to the Comanche we have restored their faith as a friend. As Indian allies we are from both the settlers, and the Indian nations so we will act as a buffer zone to warn strangers not to go into their lands without permission, or to do harm to them when they meet them on the prairies out on hunting parties. We are asked to tell others that pass that when anyone travels across Kiowa lands they are to pay tribute in tolls as the Kick-a-Poo do. We are to ask the army not to try to do battle with them on what is Kiowa and Comanche lands. The Mexicans have tried to ask the Kiowa to fight on their side of the Mexican War. The Kiowa said, "We do not want to fight a battle that makes us in the middle of two battles." This is what Red Bird told me they said. So this has been some useful time these past days and it all started with finding a lost boy as Chief Spotted Tail had done just a few years ago. This time it was a lost Kiowa boy. He was about the age of our sons. So it shows that we value the peace between us and that we value our young people's future. We thank the Lord for small miracles every day. A lost boy in a thunderstorm can do much more than any words, or empty promises in a treaty. We can change an enemies' way of thinking. They are now our good friends and allies. We are brothers in peace in the middle of a terrible war that still rages west of us. The Kiowa will leave tomorrow if the weather permits good travel. It has clouded up and it looks to be bad weather coming the next few days. We pray that it holds off to give them safe travel to their winter camps. We do part company on good terms. We will sleep better at night knowing that we did right in the sight of the Lord.

Tonight we read: PROVERBS, Chapter 3, Verses 5 and 6. "God will direct your steps."

December 2nd, 1846. Well, many days have passed and it rained **beau coups**. The Kiowa have time to settle in at Red Top mesa with the Comanche. I was glad for their sake that they were back home safe. Red Bird said that he saw their smoke signs talking with each other from the high hill on his place. The roads were now passable and we considered going to the church close to **Cross-Timbers**. It had been since August that we have gone and celebrated God's Word together. We will go and take the family and make sure that they learn of important things, and learn to go to know their neighbors no matter how far distant they live from us. I feel that we have done that by making allies recently with the Kiowa and the Comanche. We have 2 days to get ready before we are to meet again at the **Lonesome Dove* church.** We have plenty of hay to put out and the recent rains have filled up the stock ponds with plenty of good tasting water. The boys were already ahead of me and they were out early doing their chores, as boys love the good adventure of traveling to the church to meet the new people and to see some of their friends that they haven't seen for a while. They love to learn more about the Lord and they have learned to read as well as I do. I am most proud of them as they get much work done than some men do! They take little stock in foolishness, and they get the job done first for they know that work and chores comes first before play. They are quite the little men who are growing by the day. They are as tall as me and they will be taller from the looks of their pant legs getting shorter than their legs. The women have made them some new clothes for church and they will look their best in the Lord's House. Well I have to get the repairs on the roof done, as that is my chore for this day. I want to keep the rain out to keep our cabin a good and dry lodge to stay in. My finger got in the way of the hammer a few times. It is good to write and sort things out on paper so that my mind is free to think about other things that are needed to be done. It will be some good days ahead of us. Tonight we read: SECOND TIMOTHY, Chapter 2, Verse 1. "My son be strong in the grace that is in Christ Jesus."

CHAPTER THREE

The Tejanos and the Battle of Buena Vista.

December 14th, 1846. We received our answer to General Sam's letter: he has sent some of the best **Tejanos** to be horse wranglers! We are in need of some help as these horses are so many that we can not take the time we would to train them properly. We would normally train half this many in a longer period of time. These **gauchos** are the kind of horsemen that we wished we could be. Our methods are too slow, and too awkward to be consistent. We have missed our allies that have made us strong in the times that were felt helpless against Santa Anna. We instructed the men that these Mexicans are our allies, and not the same as the people that we are at war with. Their cause is the same as ours: to stop Santa Anna from ruining our way of life. Some of the men balked at our orders and we put them on Kitchen Patrol, and extra Guard Duties. One man we sent to the stockade for threatening a young Mexican wrangler. We have to be tough on them as they are also threatening our success to get the horses trained with their foolishness. We don't have time to deal with this. We went down our duty roster and we found ourselves short handed. The loss of so many soldiers to the Typhoid has made us short with the battalion out to relieve the wounded at **Saltillo** and **Palo Alto.** We went out and the gauchos had the horses split up into two groups with the most difficult kept in the smaller corral. These were mostly stallions, and stubborn mares. The gauchos have the boys let them be the only ones that feed and water the horses in the smaller corral. They used some tactics that were surprising. They rode the stallions into deep water until it is up to its neck, where it almost drowns if it does not obey. That seems cruel, but they know what works best. With them in charge we have the best chance for success. General Sam knows best, that is what makes him General Sam, and our representative to Washington City. Sarah was happy here at the fort as she felt safer, and she has made many new friends. She is able to use her many talents and not feel so alone, here.

December 20th. Many of the soldiers bring her fresh game as a gift for her good help when we were out hunting for the mustangs. She talked with a group of soldiers and she told them to pull together and act like soldiers. She praised the ones that worked with the tejanos, and she said that she would curse the ones that did not do right. She told them about the ogre woman who was evil, and about the animal called the Chupracabra that would come to get them if they did not do right. Some were quiet, and some laughed at her. They said that those stories were used to frighten little children, and that that were no fools. She put her hands on her hips and looked stern. She tapped her foot until they all got quiet. She warned them that she knew many Cherokee curses, and she was not afraid to use them on the offender that did not do right. They got quiet, and looked at the ground as I got out my duty roster to add more chores to their duties. I did not question her motives, as she has many talents that are wonderful, and some that might be terrible to find out about. I did not want to know. They do not want to find out. I always try to stay on her good side so that was that. The commander came by and made her the "commander of the kitchen." He gave her a special shirt to wear that showed her rank over them. They were to look on her as any other commander that they have, and she could use her authority to punish, or praise them as she saw fit. She makes quite the soldier, and she took it seriously as she is still a **Qualls** with all the authority that it brings. She may not interpret dreams, but she knows how to get things done. I always stay on her good side as she might outrank me one day. These are desperate times and it requires for some drastic measures if we are to succeed at winning this war, once and for good.

December 24th. We get together to celebrate Christmas Eve. All the regular duties are suspended for a few days. Only a few men are kept on guard duty with shorter shifts. All whiskey was kept locked up and only a small portion was given out to those that wanted it. It was not something we wanted as it is poison to us to drink since it makes us sick if we partake of it.

The tejanos have a fiesta planned with fireworks, music, and the wonderful Christmas tamales. The wife has been making tamales for days. It would be the first Christmas celebrated at this fort, so they were doing it up big. We all enjoy a party and this one was going to be a good one. The tejanos and their families got together and they sang a song called "La Buena Noche." It was beautiful and they sang several songs and then there were games where a hanging paper star was broken open with a colored stick. Candies of many kinds fell out and the children rushed to get a handful each. The older children got candy for the smaller ones. They called it a piñata. Their children did a play about the Christmas story and it was most touching to see how sweet it was. There was dancing, some speeches, and good hopes for the New Year. We were singing from a book of hymns. Most of all it was nice to see everyone get along, and make for a nice evening. We watched the fireworks display, and the night was lovely and clear with no mishaps for a change. It was a lovely party that I will remember for a long time. We are truly blessed, and it would be the start of a good year for us all. We all prayed a prayer together and it was the end of a good night.

January 1st, 1847. The New Year comes and we hope for the best, and for the war to be over soon. We wrote down our wishes and hopes for the New Year, and for our God to continue to bless us here. The tejanos have made some good days breaking horses. I have learned a great deal from watching them at work. Ben went back home for a few days to get the farm up to snuff as Simon's boys needed some help getting the chores done. I went along for just an afternoon to see what the place looked like. We came back home to find the barn burned down. The boys ran away and we rode up to them and asked them what has happened? They said that a stranger had slept in the barn and he had turned over the lantern. We told them that we were not angry with them, but that we wanted to talk to the stranger who did this. They said that the stranger asked to sleep in the barn and when the fire started they woke to see the barn ablaze and the stranger was gone. So we had no idea if this was intentional, or just an accident. Ben said that he would follow the tracks and bring him back to answer some tough questions. I told Ben that we would just clean this up and not waste our time hounding some unfortunate person that probably was scared out of their gourd. We forgive him for being foolish. We set about going through the ashes and we found our plow, some tools and a saddle that was still good.

We later found that our visitor has died in the barn, as we found his skeleton in the ashes. He was holding a bucket, as it was close to his remains. So it seems that his horse and our cows ran out of the barn, and he was trapped when the hayloft fell on him. We were glad that we had the proper heart, because it seems that the man was trying to put out the fire when he lost his life in the process. We sat a while and pondered it all. It seems that we have to build a new barn in the near future. We buried the man under the oak tree close to where it is nice and shady. We prayed over him and we hoped that his family would be safe. Ben rounded up the animals and we took them over to his place. The boys put the good timbers to one side, and they took what tools that were found to the over hang of the cabin. We talked to the boys and we told them that we appreciated their help and that we did not blame them for this, as it was an accident. They talked about when Deacon's son, Samson played with fire and burned down half the settlement. We told him that people make mistakes and then they have to live with that for a long time and that is punishment enough. It isn't for us to make it worse on someone for everyone breathing makes mistakes, and this poor man paid for it with his life. We have more important things to do, and we set to checking on the crops and the fields that needed tending. My head hurt and I needed to sit by the well and drink some water. I was a little overwhelmed by it all, but I held my temper, and I prayed for the dead man's family. Ben Bird came back with something from the smokehouse and we ate something decent for a meal. It helped and after I have rested, I was ready for the world! He had a positive outlook and he said that we could rebuild the barn the first chance we get. It was good to have a brother that was always so positive in his outlook. We talked with the boys to make sure that they understood that we appreciated their help, and that this could have happened under our watch, as well. Simon came over and we talked with him, and we assured him that our friendship is not harmed by this unfortunate incident. He was happy that the boys were fine and that we are still friends. He offered to help build back the barn and we accepted his offer of help. We shook hands, and he patted me on the back relieved that our friendship was not harmed. We gave him the rest of the roast that we were carving on and he went back to his place. Evening came and we headed back to the fort before the gate was closed for the night. It has been a tough day and some rest will be welcome.

Tonight we read: FIRST CORINTHIANS, Chapter 6, verse 3: "The Judgment of Angels."

January 5th, 1847. We have 87 of the horses ready for inspection. The tejanos have worked night and day to make the impossible quite possible. It seemed wonderful to see a mustang made into a fine horse for battle. They were brushed down well, their mane and tail are well groomed, and the tack was new and shiny. We have our inspection and the tejanos put them through their routines. They would be the pride of any soldier. Our commander went along and he could not find any fault with any of them. He spent almost an hour to look them over and he is most pleased that the work was accomplished. The other 20 horses are most difficult animals and they are still needed because they are needed to replace the horses lost in battle. We set to help complete the contract. It may be that we might need to catch more horses, but we find that we must make do with these stubborn nags and make lemons into lemonade. We tried our method of roping one of the back legs and trying to control the horses by being persistent. We have some luck with a few of them. Young Bull comes with Sam Bird and they try. They are younger, and through their youth they make better progress by winning the horses' confidence. They rode them one at a time down to the river and they rode them into the deep river. The water was cold and they have a short time before the cold water would cause the horse to drown. The rider has a rope tied around him so that if the horse stumbles the rider would prevail to reach the shore. They do seven of the better horses and lose two. They stop because they are tired and cold. So they help us with a minimum of loss. The lost horses are not viable, as they were a danger to the rider and to our cause. We counted eight more horses to complete the contact. We talked with the tejanos and commander Ripley Arnold. They said that we should bring these horses for food since rations might be scarce close to the battlefields. We agreed that we have to get the most out of what resources we have. So we continue to work with the horses and continue to maintain contact with the horses to keep them under our control and manageable. We hoped to get another horse or two from the unmanageable bunch. We wrote General Sam a letter to tell him what has happened lately. We went to eat supper and we were given two letters from him asking us about our time here. We sat to eat and we read his letter and tried to write him another letter to better inform him of what we are trying to do. We also tell him about the stranger that died trying to put out the fire in the barn. We tried to be more positive in our letter to be more encouraging to our friend. We told him about our wife becoming the 'commander of the kitchen,' by making use of the stubborn soldiers, and our dealing with horses that were just as contrary. He would know about both and he probably would get a good laugh out of some of these details. We had no other duties tonight so we spent some time with the family. We needed more time like this to maintain our family, as we should. Phoebe was making many new friends with the soldier's children and they are learning to read better, and play dollies together. Phoebe said that a soldier from England has a daughter named Chelsea, and she said, "You speak funny, here." She always makes me smile. Josiah and Sam Bird have made many friends among the soldiers and they are well respected by most of them. Even the young soldiers that spend so much time in the Kitchen Patrol have come around from Sarah's supervision. They just need to find a good place where they fit in well. There is no shame in doing a job well, what ever it is.

I have got a little guitar from a trade, and I have been learning to play on my off time. I wasn't too bad, as long as I don't try to sing. My wife was happy that I was doing something that was relaxing to me, and she said that I should continue learning something new. Another soldier was playing some songs and I asked him to show me how to play, and how to keep it in tune, as I should. I played the "Amazing Grace" and it was not too bad. Sarah sang, as she was very good, as she knew all the proper words. She has figured out the verses in Cherokee, and she asked me to play more. It was most lovely, in whatever words we sang to it.

Tonight we read: Revelations, Chapter 10, "Angel of Light."

January 7th. We are given orders to go to Northern Mexico with the remuda of fresh horses. We have a knot in our stomach as our boys are going too. We have hoped that we would not have to see our boys in a battle, but it looks like it is unavoidable. We head out towards the Kiowa lands and we negotiate with them to cross their lands. We offered them some blankets and a few canteens that we have a great supply of. They are happy, but they want a few of our horses too. That was a slippery slope, as we were hard pressed to keep every horse for battle use. We let go of 2, and one was one of the more spirited mares that we could not break. So that was the most that we could do. They were satisfied and that would get us a toll back also. We have made a good friendship and we have maintained it here. The Kiowa traveled along with us and they rode ahead to make sure that no one trespassed against us. We saw the smoke signs from some Comanche, and they watched us from a distance we were sure. We did not see them, but we felt that they were watching us. The boys acted like professional soldiers and they maintained the horses along with the tejanos. I made me proud how well they fit in to the patrol and their assignment here. We set up camp and we headed up the watch for the night. We were glad that we have made some strong friendships among the Kiowa, and Comanche. They kept us free from trouble and that allowed us to not worry over our horses being stolen and used by the enemy.

January 14th. Some of Chief Peta's tribe made contact with us to allow us to travel across their land. Rain came and they camped among us. Some of the soldiers were nervous, and we talked over the fire to assure them that our enemy was Santa Anna and not these braves. We made use of more of the untrained horses, as all the battles and strangers here have killed off, or scared off all the good game. They were starving and they wanted five of the horses for food. We were glad to be rid of them and they were a handful and they kept the good horses all stirred up. So are very glad to make use of them, as they turned out valuable, after all. We have a pipe ceremony, as that is required to make things proper. We are very well respected, as tradition requires us to make time to show that we are good allies. They seem to be glad that we are determined to make an end to the war, as they find it all threatening to their hunting, and their way of life. The Mexican army has taken several of their villages as hostages, making them work as slaves. They were not happy over the loss of their families, and we were a better alternative than them going to war with the whole Mexican army, and their cannons. Ben Bird did all the sign talking, and he explained their concerns, and that we were welcome as we both had a similar vision for the Mexican army to be defeated once and for all. It was a relief to the soldiers, and we are reaching for the same goals. It made for the focus to be a better outlook for us all. We tried to sleep but there was too much to think about. We have reached a place called San Angelo, where we will rest for a day to give us time to recuperate from riding 2 days in the rain with no sleep.

January 18th. We crossed the Pecos River and we found ourselves among the Apache nation. They have made their smoke signs and from what I could see the word was out about our coming here. The stood along the ridge top, and their spokesman rode out to where a bluff dropped down. He raised his talking stick high in the air. We all held up our open right hand and he motioned for our spokesman to come talk with them. Our Comanche and Kiowa allies chose a spokesman. He rode up talked with them to make sure that we were not seen as a threat. It was a relief to have allies watching our back as we have enough to deal with. The Kiowa and Comanche do not particularly like the Apaches from what I could gather. Since we share a common goal, they can tolerate us to cross as we mean them no harm. We made trade with them, and they mostly wanted fire strikers, as flint has been in short supply as their trade ties have been cut by the Mexican's interference. So they were sympathetic to our cause and they appreciated us not being against them, as they have their own problems as illness has stricken many of their camps.

Ben said that the Mexican army leaves dead bodies about, and that this has poisoned the water and made the illness have the upper hand. They held a dance to give us good fortune, and we were smart to take the time to make them feel their help and indulgence with us is appreciated. We are in a hurry, but we must follow the custom of the peoples that we visit so that they would not be fearful of us, or be angered by our presence here. They have a good fire and they wear some serious outfits when they danced, which scared off many of the Mexicans who were superstitious. Our **tejanos** made the best of it and they clapped and danced along when they were asked to join in. We watched and we shook some gourd rattles when were asked to do so. They have a spirited dance and we joined in until the moon set. We want to make some time to rest so we don't fall out of the saddle.

January 30th, 1847. We reached our forces with the supplies, and the much needed horses. They were worn thin and they needed us very badly. It was all worth it to see how much we were needed here. Ben went out and he helped the wounded, and Sam Bird helped him. Josiah went among the soldiers and helped them write letters to be sent home to their families. I have forgotten how trying it is to be in this situation, and it reminded me that I needed to pray for them more than I have. Their commander came up and he checked us over, and we have an inspection. They were a little rough on us, and we remember that we have not been in the line of fire as they have. They put us on the night patrol, and to do the duties that have been neglected, as they were overwhelmed here. We toughened up, and we got up to speed to do what needed to be done.

January 31st. We moved our camp and we were put in control of the sick. Ben Bird helped put up new tents to help keep the threat of illness down. Their old clothes and blankets are ordered burned and we looked for a good source of water that wasn't polluted by so many people. The little details are so important here, and it might just save the majority of the wounded. It was as bad as what we saw at the new fort with so many sick. We could see why the Apaches welcomed us here as most rivers were too polluted from dead horses and deceased soldiers being left in them. We set up new latrines, and that was a good move as most of their problems come from small things that have been neglected as they are spread too thin to do their proper chores. We made up new duty rosters, and those with less terrible ailments are helping where they can. We wrote out all the proper reports to tell what needs to be done. We were running out of daylight, and the night watch needed to be set.

Our new commander, Major General Zachary Taylor came and inspected us. He wore a simple uniform of a red flannel shirt, and a straw hat. They called him "the Straw Hat General" and "Old Rough and Ready." He did not want to make a target of himself by wearing a fancy uniform in battle like Santa Anna does. He is more "low key, not like a peacock strutting around." Seeing is: still believing! He was strict and fairly good-natured, and somewhat bad tempered when he was crossed. He would be a good friend to General Sam as he has a lot in common with him. I gave him the reports of the duty roster, and the progress made with the Sick Call being maintained, and some soldiers were able to go back to some of their regular duties, and that we have lost only two soldiers to illness since we have arrived here. He was pleased with our reports being in order, and that we kept him well informed. After supper, a captain walked up to me asked that I act as his secretary to write letters, and make sure that the orders are complied with, as his helper had recently died from an illness. I accepted his offer, and I was given the rank of captain. The commander sent some new orders for this week. He asked me to go out on a patrol to help scout the enemy. He asked me to pick some soldiers to make a detail to go along with him. Ben is good at this, but he was too busy from his own assignments. I accepted this task, and I asked some decent men to come along.

We went along and we followed the signs they left. They seemed to eat poorly and they have left many obvious signs that they are stressed from the type of animals they are eating. We found the remains of armadillos, some rats, crows, and a fox that were eaten. Also a coyote met a terrible fate as someone's supper. We also saw that there was a horse that was eaten, and that they left many of their saddles and tack behind. They left many tracks showing that they were mostly on foot when they traveled. Some were barefoot from their tracks. We found several abandoned wagons. There were tote sacks full of spoiled food, and several burials that were fairly new. They have burned most of what was useful, and there were signs of at least two cannons being moved along by some oxen. From the looks of things it seems like they might be on the dinner plate before it is all said and done. So when we do fight them they will be fighting us tooth and nail as they are desperate. We pray for them to find some peace in their lives so we all can go back to our lives we had before this.

February 2nd, 1847. We are headed for Fort Texas and we are found out by a passing Mexican patrol. We knew that we were getting close to trouble as we have seen buzzards overhead the past day. They hoped to over take us as we crossed over a hill to get the goods we have and the supplies they need. We were determined that we would die protecting the horses we have worked so hard to capture and train. The tejanos managed to ride up their flank and make them run for cover with their rifles cutting down two of their men. They shot at us, but their shots were not meant for us, at least for today. I do not know if we were either very brave or very foolish as we rode up to meet them like a mean dog looking for a fight. We searched the slain men to find information and letters that gave out details that might prove useful. We have ridden up a deep ravine to make the horses hidden up in some brush. It kept us from having to ride over the open prairie to catch up to them.

We have a burial detail to show the soldiers their due respect. We were able to make a place where we could rest for a bit and look over some of the captured letters. The tejanos read some of them and Ben read a few. They reached the notion that the Mexicans were calling for reinforcements to meet up at Saltillo, in Coahuila Mexico. We headed for Del Rio as our forces are meant to muster close to there in the next weeks. Commander John E. Wool is to join us with some volunteers of close to 4,000 men or so. Some are seasoned soldiers, and some are "green as a new persimmon," we are told from our commander. We remember what that was like. Since they have been the Center Division they are the men that we have come to assist with the horses and supplies. They have controlled Monterrey for over a year, and marched on to do God's will on earth. I hoped that we are doing the right thing by being here in this place. There is no doubt that this is all coming to a head, and it might be the last battle I get to witness or write about. I have dreamed about it most nights since we have been gone. I missed the wife. My boys were sent in a scouting detachment with Major General Taylor. I chewed my fingers to the quick as I was on guard duty until daybreak. If anything happened to them I would blame myself for the rest of my life. We expected the Mexicans to return with reinforcements, but they did not, for they must have run for cover and kept going as the wind blows the leaves. We still have the Apaches up in the near **mesas** keeping watch. They are to make the smoke signs if they spot trouble coming our way. Today it was so windy that we could not have seen a single sign if we wanted to. Hopefully we will be sharp and not get into a hornet's nest like today. We do a great deal of praying in between doing our regular duties. I wish to be back home and not die out here in this lonesome place.

We read FIRST SAMUEL, Chapter 27, "David flees King Saul."

February 10th. We have moved to a new place that is green and fresh after a good day of rain. The ill have returned to health and we have not lost any more soldiers to illness. The boys are back and they are excited to have scouted the enemy positions. They covered themselves in clay and brush like we do when we go deer hunting. Commander Taylor was impressed and he also learned to 'hide in plain sight' from some real Cherokees. He has a good sense of adventure and the boys made a good impression on him as they were smiling from ear to ear. They made reports that the enemy was starting to muster close to Aqua Nueva. He said that some Texas Rangers came to their camp and they are among those supporting us as well as some men under command of Joseph Lane of the Second Indiana Brigade. They are very impressive and we feel that we are part of something bigger than we could understand, but that the Lord would make us all strong, and brave to do proper battle. Also, this evening a commander named Jefferson Davis came here and he has some stout riflemen from Mississippi. They went through their maneuvers and they are some soldiers here that would out do Santa Anna any day. We were in good company and there is going to be some real reckoning here. Commander Taylor conducted an inspection and he was well pleased that there is such talent here. I walked along with him and made notes as he asked, and I gave him a complete roster of men with their names clearly printed and their duties assigned well. I spent most of the afternoon going over the details and it allowed the commander to make plans for tomorrow's duties. We prayed for wisdom to be worthy to fight with these great men. Tonight we read about King David, and his Mighty Men. We find much wisdom in reading about how he dealt with his problems. FIRST SAMUEL, Chapter 28. Our nerves are settled and we can better rest now.

February 12th. We are order to go to Fort Texas with some wagons to get supplies. We are to get as much gunpowder and cannon balls as we could get. Some Texas Rangers went with us to maintain our security, as they know the best and fastest way to get here and back. I thought that Del Rio would be closer but according to the Rangers there are many spies for Santa Anna there. So going a longer route is the safer way to go, it seems. Our boys stayed with commander Taylor's group and he has them on a detail to deliver goods among the camps. Some need new tack and blankets and it was good for them to stay busy and meet all the different groups that represented us. Some tejanos came to join our group, and it was more balanced that way. They brought some of the captured saddles, and tack to make us blend in better as we traveled about. We were told to let our beard grow out and not be clean shaven, or have our boots well shined, as that was what told off on Santa Anna when we helped capture him the first time twelve years ago at San Jacinto.

We dressed in plain clothes like we were some Mexican horse wranglers. It was safer this way and we kept our heads down and tried not to ride like a Texan, or as a good soldier. We slouched in the saddle and we looked as bad as a scarecrow riding past. We got past several patrols in one day and they thought us to be working for them, as the tejanos did all the talking, and we did all the toting. We did not look them in the eyes, as a servant would do. We passed by their sentries and we made progress better than we could hope. We later stopped and rested the horses and we threw up. We weren't the only ones that did. There was hardly a soldier here that did not have some kind of stomach trouble. We washed our face in a river and it was better after we got a chance to rest. We made time to pray and we encouraged others to do the same. It was the wise thing to do.

February 14, 1847. We arrived at the fort and we showed the sentry, and the Officer of the Day, our written orders for supplies of powder, cannon balls, and fuses. He tried to write us up for being out of uniform, and unkept. We saluted him and told him that our orders were to get past the enemy and not stand out as a threat. He considered it and he asked us to go to the quartermaster and get a regular uniform, and to go to the horse trough and clean up properly. We obliged as he was missing the whole point of 'hiding in plain sight.' He has been in the security of this fort and he has not ventured more than five miles out from the looks of him. He was greener than some of those persimmons. We felt more like a human being, and it was probably for the sake of everyone within a mile of the fort. We dipped our clothes in the water and we put them in the wagon to dry. I felt much better and I was probably better to be around. We were fed some decent food and we are to rest here for two days and to return back to our company. We had no regular duties so we took the time to talk with some of the soldiers. There was a group that met to read the Bible, so I asked if I could join in and take turns reading some scriptures. This evening we read: SECOND CORINTHIANS, Chapter 9, verse 8: "God is able."

February 18th, 1847. We have left **Fort Texas**, and head towards **Buena Vista** with the needed supplies. We pass a patrol and they look us over and they see that our wagon ruts are very deep. Our wagon tarp is pulled back and some cowhides are removed. We have to shoot and hope that their rifle fire does not set all our gunpowder off. The tejanos ride them to the river and they make them our prisoner, other wise they would drown. They tie them to some trees and they question them using some serious pressure to get them to talk. They refuse to talk, so we go through their saddlebags and get some information written as orders, and some letters soldiers have written for home, to take back to our commander. We took their horses and their gear and we left them tied to a tree. They will get loose by at least daybreak and give us time to get away. Since they have no horses they won't be going very far, very fast. One of the men wanted to kill them, and I thought it not honorable to kill unless we are hard pressed and our life was in jeopardy. This was the Cherokee way, and the way that a good Christian should do. We rode on without any more trouble and we rested the horses, as they were weary from all the burden they were under. We were feeling much the same way. We make our way to a camp and we felt safer from any patrol that might find us. We met a Texas Ranger named Major Ben McCulloch. He took the information and he asked us to go along on a scouting party. We were obliged and we went along to find the enemy position. We went along a ridge and we felt that we have found where they were camped. We watched but we did not see Santa Anna as we have hope to. He might find us soon enough. That was that.

February 22nd. We stay on edge as this place looks dangerous with all the bushes, and the high bluffs close by. This is not the flat prairie we are use to, where you can see for miles ahead. We have a group of soldiers on point, in advance of our wagons, so we would not be ambushed, or caught off guard. We still kept our eyes peeled looking at the horizon. The word was that we were at a disadvantage being greatly outnumbered at least 4 to 1. I felt it might be worse than those odds as we were always the ' little dog in a big dog fight.' It was much as we were back at San Jacinto, fighting the same battle, with the prize being the possible capture of Santa Anna, his soldiers, horses, and his ammunition depot. We would not be so bold to think that lightning would strike twice for us, to hit the same mark. But determined persons can work wonders, if they can have faith, and hope in God.

Commander Taylor's assessment that some of the persons that helped defeat and capture Santa Anna, might have some insight into his weaknesses and strengths. We sat down and wrote down some thoughts for the commander. We talked over our thoughts each night but we are not allowed to make any campfires, or cook our food for over a day. We then thought over what we knew of Santa Anna from our own past experiences. There was much to consider to give insight into what makes him the success that he has been. But how long will he keep things stirred up between us? We have tripled the guard, and moved the watch line 500 paces out from where it normally would be. We climbed out and set the watch from the bluff, high up. There was a moon, but it soon became rainy, and it was hard to see. It turned windy and it would be difficult to make a decent fire in this valley. We would do what we must, and sleep was a fair commodity for us for a while. Our time has come to watch over the wagons, and make sure that they do not become the property of the enemy. We kept a good watch, and fortunately there was nothing more than some coyotes howling in the distance over the thunder and lightning. The next morning we took the remudas down to the river to water them and we had the men groom the horses well. They were some handsome horses.

We had a rider come up in a hurry. He was a scout telling us that Santa Anna was spotted over twenty-five miles away! It was exciting and scary, to wonder if we would get to tangle with him. He was a half a day's ride away, and it might be until the weekend that we catch up to him. He would not be caught unawares this time, if he has learned anything from last time. Twelve years have passed, and a fox would grow smarter in that time. He was no fool, but he was so smart that he thought that he was infallible, that what ever he did he did it well. He was too good for all our sakes. I would like to think that I was so smart, but that I was more humble in my approach to things. I would hope that anything I did would be a stumbling block to anyone else. There would be the Devil to pay, if I did act that way. We got our orders, and we left out, and pulled up our tent stakes. We covered up the signs of our campfire, and drug brush, and tree limbs behind our horses to hide our tracks, much like we did when we were living with the east Texas Cherokee. Our detachment joined General Scott's forces. We felt more secure being part of a battalion of soldiers.

We all sent our recommendations on capturing Santa Anna to the general Scott's aid for his consideration, so he could brief him in the evening. We got extra rations for our work, as we might not be able to eat well the next two days of the campaign. We stayed to a strict duty roster, which gave us little time to worry over too many things. We were called to muster, and we got our orders to leave the camp intact as a ploy. We left out in a hurry, leaving the campfires going. There were some men that used clothes stuffed with straw like they are bedded down, to look like more people are left in our camp. It was worth an effort to make us look like more forces were here. Dawn broke as we traveled along.

February 23, 1847. It is terribly muddy and our gear is all wet and we have to lay it out to dry. This morning I looked up and I saw an eagle fly over. It is much like a dream I've had a number of times. It flew over and it swooped down and picked up a snake in its claws. It continued on until it disappeared towards the rising sun. I felt like this would be the day that we see battle. I prayed to be strong, and not be afraid if it is so. I thought about my boys and I hoped for them to be safe. We did not have any coffee and many of us felt bad, so we have to tough it out and leave in a hurry.

We moved our forces east, then north along the river bend. We took what we could carry, and left the old, tired horses in the picket line. Most of them were battle scarred, lame, and gun shy from all the battles, so they served a better purpose this way. A few older men, and boys stayed behind to make bigger fires from some of the broken down wagons. They do the mock sentry duty for appearances to anyone scouting our position. The wind and the wet ground kept the dust clouds down, and out of sight, so we traveled at a quick pace, but not at a full gallop as it was so muddy that the horse might stumble down a slope. As we came to the place where the Mexican camp was, it was much as it was at San Jacinto. The river was deep there, and it had them boxed in.

We kept our horses, and artillery in its proper place on a ridge, where we could force them into the riverbank, up against the high wall of a ravine. We were riding up their flank, so we could divide their men if they opposed us. They were startled that we had caught them as they were changing sentries. We took them on and we are fired upon. There were many Texans wounded, but still fighting because they were determined to win. Some of our men moved along in the point position. They were killed by a sniper with a new Mexican rifle hiding out on the ridge in the brush. Ben Bird fired some long arrows with fire lit to their tips. It burned the dead brush where the man was hiding. He was fired upon and he fell into the river. He was later found hidden away downstream. He is patched up and taken away to be questioned about their troop movements. The battle went on for several hours, and many of their soldiers were captured, and put under our control. A number of bullets came close to us, but we have been shot before, and our fear of death was overwhelmed by gaining control of their camps. We backed off and made plans to regroup to the east. Our cannons moved in where we were staged. The cannons fired, and it was the shot that took out their powder magazine that settled it as it was deafening. Our ears rang and it was troublesome, as it was hard to understand commands. The main thing is that the Mexicans were not able to rally against us as we got the upper hand against being so terribly outnumbered. More of their soldiers came like red ants after you step into an ant bed. We might be in over our head, but we have to wait it out to see when our reinforcements come here to help. Their cannon return fire and we hug the ground as it hits all around us. We dig into what might be our own graves. A long time passes and we get ill from stress. More of our soldiers come and they bring fresh cannon fire to relieve us, and we drag ourselves along the ground as **grapeshot** is all over the place. We picked up handfuls of it and stuck it in our pockets, as we might be needing it for later. Some tejanos came and they relieved us and we went back past the front line as the relief soldiers pushed past us and advanced 1000 paces from where we were. I tried to stand and realized that I had been shot in the left leg and it seemed broken. It explains why I was throwing up so bad early on. I could not hear commands and they drug me onto a wagon for the wounded and dead. I cried and I prayed for my boys that I have taken them into the middle of this mess. Their mothers will kill me worse than Santa Anna if they are wounded or killed here! They put a bandanna over my mouth to shut me up as I was talking crazy and giving away our position. So I shut up and quit my crazy talking, so then the gag was removed.

I slept for some time 4 miles behind the lines and I wake to hear that they are many dead on both sides. I cry out, and I see that there are people worse off than me. Then I feel guilty that I am so selfish to just think about myself when so many others have lost their lives. I woke in the late evening. I was not aware of anything around me. I could be dead for all I know, and not realize it.

Ben Bird came along and poured water on my face to wake me to my senses. He said that the boys were a little bruised, and scared, but alive. I can back to my self and realized that I had to get a grip over my fear and get back to showing my warrior spirit again. My leg was dressed out in a splint, and I was assigned tent duties for the commander to write down the totals of the casualties and wounded. The count kept coming in as the reports were filed and it was overwhelming to consider how bad it is here! It was a nightmare that we could not wake up from, and we feared that this was only the beginning of terrible battle that might last for days. The boys came to get patched up and they set besides me, and they were bandaged and had burns on them from a cannon blast. It was bad, but at least we are all alive. After a few hours of sleep I was more like myself again, and my pain was bad enough to bring me back to reality. The good medicine was given out and I felt much better.

Reports came in and I was able to complete my findings to the commander. The count I came to was around 4.700 of our men were against over 20,000 of theirs! I threw up again when I thought about what a mad dogfight we were in! Three of us counted the roster and we renumbered it to make sure it was correct. We counted 267 of our men dead, and 456 wounded. 23 are missing and unaccounted for. On the Mexican side the tally was 594 men dead, 1,039 wounded, 1,800 possibly missing, and 294 captured as our prisoner. This was all overwhelming and hard to see what good cause would be worth the loss of so many lives: it was because of one man's goal to rival Napoleon! Well he has done that and we hope he sleeps well because none of us have lately.

Two other men looked it over and it was proper and as close as we could get it. A wagon was torn up to make a decent fire, as it is still too wet here to find any good wood that hasn't been soaked by the previous rains. We have a chance to eat something and the strong coffee was made. It was good and stout as any **Louisiana Coffee** I have ever drank. I felt much better and it was the start of things becoming right again. My boys came up to visit and they were sore and stiff so we walked them around to loosen them up. I have made a crutch from a green tree branch. It hurt to stand, but it is going to hurt for a while even if I sit. I remember how General Sam suffered so and now I know how he must have felt. We talked with the boys and we told them that we were proud of them and that they lived up to their name.

We grew tired and set down on a large stone fence. A few feet from us was a dead soldier, and we have the men take him to the field where the dead are being kept, to hold down the threat of disease, as we have seen how not tending to the dead has poisoned this land. The boys took us down about half a mile and we tried to talk about something else, but the subject of death stayed in our minds. We found ourselves talking about it to them as a way to clear the air and get it out of our minds. The boys are ordered to go and help with burial details. They would have made many bonfires but it is much too wet to have any dry wood to burn with out burning many good wagons that are needed for better purposes. There was a detail to go out and spread lime over the dead as it was much needed. We are still in shock and we are not alone. There are prayer meetings in the mess tent after supper and it was crowded with as many as could fit. People talked a great deal and I just listened intently, and tried to make sense of this mess. They had us 4 men to every 1 of ours. I felt sick when I thought of how we were so out numbered! This is madness and we need to be back home with our family where things are normal, and the life is much better, even on the bad days.

I felt foolish, feeling sorry for myself when so many are lost on both sides!

The question was: where is Santa Anna? We figured he is dead, or at the worst, he has escaped, somehow. We kept having our thoughts of our other battle against him, and we wondered what the outcome would be for this battle? We knew we had won, but without Santa Anna, it would be a hollow victory. Our ears still rang, and we wondered how anyone would be able to hear the bugle calls, or the commands. Ben Bird was tending to the wounded, and he came to check on me. I was just relieved that there were many survivors in our regiment considering the situation here. Once things were situated, the commanders came and sorted it all out. The picket lines were set for prisoners, and captured goods were piled up into wagons. I hobbled around to help write letters for those that could not write, and that was the best medicine for me. I reported to the commander's tent, and he asked me to rest, as he looked as bad as I felt. I poured him some coffee, and I brought some tobacco that was given me for writing a letter. He was pleased to see we thought of him well after what we have been through. This was not his doing as he was just put in charge of this mess. A captain came and reported that a number of prisoners were being brought in for his review. He made the following report, and General Taylor perked up: he knew this was some good news!

A farmhouse, a large **hacienda** was the focus of the battle as it was rich with goods that we needed, and it gave some cover from the battle as it set upon the ridge. This single farmhouse was now being coveted by both armies. The Mexicans called a truce and asked the Federals to surrender. Why admit defeat when you are the winner? It was a ploy for them to escape. It would be the best to take the hacienda under our control as it is very close by and it should be seized for its hayfield, and for it as a base of operations. It was there that a peasant farmer came into play. He was very nervous. This one wore simple clothes, and he stood out by his shiny and fancy boots! These were some boots that are much too fancy for a simple hay farmer. It was **Santa Anna** again, play-acting to a captive audience. He is a wily old fox, and as slippery as a wet rope. As he walked along, his men were so loyal they saluted, and some bowed in respect. Something that was not typical on a regular battlefield. We never saluted a commander out in the field, as it was like putting a target on their back. When the woodpile was taken down to light the night fires, Santa Anna's fancy uniform was found hidden under the pile. So it was a full day that had its reward. We were tired, and sick from the smell of death. Many more helped to spread lime and to quickly bury the dead. Our ears did not ring so bad now, but my leg really hurt worse than anything else. We said some prayers over them, as our enemy was worthy of respect. Still, we were sick to our stomach, like we drank some bad water. It was just our nerves, and some passed around a bottle to soothe some nerves. It sounded good, but not what I needed. I poured some over my wounds, and that was good enough. I wanted to be back home, and escape this place, as we were here to deliver horses, not dance with the Devil. Still there was celebration, and the duty roster was filled, and we had guard duty tonight. We are to sit and help keep watch from a large stone that sat high enough to keep watch over the valley. We are told to sleep for a while. Lightning does strike twice, and we were in its path both times. So we must be careful where we stand. We can hardly stand so we had better sit more these days.

Today we had reinforcements come to relieve us of duty. I had a headache that made it difficult to stand up for long. It seems that others are suffering a similar problem. There was a sick call, and many of us made our way to the wagons to be taken back to Fort Texas. The explosion of the ammunition depot has caused many to have problems standing, hearing, and riding a horse. We have had a difficult time doing our duties, and then trying to rest very well last night. We just felt that it has been some trying days and that there has been some real stress trying to catch up to Santa Anna. Now it is catching up to him, all the stress he has put us all under with his vanity to win.

Now that he is caught like a grasshopper in a spider web. There have been droves of Mexican soldiers surrendering, because the fight has left them. They have no heart for battle, and neither do I. Also some have come back with more fight stronger than ever before. So there is a need for some healing here to reason between us to get this settled once and for all. Only God could heal this.

We got orders to rest, and leave back for home tomorrow, as our duty is completed here. That is fine because there were some big war drums beating in my head all day. The field doctor said that many of us have broken eardrums from the blast. We have cotton in our ears, and a concussion in our heads. So they wrapped our heads with a bandage, and put us in a wagon for home. Ben Bird has a hurt arm but he has made himself busy so he did not have time to worry about anything. He found a spider web and put it into his wound to stop it from bleeding. He was farther away from the blast, and the cannon fire. We were just glad that it was over. Ben made a big kettle of mesquite leaf tea, and he gave it to a number of others, and it seemed to give them some relief. He also has made some willow bark tea, and that was useful to be able to think again without head troubles. Santa Anna must have a bigger headache than all of us put together, so we do not envy him at all. He was a sad, pathetic figure, and he was not the former soldier we remembered. He looked old and tired, and more worn than the clothes he wore as a disguise. He stands like a sore thumb, and like a sore thumb he has been a real pain. I hope that it was all worth it from the terrible looks of things.

We got close to Fort Texas, where we will rest a few days and then go home to be with our family again. This will be the best medicine to have hugs from the wife and children. We are given our leave, and signed the sick roster to be free of our regular duties for this battle. We are to be sent home along with our sons. Ben Bird has fulfilled his obligation also, and the Commander has signed the orders with a letter of accommodation for us serving Texas, and then to serve with the Federal States. We have to go and allow more able-bodied soldiers take over here. Santa Anna was marched around for us to get a good look at him. The shoe was on the other foot now as this is how the captured Commander Bowie was treated before he died so terribly at their hands. We felt that peace would be ours now. If not now, but before the year would be out there will be a lasting treaty that would put **Valesco** to shame. Santa Anna is taken away, and we are glad that he is not our problem any longer. His commanders will be mad as hornets as we have kicked the tree, hive and all.

Santa Anna in disguise.

CHAPTER FOUR

The return home from war.

March 2, 1847. We have a chance to rest a few weeks and we head home. We wanted to be back home again and look across our fields. It will be good to cross back over the black land prairies and be in the land of the Comanche and Kiowa again. They will be a welcome sight. Some might not see it that way, but we know that they are our true allies. After what we have been through we have a greater appreciation of our allies that we have before. The tejanos have proved that from the git-go. The Apache have been great too. We have been unlikely allies with a similar cause as we were with the Comanche, and Kiowa. We are not the normal allies, but dire situations have made us go beyond our fear, and ignorance of each other. We have written many letters to General Sam. We knew that he would appreciate some of our insight over the Buena Vista Battle. It was something to be proud of and it was also a day we hope we soon could forget. We have hoped to live down our other battles, but they live long into our memories. Talking about it in a letter to General Sam might give us some consolation so that that when we remember it we will be able to live with the events of that day. We are proud and humbled at the same time. We will rest and not have any cares for a while. There was a ball game and we watched them do something like Lacrosse. It was a nice distraction, and we rooted for our team made from some of the infantry under our commander, Zachary Taylor. This was the time for the youth, as I felt very old and tired beyond my years.

March 20, 1847. It is the day of the Winter Count. We have an invitation from the Apaches to visit them again. Since we are victorious in battle they would know that their land is now healed, and that their hunting will be better, and illness will leave their land, and water. They have a ceremony to honor the new children born after the last spring. They are held up high and given their names that they will be known by. They are passed around among the people so that they will be well known to them. We took each child and we looked it over like we were having an army inspection. They were each handsome and a wonder to behold. After seeing so much death it was great to celebrate life again. It gave us some consolation, and it gave us time to pause to think about the fact that life was going to continue after this. We will continue our lives and we will celebrate the small things as well as the large events. We later sat in their council house and we talked among ourselves and we answered their questions that they posed. It was an honor to be among them as they are a great nation. They honor us with a grand dance for fighting against great odds.

We are told of their view of the battle, and that they feared the cannons that were packed with 2 cannon balls, and all the smoke and noise that rose from the battle. Ben tells me that they have watched us fight from the top of a **mesa**, and they thought that we were crazy, like we are a **contrary.** We were greatly out numbered, and we fought like madmen to win against all odds. They are almost proud of us, if I could venture to say it. They have the big ceremony and they make the great dance with all the dancers and medicine men and their elders. They throw salt into all the four directions, and they burned many bundles of sage to help heal the earth from all the death it has witnessed. The Apache have a pipe ceremony and they make the boys part of it. They cough hard and they try to be brave. Sam Bird passes out from the smoke in their lodge. He has lost a great deal of blood, and he is still too weak, that is why we had him riding in a wagon, instead of on horseback. They killed a deer and have him eat its liver. He did not want to, but we encouraged him not to anger their medicine man. It was for his benefit, to make him stronger. It was no worse than we when hunted buffalo and ate the heart to make us brave and strong. They offered us some and we ate a bite of it and passed it along to the boys. Sam Bird ate most of it, and he felt worse for it. It was not enough as it was deemed proper to have a sweat lodge ceremony. He was put in the sweat lodge, along with the rest of us that fought in battle. We went along with their plans, as it was the custom to be appreciative to be honored in such a way. It felt terribly hot to the point of passing out and we were carried to the river's edge and put into the cold water to be revived. We were given shirts with painted signs on them to wear for good medicine. We felt very much alive and we will feel better from now on.

March 21st. It is good to be alive, and that our boys were not terribly hurt as some were. So we can count ourselves fortunate to be alive. Now we will enjoy everyday and celebrate the small things that come our way, and not take things for granted. We rested and we leave for home the next morning. We were so excited that we could hardly sleep. To see our wife, and our home again! The chores would seem like nothing, and the hardships we thought were bad seem not so, now. We traveled through the place of the Comanche and Kiowa. They saw our painted shirts and they marched us through their camps as heroes. They put turkey feather headdresses on us and painted our faces. They brought out the drums and they danced like there was no tomorrow. As much as we want to be home we have to stay here for a night to rest and be their honored guests. We sat back and ate a big feast of dried buffalo meat, corn from their corncrib. Their maidens danced for us and they made a good show of it. We were looking forward to just being home a few days, and not to sit a horse for hours and hours. We just sat back and we watched their ceremonies and we wondered how we came to this place in our life. It must be part of God's infinite plan for us to be a better steward of this land. They showed us their fields, and we thought that if they had a plow or two that they could feed their families better. I will ask Simon about getting them a plow to see if it might help them be more fruitful. Their **Qualls** came and sat besides us. Last time we were here she was mean and fierce for a woman. She sat politely and she never had a harsh word for us. She gave us a gourd full of water. She talked through Ben as an interpreter and she asked about my wife as she has heard that she was a **Qualls** too. So we are in good company and we made the most of our time with them. We sat in the place of honor and we respected their right to celebrate. There may be other battles here, but our time of fighting is over. We will just trade horses, and farm our land. That will be enough. Just to live and cherish each day.

March 25th. We are home again and the wife is most happy. She had cut her hair off fearing that I was dead because I was gone so long. I told her that her hair will grow back, as I am very much alive. She has no reason to morn me anytime soon. Phoebe runs down the road as she caught sight of us. I held her in my arms, and the boys ran up and kissed her. The dogs and cattle run in circles, as they know we are back. They know who loves them and it is a sight for sore eyes. Everyone here gets word that we are back and Simon comes to greet us. They want to celebrate us home, and I just want to rest. I am glad that they are happy that we are alive, and I let them make a fuss over us, as they do not understand what an ordeal we have been through these past weeks. We indulge them to visit and bring us gifts of food, and a new, handsome saddle was mine as the old one was very worn looking. I accepted it and I patted my friend on the back to show appreciation. They showed us where the barn was rebuilt, and that was present enough! Some army and some of the settlers from the Dove came here while we were gone and built it back better than ever. So there were many nice surprises. I just got down and lay in the dirt to show that I was thankful to be home. It seemed crazy to the others, but they would not understand how hard I have fought to have this place. The shade of the well was so inviting. I just sat there and rested all evening. I watched the wind blow the leaves of the gourd plants and the gourds swayed in the wind. The sun felt good on my face and I was ready to enjoy some days here at home. I thank God for all these little things that have made the trip home all worth it. Most of all we were alive and that is what counts the most.

March 28, 1847-It has rained for days, and we appreciate having too much of what we pray for, so often. The wind has blown down the windmill, and broke many trees. The river crossing to the fort is flooded terribly where it will be two weeks before we could cross over the Clear Fork. We have not been able to get the horses out to stretch their legs too much, and the boys are getting tired of being indoors. I don't blame them. I have took the time to work on their writing their letters better, and reading some to make them smart enough to write a bill of sale, or read a newspaper to know what is going on. We are patient, and the boys tried our patience.

March 30th. We have been ready to get out and look things over here. It is very wet, but we took them to the river, and some of it has gone down, as there was brush, and driftwood high into some trees along the bank. Much of the black dirt was washed away, and there was some interesting stones washed up that have been buried for a long time. They look like some of the shells like we saw at Galveston, years ago. Also there were large fish bones about. They had turned black from age. They were many about, so full of minerals, and shiny like glass! There were wonders all around the sandy ground, and it was a matter of what you wanted to pick up. The sea has been gone from here long since, and this recent flood has *uncovered something that only Noah and his ark might have seen!* We got a lasso off the horse and tied it to the saddle horn, and let the boys go down the side of the ravine, to what was an ancient beach. They brought back some real treasures that are most curious, and interesting. This has perked them up, and has kept them from fighting too much. We only allowed them to get what they could carry home, as some items were so big they could not be loaded up to take home. We told the boys we could get a wagon to come back and get some of these things when the ground dried out a bit more. There was much driftwood about, and it would not be a total waste of time to come back. It was good to see the boys excited about something, and some work could come out of it also. We were just in need of some outdoor activity ourselves, as we have become **barn spoiled**, living indoors, under a roof so often. We got home and showed the women our treasures. They enjoy collecting stones to put around the well, and where they plant the gourds. We took turns after dinner trying to figure out what some of these things were. One stone looked like a coiled up snake, as we found a small one farming sometime before. This time the stone was several feet across, and the boys took great care bringing it back home in one piece. It was a beauty, and a wonder of creation to see it. We brought back the smaller seashells, made from stone. The women were glad we were back, as we had tarried too long, as we were glad to be out of the house. The women have been busy cooking and cleaning things with us being out of the way. **Sarah** made us hang up our boots on the pegs, so we would not bring clay, and sand into her clean house. We ate on the front porch and the women had a fit over what the boys have brought home. I gave Phoebe the heart-shaped shellfish, and she marveled over the star pattern on it that looked like a strange sand dollar. She sat with it in her lap all evening, and she slept with it beside her bed. The boys slept on the floor, as they were tired out from toting the large stone so far. We watched the fire and drank coffee. We made plans to do something useful. I told Ben Bird we would go out in a few days and get that driftwood for firewood, and for some furniture we could build from it as Simon the blacksmith has done. There was plenty to do, but the ground was too wet to plow, or to do much of anything else. Tonight we dream of the things we will do as the weather will allow. We will draw out the land to map out our crops, and which fields are useful this year.

Fossil shells from the flood.

April 5th. It is dry enough to get out to do something outdoors. We took the wagons out and picked up driftwood. Since my leg was finally out of a splint I was ready to get out and about. I hobbled about and I looked for a good reason to get out. I used a walking stick like General Sam to keep from falling down the steep hill. The boys were distracted wanting to look for treasures, but we told them we had to fill up both wagons, and tied down the loads before we could look for goodies made from stone. The boys went to work and had the wagons loaded up good. We had the axes busy chopping the wood to fit the wagon, and a few stumps looked useful for a table-top. Now we had the chores finished, it was time to rest for an hour. The boys were ready to stomp around to look for the treasures, so we sat and watched them. They ran around like crazy, and we laughed at them being so funny. They brought back some of the black fish bones that were quite large, and more shells for their mother's garden. I told them to find something for Phoebe.

They came back with a flat rock that had the clear outline of a brown fish. There were some most strange things here, and we will have to have a pow-wow here sometimes, to bring our Indian brothers here. We made the boys rest for an hour, and we kept watch while they slept. I hitched the horses back and we left for home. My stomach growled like I was in church. The boys laughed at me saying it was that bear bacon we have eaten. I would enjoy some bear bacon right now, but it is time to unload, and clean up. We ate like it was our last meal. Later we took the map out and plotted our fields. We planted some squash from the seed stocks, and there was much to do. We walked along with the planting stick and poked a hole in the ground, and the boys followed planting the seed, and covering the hole. It was late afternoon and we finished the field. We had more seed, so we planted another field. Our corn was coming up nice, and it was not washed out from all the rain we had. It was late and we cleaned up at the horse trough. We brought the fan of the windmill into the barn, to fix it back. It might be a job for Simon to do, as we are all thumbs sometimes. Some rest is in order, and our eyes are too tired to write anymore today. Sleep will be welcome.

April 8th. We went out and looked at the corn. Some buffalo have run through our fields, so we have to either run them off, or hunt them. One of **Ben**'s best fields have been stomped on, so he was mad as some hornets. I learned some Cherokee words I have never heard before! He seldom gets mad, and he was all fired up today. It looks worse that it is, and most times it will come back stronger from all the manure they have left. I was staying out of his way, and I toted extra ammunition, my wagon, and an extra horse. He was on foot, and we just tried to keep up. The boys just were quiet, and in awe of his bold trek across the prairie. Well he found them several miles away, and he got out his arrows, and then a rifle. He cut down a quantity of them where we would have four a piece to butcher. Josiah took the horse and got the women to help butcher the slain animals. They were surprised at the zeal that the quiet **Ben** took to fill up the smoke house for both of us. The women showed the boys how to get started, and what not to do. The boys had to do the heart removal, and the liver is what the women like best. So it was good we had got out early, as it would be an all-day-thing to butcher so many animals. The boys were good workers, as they like to eat a good steak, and they did not mind the time it took to do things right. Some vultures were flying overhead, and that brought some Kiowa that were out on a hunting party. We offered them two of the slain animals, and they took the ones we had not yet butchered. We were pleased that they came along, so nothing was going to waste. They gave us some fine flints, and a nice pinto pony, as a trade. They made a **travois** in a short time, and it loaded up headed for home. They sang a happy hunting song, and shouted their "thanks" where it carried over the prairie for miles. It was a pleasant song, even though I did not know most of the words. So what started off as something bad, made us benefit as the day wore on. Ben was smiling now that he had the nice flints that were like black and red glass; and the strong horse that would be good to ride, or put behind a plow. So maybe we will look on things as a mixed blessing when trouble arises, and wait and be more patient in the future, when things go wrong.

April 24th, 1847-We have been unloading the smokehouse today. We brought Simon some of the good smoked meat, since he has been so busy making iron implements. He was proud to get a nice smoked roast. He took his knife, and cut off some pieces to eat, and he cut some for his wife and children. They ate heartily. Simon has made a new plow, and we offered him to barter for it, if he felt the meat was good enough. He had not had much time to hunt, and his family needed something beside salt pork to eat. They were happy, and they said it would be a fair trade for some roasts, or some tasty steaks from a shoulder, or two. We said three complete shoulders would feed them for a month, and they agreed. We shook hands on it, and it was a done-deal. The boys will bring the shoulders of meat, and bring back the plow this evening. We have to teach them about bartering, and ways to make a good trade, since they are getting more grown by the day. We enjoyed our visit. Simon's wife got out their homemade fiddle to play for us, and she played joyful music for our benefit. The boys clapped, and Simon danced for us. We danced too, and they laughed, and clapped, and enjoyed being together. It got to be early afternoon, so we had to head home to tell the boys what we wanted them to do. They were happy to drive the wagon over to visit and Simon's, as he would be showing them a lesson in working iron, as he often does. I like that the boys are so smart, and it is good for them to be independent from us, sometimes. They will learn to wrought iron, tame horses, and hunt, so they will be well rounded in their knowledge. We told the wife of our day, and she hated that she missed the music. I will get her out more, and maybe it will be dry enough to go to the fort this week. She mentioned for us to go to church next third Sunday of the month. We promised to get our act together, and do more for her, as we do for others. I told her of the trade for the plow, and she hugged me for being wise. We took Phoebe out to teach her to ride better, and she had a great time. Sarah rode along, and she knew her way around a horse since she was old enough to set one. We enjoyed the day and we rode until it was dark. We crossed paths with the boys, and they rode with us back home. We got cleaned up, and ate a light supper of steak sandwiches, which Simon had showed us. We read the Bible out loud, and the boys took turns reading out loud.

We read FIRST CORINTHIANS, Chapter One. "God will give you wisdom."

May first. We were awakened by the sound of our horses being stolen. The dogs were barking, and they had got someone by the **breeches**. It was other deserters from the Mexican army. It seems that we are Easy-Pickens for them since we live so far out on the prairie. We caught one varmint, and we rode hard to catch the others. One fell from his horse and he appeared to be sick, as he could hardly stand up. He was to weak to fight back, so we let him be. The other stopped riding hard as he could hardly sit a horse. He knew that we would be terribly angry when we did catch up to him. It all seemed so odd, so we made a smudge fire to call for help. Ben Bird was up early, so he came in a short time. The boys had come too, and brought the others bound in the wagon. We secured the prisoners, and searched them for weapons. Ben Bird asked them in Spanish, "What were they up to?" They replied that they were left for dead, as they were too sick to be any use to their army. We offered to help them as long as they did not take arms against us, or for them to try to harm us in the process. They swore to be peaceful, if we could just help them. We saw vultures circling a few miles away. We rode to their camp and there were four dead there that we buried. Ben Bird tended to the men, and he pitched a wall tent that the boys always kept in the wagon bed. It seems that their foodstuffs were spoiled, and they had drank bad water. Their foodstuffs were not kept in barrels, and the rain had kept them wet, and soured. It was too poor to eat in those wet tote sacks. We burned all that, to keep someone else from eating the bad food. The smoke brought two **Texas Rangers** that were out on patrol, looking for trouble. We told them of what had been going on, and that the men had stolen our horses. They offered to hang the men, and we said that were weren't in the mood for revenge, especially after burying their dead, and these men were not far from death. Something would not be right about that. They shook their heads, and we insisted that they were treated well. We told them we had done so after the Battle of San Jacinto, and we remembered how to talk over the events following the battle. We told them of our plans to help the sick men. They were weak that they are only a threat to themselves, and no one else. The boys rode back to tell the women of where we were. They rode back with some good broth in a kettle, and some full medicine pouches sent by the women. They are afraid of some illness, as children, they had seen the Typhoid, and Small Pox at New Orleans, among the Irish immigrants the Cherokee encountered during their southern move to east Texas. So it was best that we were away from the cabin for some time, to give them some peace. We told the boys to go back home, and help them, as they had no contact with anyone. It just seemed to be food poisoning, and that was all, we all agreed. So the boys brought them back the news, and they will stay close to home to help them tend to things, and to settle their nerves over worrying too much. We stayed and talked over the news we have heard, and asked about the latest on the war at Del Norte. Ben Bird asked the Mexicans what they knew, and they had some insight into recent events that we had not known, and they would not say too much more. They have been through a great deal, and they have suffered enough. We let them rest and watched over them in case they need our help. We did for them what we could with what little we have.

One of the Mexican soldiers died last night, and we gave him a good burial. The other man was stronger, but understandably sad over the death of his friend. We allowed him to say some words over his friend's grave, and the Rangers felt it was time to take him to Bird's Fort. We would go with them to ensure the prisoner's safety. I was fairly sure that he was safe, but I wanted to make a report to Captain Patterson, and let him know what I knew of these Mexican deserters, and the "stragglers" we keep finding. We made the fort by evening, so we had time to report, and to get a load of coal, and iron that Simon had ordered. The quartermaster asked us to bring more horses, as many are going to be needed for the war across the Rio Grande. We told him we have seen some in a canyon not too far away, and that we would catch them the first chance we had. He said to bring, any, or all we find, and we will, when we can catch our breath! We stopped and bought something for the wife, and children, since they have been so helpful, and not complaining when times were difficult. They deserved a reward, and we had some money coming from the last horses we have sold. We also got some trade goods that might come in handy, in a pinch. We made it home by nightfall, and the wives, and our boys were glad that we were back home, and safe. It was nice to be under a roof again, and to have the love of our family, and a warm hearth to sleep by.

Tonight, we read: HEBREWS Chapter 13, verse 5: "God will never leave you, or forsake you!"

CHAPTER FIVE

William Goyens: a freed slave like Andrew.

May 5th, 1847. We went to Bird's Fort to take the windmill blade to be fixed. Simon has been too busy making new wagons to sell. We got word that they were building a new fort west of here. It was pushing towards the old Wichita's land, and the land that is part of the **Comancheria**. I wonder what **Chief Peta** will think of new fort. It might not set well with his tribe. This fort has been outgrown for a while since trade days have been so overcrowded. There were many, many new settlers here, and it was funny how green they looked! That might have been me at some point, but it has been twelve years ago when I came from Louisiana to **Nacogdoches**, with **Delephine to talk with General Houston**. It is awkward how so many people stared at me, and Ben Bird walking around. We wish we could sit a few of them down like we were in a council, and educate some of them about living out, and dealing with some of the people that we know as good friends. Then they would have something to stare about! We went to the Officer of the Day, and Captain Patterson had a guest: it was Commander **William Goyens**! He was a sight for sore eyes. He looked great, and that life has been good for him. He said he has a daughter now, and we caught up on the latest. We all went to a café set up in place of the regular commissary. We wanted something good to eat, and have a place to get out of the captain's hair. The captain mentioned the horses we have promised, and we told him he would have them before the next trade day. The war effort has taken many horses away from here, and many more are needed for people that are living in this area. They offered top dollar, or trade, as always. We would come through for them with more than they would expect. Commander Goyens asked to go with us back to our homesteads, and to go round up the horses this week. We agreed, but worried that we had not given the women any notice of visitors coming. Other than that we were fine. We went over the Trinity River crossing for home. The wife was happy to see him, and the boys went to get Sam Bird, Ke-Ke, and little Jacy. So we would have a celebration today. We showed the commander around, and he asked us to call him, "William" from now on, as we are both out of the army now. So "William" it is. He was most impressed over our fields of corn, and squash. He liked our smokehouse, and we promised him some goods to take with him when he leaves in a week. He asked if he could join in on the capture of the wild horses. He is the one that could still teach us about horses, so we agreed. It was exciting to see our old friend again. **Phoebe** took a liking to William, and he enjoyed her, as he has a daughter of his own. She sat on his knee, and she was so sweet, and a bit of a pest asking so many questions. She asked some interesting ones. That is why she is so smart. He held little Jacy, and she felt of his face, and his beard. She laughed, and was very sweet, and wonderful. William smiled over all the children's attention. William said that his store, hotel, and livery stable, has made him richer beyond his dreams. We could see that, because he has employed over half of Nacogdoches with his business sense. He worked harder than any two men I have seen. He has taught me a great deal as a mentor to me. So it is only fair that he has prospered so well. Again he could teach me a few things, so I listen, and take note of any suggestions, or comments he has. He wasn't made commander because he was good looking. He has taught me as much as Ben Bird. Well we visited and went to bed early, as we are to go out and catch some horses tomorrow. William told Phoebe a bedtime story about our days living in east Texas, with the Cherokee. He told her of the time I had to catch some ponies for my future father-in-law, Chief Bowles, to make him happy. She laughed when he told the part about me roping the wild horse, and the horse ran off and dragged me over the cactus patch with me holding on for dear life. He can tell a story better than me, anytime. Sarah laughed as she heard William tell it, and it was a funny picture to see. I think I still have stickers in me from that day. It was all a small price to pay to enjoy my life as it is today. Thank the good Lord I survived to see these days. It is a wonder that I am here to tell it, at all. The wonders never cease, on a daily basis. Tonight we read FIRST CORINTHIANS, First Chapter, verse 30.

"God will give you Wisdom."

We went out early before daybreak and built a corral from some of the broken tree limbs that are all over. We found some stout ones, and we found a circle of cedar trees and cut the lower limbs off to use them as ready vertical set posts.

They formed a natural corral, and we added the broken limbs as horizontal cross members. We left the front barely open, and covered the rest with the cedar limbs we have just removed to hide the fence's cross members. We went out and caught some colts without too much trouble. The mare's followed close and tried to nip at us as we tried to wrangle them into the corral. We kept them fed with some oats we got at the fort, as an enticement. Other horses came by afternoon, as a spring fed creek was close by. We used a rope lasso to keep them pent up horses back from the opening. We put more cross members in front of the corral to make it hard for any horses to avoid the rope barrier. We were attentive and hid as much as we could and stayed down wind from being detected. By the end of the day we had seven horses: four colts, and three mares, and no stallions dumb enough to be captured yet. We kept watch for trouble of any deserters, or stragglers, or thieves. We kept a good watch and built a fire behind the corral to make the coyotes stay away from our colts, as they could sneak in below the barriers if they wanted. We put more limbs around to fill in the spaces, and it was more secure. We took turns keeping watch, and we ate beef jerky, and slept under the stars. It was a full moon so we had plenty of light to keep the good watch over things. The coyotes howled all night, and yipped at each other from afar. It sounded like my attempt to sing something. Well we did keep a watch while we both got some sleep. I wish now that the boys were here to help out, but we were afraid not to leave the farm guarded with so many deserters about these days. We managed to get four and a half hours of sleep and that will have to do for the next day or so. It made for a long day Wednesday. William asked me to rest from noon to four, and then he would rest. We had finally caught a stallion that was tempted to join the others, and it will be a matter of time before others will try to vie for the mares' attention. We took turns keeping watch to make sure no one takes our horses from under our nose.

May 8th. So it is worth the loss of real sleep for another day. Ten horses will bring ten month's of our old army wages. We were laughing about how hard we worked to make ten dollars a month, and now we can make that in a few days, if we don't mind getting less sleep. Some Kiowa came to check us out, and they brought us three horses since we have shared the buffalo hunt with them, so we had three more "ten dollar army horses." That might have been those Kiowa talking to each other, instead of coyotes' yipping all night. It seems they have been watching us trying to catch horses and felt we needed a few more. We could get more at the fort to sell them to the new settlers, but the army needs them worse for their **remudas.** At least we don't have to break them. That makes them sold cheaper than normal. William was telling me how funny I looked being dragged through the brush, thorns, and cactus, when I first tried to catch some horses. He was hiding in the brush with the elders of the tribe judging me to see if I was worthy to join the tribe, when he first met me at the Cherokee camp, years ago. Now it was the Kiowa watching us, and they probably think that we are amateurs compared to them. It makes it that more embarrassing now that I think about it. I told Goyens what I thought. Goyens laughed, and I laughed too, because it must have been quite a sight to see a green horn trying to rope a wild pinto pony. We have come a far cry from there, but we still have some things to learn. It is my turn for the watch, so it will be easier with the Kiowa helping scare off intruders that come close by. We both slept like babies, and made up for lost time on sawing some logs, snoring big time.

William Goyens

May 10th. The trees were full of birds this morning, and hearing them chirp happily made it nice to drink some coffee, and to talk about our plans for the future to an old friend. We went to the fort to sell our horses. We got a trade voucher, in lieu of payment, as money is still scarce around here. Something in trade is better than nothing to put in the pot! We got sixty dollars each and it was enough to get us by until next year, in case the corn crop is not good enough. William Goyens was happy just to be out on the prairie, and the trade was good for some good relations with the army, which has asked him to scout for them, and for him to bring General Sam back around here again. He needs to come out here and spend some days like we have. We have a new governor named George Wood. We wonder what he will be like, if he would remember to include the Tejanos in his government. In San Antonio the Tejanos have lost much of their power in government, and many new settlers who have not fought in any battles, or spilled a drop of their own blood, are talking the reigns of power! It makes me shudder to think what might follow in the new politics, and how it might affect the price of our crops at the gristmill, or our peace at home. We chewed the fat about that one all the way back to the fort, and it was the talk all over the fort, everywhere we went. Mister Goyens had made many new friends here, and he seems to never meet a stranger, as he is so out-going. He has people scratching their heads and thinking as he was speaking to just a few persons, and he now has a sizable crowd about him. He would make a good preacher from the way he spoke so well. People were asking him questions on everything from horses to politics, and he was sharp as ever. It is easy to see how he is a deacon, and an elder in his church. A few had criticism for him, and he answered them in a calm, confident tone, that spoke with authority. So that was that. Those people lost their thunder, and others came to hear him speak close to the front gate.

May 14th. We went out among the corn to see the full ears formed from the tassels. The boys gave him the tour, and they were showing him the highlights of the crops, and they showed him their stone treasures that they keep in the gourd patch. He was impressed, and asked to see the place where all these things were found. We saddled up and took him there to spend the afternoon. We walked along and looked at the place where the river was so high before. Now it was a tame little brook that went along a sandy river bottom. It was plain to see the driftwood that was lodged in the top of some trees, and bushes. William called the strange stones "fossils." He said that these were the remains of past animals that were so old that they turned to stone.

These were full of minerals. He picked up a heart shaped stone, and said it was a sea urchin, much like you might find at the gulf coast. It was exciting to think that that coast has moved three hundred miles southeast of here. He saw the big black fish bones, and said that this was some mighty beastie that ruled over the water at one time. There were some large teeth about, and he said that this thing would make a 100-pound garfish look like a puppy in comparison! It made for some lively discussion. He put a few stones in his saddlebag to take home for his children, as a gift for them. The boys brought him a few cone shaped fish teeth from the ground, and they were much like an alligator's. Goyens stepped it out, and he figures this animal was over 40 feet long! We thought an eight-foot gator was bad, back in Louisiana. This one trumped it as a "biddy." We pondered it all, and we got very hungry. We caught a few rabbits and cooked them over the fire. Goyens showed the boys how to make a better fire that burned hotter, with less wood. He dug out a small fire pit and showed them how to pick out the best kindling wood. He was a blacksmith as a youth, so he knows many such tricks of the trade. So there is always a lesson to be learned, no matter what you think you know. We brought a few rabbits home for the women, and we settled in for the night. Goyens went out with his horse and rode for a while to have some time alone. He came back the next morning, and he helped me put the fan back on to the windmill. The women cooked us some boiled eggs, and we sat under the shade and enjoyed them. Red Bird rode up and he said that some buffalo had crossed his northwestern fields, and that we ought to get a few of them. Goyens was for it as he was always ready for something to do. We let him lead the way, and he tracked them to the Clear Fork. We killed one a piece, and it was a good hunt. The rest we will save for another time. The boys cut out their hearts and we had to eat a few bites from each, as we had done in the past. The livers we cut out for the women to have, as it is their favorite part of the hunt. We made some travois and went back home. The women danced around, as we have been good hunters. We gave them the livers. We moved the travois downwind of the house, to the smoke house. There, Goyens showed the boys how to butcher the animals more efficiently. He divided up the meat into quarters, and left the other butchering for later. He cut the best flank pieces into strips, and he hung them on the meat hooks, and we put the rest into barrels to cure out. We put the mesquite to burn with some pecan wood. It all smelled so good. The ladies had a shoulder roast cooking in a pot, and it was all very good. No one will go hungry around here. Goyens said that he needed to get back home tomorrow as the steam ship was leaving tomorrow, if the river was high enough to go. It looked like a good rain was coming, so it was good timing, but we hated to see our good friend Goyens leave.

May 16th. Our friend has left for home as the rain brought the river up high enough to float a big boat. He gave us a letter from General Sam, and it was quite an ear full as he wrote on the front and back of five pages. He said for us not to worry about him, or his family. He would visit at a time that was good for us, and that we should write him more often. We will, and we will invite him to see the new fort being built to honor commander Worth. He said that James Knox Polk is now the president of Federal States. He said that he has worked with him, and that he is a decent, and just man. We took the letter and put it in our Bible for safekeeping.

May 26th. We went to trade day at the fort. It was busy as usual, and we found us a spot to set up our goods. The women had made some nice clay pots, and they have made some nice shirts to sell. I could not see how they do all the things that they can do. They keep us well dressed and have time to sew enough to sell. We had two extra horses for trade that are gentle, as the boys have trained it to be so. Sam Bird has taught Josiah to be a great horseman, as he was not always very good in the saddle. There were many lookers, but none had enough money to pay what they were worth. Josiah considered some money with a fair saddle for trade, and he asked me if I thought it was fair. I said that it was up to him, and that it seemed good to me. They agreed, and they shook hands as fair gentlemen. Josiah wrote out a bill of sale as I have showed him. He put his stamp at the bottom, shaped like a star with crossed arrows under it. He had carved a small piece of cedar and he used some ink to print it. He has practiced carving on a piece of cut potato to get the design right. It looked smart, and it stands out as a good idea. He wore the stamp around his neck, tied to a leather string. I liked that he was so bright to think of such things. So the boys can teach and learn from each other, and they could show me a few lessons sometimes. All the shirts were sold, and there were orders for others to fit some that were tall and had trouble getting clothes that fit well. They paid up front, and the ladies used a string and a ruler to write down their measurements. They put the string around certain points and then measured the string on the yardstick. They too were very sharp and I marveled over the company I keep. They paid up front, and it was nice to see that we were all good businessmen and women. The boys have brought their fossils, and sold a few of the small ones for a silver dollar each. They kept the large stone seashell in the back of the wagon.

They sold tickets from a cut piece of paper with Josiah's stamp on it. They have made 3 dollars selling tickets for a dime a piece. An educated man caught sight of the coiled-shaped fossil, and he offered twenty silver dollars to buy it! It was a lot of money these days, and Josiah said, "No thanks." The man named Doctor Ken Steigman offered the same money to see where the boys found it, and he asked me if we could show him our secret meeting place by the river. I met the man, and he worked for a museum up north, and he was looking to find something unusual to bring back from Texas. I thought it over, and I agreed. The wife did not like strangers going over the Comanche and Kiowa's land. I told the man I would show him the place, if he would be careful and considerate of where he was. He is to buy some trade goods if he was to go to Indian lands. I told him it was the way to go there and pay for safe passage back and forth. He asked me to go with him to pick up some trade goods inside the trading post. He bought a good many knives, and iron pots, and the usual glass pony beads. He seemed to have plenty of money, and I was surprised how he could get so much in goods with real money in his hands. This looked to be a profitable day, so we thought it all over, and finally the wife agreed. Ben Bird did not like taking the stranger to the meeting place. I told him that a museum collects treasures for people to ponder, and appreciate the wonder of it. It was as when the people paid to see Josiah's fossils in the back of the wagon. He still was not happy with me today, as he feared trouble might grow out of it. I was sad that my brother was mad at me, and I just left him alone until he felt ready to talk with me. Still I did not like it when he would not speak for a while. The man rode back with us and he had hired a wagon to bring back some stones from the river. He had hired a few men to go with us, and I told them not to raise weapons upon any Indians we meet, or they could not come with us. We would all die if they did. They said they would be peaceful, and just do digging as they were told. That seemed to pacify Ben Bird, and he spoke to me, finally. I was relieved, as I was not used to my brother being angry with me, as it was an uncommon event. They made their way to our cabin, and they are to stay in the barn. The man pitched a tent and stayed there. The men seemed fine in the barn. We went to bed early, as we are to leave out early in the morning.

Tonight we read: FIRST PETER, Chapter 5: "Membership in the body of Christ."

We went out in the morning after the men helped us do the chores. We went out and made it close to the meeting place, and some Kiowa stopped us. They raised their lance in the air, and we made the trade signs. I told the men to keep away from their guns. Ben Bird did all the negotiations, and they seemed a bit leery of it all. I showed them a fossil stone that we looked for, and they nodded knowing what we were looking for. We brought out all the trade goods, and they picked what they wanted, and then they pointed the way to travel to find the bend in the river. We went on and they followed at a distance and watched us. The men were nervous, and I told them to act right, and all will be well as guests on their land. They did so and set to picking up some stones that Doctor Steigman has directed. I showed him the place where the large fish bones were. I told him that it was over 40 feet long, and his jaw dropped when I showed him the giant outline of the great skeleton of the ancient alligator. He just about shook, and fell over when he saw it. He did not believe his eyes. He said that he had heard of such things, but has never seen this in its natural state. It was laid out as it was in its life. I have seen a smaller one in the side of a creek bank much farther out when I was looking for some horses. I asked him not to go past where we have agreed to stay for his own safety, since he was a green horn. He did some drawings, and I offered to do one for him. Farther down we found the skull of the beastie. It looked much like a horse's head, as it was broad, and flat on top. It had deep-set eyes, and several rows of long teeth that were most frightening. The bottom jaw was close by, and we put them together after a little work. It made the bad bear look like a kitty cat! We think Doctor Steigman got his money's worth, as he had found more than just some sea urchins, and clamshells. He said several times, "this is remarkable!" He wrote down a ton of notes, and we stepped out the length of the beastie, and it was over 47 feet long, not counting the head, which was at least five feet long. Josiah lay next to it and he was just a little taller than it was. There were several pieces of other beasties that the rain has uncovered. So there was much to wonder, as this was a most fearful creature in its time. Doctor Steigman's helpers were just besides themselves trying to figure it all out. They were impatient as he did several drawings before he would let the men move anything. I made two drawings and Dr. Steigman asked to have one for his records. We had an interesting day, and the men were packing up the treasures in wooden crates packed with buffalo grass for padding. The Kiowa watched from a hilltop, and they seemed amused that they profited from some rocks that lay abundant on the ground. We got packed up, and the doctor asked to stay another day as the sun was setting. Ben Bird said it would not be a good idea to push the Kiowa's patience. So that was that, and we headed back home with all the new found treasures. We can't wait to show the women what we have found.

The Ancient Alligator.

June 1st, 1847. The good doctor has left and we can get back to normal. We have a tidy sum of money put back from this month, and the corn crop is getting close to being ready for harvest. The blue corn quickened, and we went out and the whole family was out with baskets ready to fill. We have a full day and it was a relief to see the fruit of our efforts in the corncrib. The corncrib filled up, and we might have to build another to accommodate the yellow corn. It is a nice problem to have, and with the money Doctor Steigman gave us, there was the chance to build a nice one. We went to Simon's and bought some of his metal hinges, and we found we have a good many nails left over. He had a pile of lumber he did not need, so we gave him some baskets of corn, and he was happy with the barter. We loaded up the wagon and headed home. His boys came along to help us. We had the boys dig out all the dirt for the crib. We supervised, and saved on our bad back. We had much progress, and the ladies had a supper of **ma'chu** made of blue and yellow corn. The boys dug down fifteen feet, and hit a big layer of sandstone, so it was time to stop digging. We made a ladder to bring baskets of dirt up, and we used some fieldstones to shore up the sides of the walls. We mixed some mortar and set it all together. We said that this would also make a good storm cellar if we needed it. It was a nice dry place, and the work was done in no time since we had so much help. We dug out a small fire pit in the bottom, in case we needed it for the future. The boys dug post poles, and we found some cedar poles from some trees broken by a storm. We helped set the poles and placed rocks around them to secure them. The rest of the lumber was just enough to make a nice shack above it to make it good and dry. We made progress and it was past dark when we came inside. The roof would be left for tomorrow morning.

We read the Epistle of JUDE. "DO NOT embrace, or listen to heretics."

June 2. Well the heavy rain came early this morning and our corncrib is now our new **cistern**. It goes that way sometimes, and we will just take the other corn to the gristmill. We went out and surveyed it, and it looked to be holding up well. We went on and it was too wet to work outside, and the corn will plump up a bit from some rain. We got cleaned up so we would not ruin the clean cabin, so we would not have to sleep in the barn for crossing the wife. It continued to rain so we sit inside and try to do something useful. We took time to do some reading, and to write General Sam a letter as we have promised to do. We told him of some of our recent events, and that we have been busy to do as we have promised in the Great Council, to promote goodwill, and trade between us, the army, and the local tribes. I hope he does not think us too bold to bring the doctor on to Kiowa lands, and to bring out the strange remains of the ancient animal for the museum. I have sent him a drawing I did of it, and he will be interested in something besides politics for a change. We gave him much encouragement, and asked him to come here before the fall comes, to stay, and visit with us. I did invite him to bring the family, and I sent him our well wishes for his good health, as he suffers from his battle wounds so much. We tried to be upbeat, and tell him the story of the bad bear, and something that might make him laugh. It is easier to laugh than cry sometimes, and our good friend needs some encouragement since he lost his bid to be governor. In his letter he did not have good words for him and that he had some terrible plans to implement when he got into office. I gritted my teeth as I read some of his words, and it did not sound like the General Sam that I know. I read the letter to the wife to get her impressions, and she laughed at me, as my words "seem like a delirious person," she said. Well I can ramble on, but it can make for a good read for our friend, who loves to get letters. I added some things about William Goyen's visit, and we managed to write four pages for him to read. I wrote out some scriptures that I found comforting, and I thought it was a good way to end it on a positive note.

June 6th. It has dried out enough to harvest the corn. Members of the farmers co-operative came and helped us harvest our crop and they took it to the gristmill so it would not rot from all the rain. We are to go tomorrow and help another farmer take in their crop, and it was pleasant to have some many hands being helpful. We felt fortunate to get the job done in a few hours, and the corn was taken to the mill to get them busy, before things get bogged down in line waiting. We asked, "Who can we help?" It was to go to the Torian's to help them raise a barn. We got all our tools and put them together to have them ready. We took half a keg of nails we had in the barn, and we brought a few good hens for their egg production. The wife would go with us and she brought some things as a gift for them. The boys put out plenty of hay, and made sure that the pond was cleaned of lily pads for the cattle to drink better. We left out, and hoped to have a clear day to work tomorrow. We set up some tents at their place to make sure we would be up early to get things started. We visited a while, and then we turned in early.

Tonight we read: SECOND CORINTHIANS, Chapter 12, Verse 9. "God's Grace is sufficient."

CHAPTER SIX

The Good and Bad Neighbors.

June 7th, 1847. We went out to the barn raising at the Torian's place. We had permission to cut down a stand of persimmon trees for roof gables and porch supports. We let the younger men swing the axes, and we helped plan out the foundation. Ben Bird took a forked green stick and he walked about to find some water on their property. After some walking he found just the right place for a well to be dug. Some people were putting stone in the bed of some wagons for their fireplace, and their well. We asked Torian's wife which design she wanted for her home, as we had ideas for two different cabins that were popular. She was happy with either one, so we told her of the design that we used for our home, and that it has served us well. I stepped it out, and we put down stakes to mark it off. We told her it should face the east, for the benefit of the sunrise to light the kitchen well, and the rooms would be cooler in the summer. She agreed, and we set about to cut some logs for her cabin. They needed something more than a barn to stay in. She chose a stand of trees that did not shade the house, and that would make way for her rose, and herb gardens. We obliged to do as she wished. In a few hours there were the foundations of a nice comfortable home. Several men continued to cut the trees we marked, and several others used wedges to split several large logs. Another man used a double axe to knock the bark off the top and bottom of the log lengthwise to make it flat like it was an Indian bow. Another man marked where the notches went to secure the logs to each other. It was all well and done, with the roof left for the last day. A man drilled a hole into the log, and a hardwood peg was hammered in place. A stonemason was putting together a nice fireplace that was red and yellow sandstone. Mrs. Lucinda Torian said her last fireplace had a mud, and stick base, and that it had kept the house very smoky on some windy days. She cried, and she was happy with the nice cabin for their new home. The women have put together a nice quilt for her as their gift, and they had some seed pots full of flower seeds for her. John Torian helped stack the logs, and he was piling up stones for the hearth, and fireplace. The boys were helping dig the well, and they took turns when they tired out. The well was close to the house, and it would not be too terrible to haul water for either of them. We put up the roof gables and then helped stack the logs. It all came together well as most had helped build a good many cabins. It would be better than the tent that they had been staying in. We had enough wood the make a shelter for their animals, and it was fitting that they enjoy some protection from the elements, too. More people came to help. It was good as we were all tired out. They took up the slack, and they have brought food, so we were all encouraged by them being late, like the "workers in the vineyard." We cleaned up, and ate something good, and we felt invigorated to do more. We rested for an hour and then we helped with the well. The younger people had it dug out about fifteen feet, and then they hit the water table. The water was clear, and sweet. It was not salty, or bad tasting with Sulphur as some do in this area. So everything was going to plan. The new arrivals took over, and they placed the stones in the sides of the well, as it would be more solid, and cleaner that way. We sat and made shingles with a spoke shaver, and a machete. We made a dozen or so then turned it over to another man, as we were tired, and it is dangerous to do when you get too tired. We were told to rest, and we looked over the handiwork of our day's labor. Thirty-eight persons did a good job here, today. We would spend the night and finish up the details by tomorrow afternoon. It was nice to meet so many new people that have joined the church, and they were some good, decent folks.

We read, Matthew Chapter 20—"The Workers in the Vineyard."

June 10th, 1847. We are still tired form our days working on the cabin. We had to catch up on our chores, and get things accomplished here. Our cow had a new calf, and she was bossy. She butted me with her head, when I turned my back to put out some hay. We will call her "Bossy" from now on. My back did not feel so bad now, as it was quite painful from her. I am sorry that I complained. She was such a sweet cow, until today. I warned the boys to watch out for her contempt for anyone close to her new baby. I will get a mule to put in with her, to keep her company, so she would feel better protected. We went around and found plenty to do. We took some broken limbs, and sawed them to fit inside the chicken house to give the birds a place to roost off the ground. The boys came by and had the idea to go fishing tomorrow, if it was good weather. I agreed, as they acted very well at the house-raising, and they were some good carpenters these days. I told the wife, and she liked the idea of a big fish to eat. Josiah said that Young Bull had told him of a great place on the Clear Fork to fish, and I remembered seeing a number of good spots when I was scouting some horses. Hard work deserves some reward, so late in the evening the boys dug some worms, and caught some grasshoppers, and put them into some gourds for safekeeping. They got their fish spear, and trotlines, and fishing poles put together, and ready for the big day. Ben Bird wanted to stay here to keep an eye on things, and Ke-Ke stayed with Sarah. They encouraged Ben Bird to come along, as he needed to get out and have some fun. We did not twist his arm, as we had failed to properly ask him to come along, as we should have. The wife pointed out that my social skills were not always proper, and that I should work on that issue. So I had to make it up to my brother, and do right by him, and not take him for granted so much. We went to look at horses in the barn, and we talked and made good talk about our plans on the Clear Fork. I showed him the new calf, and he wanted to have the boys make a name for the new bull calf. There was much to do to get ready, and we put everything in the wagon, including the boy's tent, and some bait that they have secured.

We turned in early to get a good start. I was too tired to be any good to read the Bible well.

We headed out early before sunrise, and made our way to the Clear Fork. We saw some **wigwams** past the bend of the river. It was Red Sun's people camping out to find some horses. Some dogs barked and their sons all came out and they greeted us. Sam Bird told them of our plans to go fishing today. Their fathers came out, and they agreed that it would be a good day to fish together. The boys took out their fishing kits and the Kick-a-poo laughed, as they did not use a spear, or a cane pole to fish with. They did use trotlines, sometimes. They caught them with their bare hands! I laughed, and Young Bull showed us the creek side where the water was clear and the big catfish was poking its head outside its hole in the bank. It was scary looking, and it was huge for a fish. It probably weighed at least sixty pounds! No wonder they did not try to spear it. Young Bull got into the water so he did not stir up the silt, and he stuck his head and arms into the hole in the bank. He struggled for a moment, and pulled up the most ugly catfish there ever was! Ben Bird laughed as the boy struggled up the bank with the huge fish. We helped him so he would not fall back into the water, fish, and all. There were some stones piled up to mark their campsite, and Young Bull posed, and grinned over his triumph over the monster fish. He was so proud of himself. I had to draw this to show the wife, as she would think that I was telling a tall tale. We might try some smaller fish, as their fins can be poisonous if they catch you the wrong way, and fin you. I think some smaller ones would be safer, and less likely to drown me if I took a liking to invite it to our supper. Ben Bird went down and he tried his hand at catching a catfish, and it was a smaller one. It got away, and it finned him. He got sick from the poison, and we put muddy clay on his arm to draw out the poison. We patted him on the back, and we told him how brave he is. He recovered later determined to catch a fish, and not be wounded for nothing. He went into the water, and caught a fish bigger than the one that had escaped him earlier. I was nervous after I saw my brother wounded. I got up my courage, and I managed to catch a smaller one, without any problems. The boys caught smaller fish. They tied ropes under their arms so they could craw into a big fish hole. The other boys would pull them out if they were under the water too long. Josiah went under, and Sam Bird too. They other boys pulled them out, and they had fish under both their arms. They were good eating size, and they were most proud. The Kick-a-Poo did the Fish Dance to celebrate a good catch, today. We had a barrel for water, and we put the fish in the barrel to keep them fresh until we got home. We thanked our friends for the great day together, and for their instruction on how to properly catch a real fish. We parted company on good terms, and left for home. The women were happy for something to put in the cooking pot, and they praised us for being good men, and coming home safe. Ben Bird was in good spirits, so we made sure that he got his choice of fish first. It smelled good to have something nice to eat, and to be appreciated for being a decent husband.

Young Bull and the big catfish.

June 10th, 1847. Yesterday we went to the fort and we heard that they needed men to work on the new fort northwest of here. We felt inclined that a few extra dollars for the money pot was a good idea. The boys were hired too as they were big enough to be some good as a carpenter's apprentice. They have made themselves useful as they have built some smaller forts as play houses, and chicken pens for the biddies against the bad rooster. We were hired to work for two weeks putting out fence lines, and the houses of the latrines. Not a great job, but something that is important to do. Last night we made some plans on paper, and we talked with the chief carpenter. He liked it, and he asked me to work with him as an assistant, instead, as he saw that I could read and write well, from all my notes and details. It paid more and it was easier on my back, so I was happy. Captain Patterson rode by and he was talking to the head carpenter, Sergeant Stark. That might have made the difference having him put in a good word for me. The wives offered to cook for the men, and they were happy to have something beside army food. The women offered to do that for no pay, as they want the army to know they are happy to have their protection from the varmints that have been crossing our paths lately. It also is good for the army to see that some Indians are friendly to them if they act proper, and presentable, as they should. It was nice as the wife was able to help and be close by if we needed her. We missed her when we were gone so much. Phoebe tended to Jacy, and they played in the tents that were set up to rest in. They were playing in the dirt. Phoebe was drawing her letters and numbers out with a pointed stick. I stopped and gave her a few pointers since it was my rest time. They asked me what I have been doing today, and they brought me my lunch pail. I held Jacy on my knee and told them about my day. Jacy fell asleep, and I soon I felt the need to close my eyes for half an hour. Jacy and Phoebe took a nap. I sat in the chair and fell asleep. Josiah came and woke me up. He said that he was working with a surveyor. He was excited to learn something new to do. It was good to see him enjoying work, and learn a good paying job. I patted him on the back and he told me that they have helped lay out the perimeter of the walls, the larger barracks area, and double-sized mess hall. He had been out since before sunrise, so I expected him to be all wore out. He talked nonstop, telling me all the details. We went and had a cup of coffee, and then I have to get back to work. The chief carpenter asked me to look over the plans for tomorrow and give him a report over what would be best to do next. I said that the quartermaster needed to have a larger pen for the horses, and that the source of water needed to be larger for when the summer heat comes. He made notes of my suggestions and he made me take the other plans to look at tonight to see what might need a little help. I agreed, and went out to check the status of the jobs that are set to be done for today. Things were going smoothly, and we wrote down some ideas for tomorrow. Simon was there putting up some ironwork for their stockade. So many people were here using their talents to help make this a decent place to live. The wife was finished for the day, and we went for a walk. The moon was coming up, and the evening stars were bright. We walked together and held hands. It was nice to see so much accomplished, and be appreciated well. Life is good. We are so blessed. Tonight we read: Ecclesiastes Chapter 5, verse 2, "Gracious Words."

June 26th. Our job here is finished. The fort is fairly well set out, and it will be up to the soldiers to finish it out by the end of the year. They paid us in real silver, and we were most happy. We needed to get back home and tend to things, as it was too much to ask Simon to do our chores for this long. The farm looked great, and it was wonderful to be under our own roof. The cattle ran around in circles as they recognized us. The dogs ran up and we petted them, and they were most spoiled now that we were home. We went to bed early and we wanted to sleep solid without the sound of someone sawing a log to wake us up at the oddest hours. This time it was my chance to really sleep, and snore like I was sawing a log. It was nice to sit in my chair, and be at my own table, and sleep in my own bed. Home is a good place to be, and I look forward to our days together.

June 27th, 1847. The rains came and made it cool off and make us take shelter in the barn. It thundered and lightning, and then it hailed for half an hour. It was the size of mustang grapes. Covering the ground. It stopped, and then we went out to look at our crops. They were beat down, and we would not be bringing in any wheat this season. It is good that our horse trade made up for our short falls, and there was always a chance to work at the fort on odd jobs that they needed done. So we will proper in spite of what happens.

We went out and found that some people were camping on our land, so we paid them a visit. They thought that the field that they were camping on was free land, or that it did not belong to anyone. We showed them our land certificate, and that we had earned the extra land as our service for fighting at San Jacinto. We have let those fields lie fallow, as it had been farmed for seven years straight. They had made their mind to buy it from us, and we told them that it was not for sale, and that the local tribes do not want strangers living here without their consent. We are the buffer between the settlement and their lands, and they do not want trouble. The people threw rocks at us, and tried to chase us off, and we had to duck out of the way of trouble. They brought out an **escarpito,** and pointed it our way. This is what scares us is that people will come here with no regard of anyone, but themselves, and have ill will towards us, and our Indian Brothers. We considered violence toward them. We then desired to give them time to cool off. We would talk with them tomorrow after they had time to rest, and reconsider their stand against us.

Sergeant Stark came by tonight to ask us to come work for him a few days. I told him yes, and then he heard of our trouble with the squatters on our land. He sent a detail of soldiers down to talk with the men, and they broke the strangers' camp, and he promised to take them back to the fort in iron manacles. It seems that they are wanted by the Texas Rangers. The Sergeant had a warrant paper listing them as thieves that had robbed several wagons, and stole a number of horses. The Sergeant wanted to hang them from the big oak tree. I said that it was not proper to curse our land with spilled blood, if it was not necessary to do so. The Sergeant decided to put them to a work detail, as they were now his prisoners. I said that I would still like to help at the new fort, and that I had some good ideas for the stonewall that needed to be built. I showed him the ruined wheat, and that I could use another job this season. Since the men were spared their lives, they were more willing to listen to reason this time. They apologized, and fell at my feet to ask for my forgiveness. I forgave them for hitting me with rocks, and that my head still hurt. They would have to do as I have asked or my word would mean their former sentence would be implemented. Perhaps they just needed some hard work and a chance to redeem themselves. It would be a chance to get their life back in line. It was fair and just to make use of their youth, and their foolishness should not mean their death. The wife was pleased that I spared the foolish men, and that I did not spill blood as Lamar's soldiers have done to the Cherokee in east Texas. She cried, but she was happy. She missed her father Chief Bowles. She was pleased that we acted in a just manner, as he would have done. He taught us a great deal about being fair, and about how to handle trouble. It has been almost seven years since her father was murdered, and she spoke fondly of him to the boys. I hugged and kissed her. She went to stay with Ke-Ke for a few days. We went to the fort with the Sergeant, and helped put the men in the stockade. They were the first to be there. They will not be the last, unfortunately. We read tonight: GALATIANS Chapter 5, Verses 19-21. "Evil Neighbors."

June 30th. We reported to the new fort, and Sergeant Stark made us welcome, and had coffee brought to us. We sat down and wrote notes on the things he wanted to be accomplished. He said that one of the men we helped captured was in the infirmary from fighting the others. There were other men in the stockade for various offences, mostly from drinking too much. It seems that we are to get them busy doing so stonework for the walls of the fort, and various places. They were chained at their ankles, so they could not run away. We went out and they were to pick up as much stone as we could find. We had a first sergeant keeping an eye on them as we directed their work detail. We took two wagons to a rocky hill and they picked up sandstone, and iron rock that would work nicely somewhere. We filled up both wagons by early afternoon. One man thought it best to get away, and he got a rifle butt to his leg by the sergeant. We felt that it was not good to be so abusive to the man, but he did keep the others from complaining so much for the rest of the day.

We went out to the same hill, and then emptied the wagons twice. Then we sent the men to clean up and have some supper. They were too tired to be any more trouble, and they will have a week of this duty. We did not mind doing this job as it was good as any, and it paid well to put troublemakers to a work detail. One of the men told me that he appreciated that we saved him from being hung for his mistakes. We thought this a better way to punish him, as we all have made mistakes, some more terrible than others.

July 6th, 1847. The men finished their work and the stone hill seemed not as tall as it once was. They had worked with the stonemason, and they had learned about laying out some of the walls to the fort, and gunpowder magazine. One of the men has asked me for advice, and I told him that being a farmer was a good occupation for a young man. I have seen a change over some of the men, and this one seemed to be the best of them all. I told him that I needed help to get the fields ready for the fall planting, and that he could come work for me, if he did not mind sleeping in the barn. He agreed, and he enjoyed having a chance to redeem himself. I thought it the Christian thing to do, to help encourage him, as he has not enjoyed the benefit of this before. People helped me when I needed help. I told him that when I came to Texas I was found half dead, and the Cherokee took me in. He would get the benefit of a share in the profits of the fall harvest. He liked that and we shook hands on it. I drew up a paper detailing the terms of our agreement, and Sergeant Stark witnessed it being signed by us. He was pleased that something good had come of this young man. So it was a good day, and the young man named Troy came to live in our barn for this next season. He got what few possessions he had together and we left out. I brought him home and introduced him to my family. They were shy at first and then they asked him some questions about himself. He answered, and they felt more comfortable around him. The boys took him and showed him the farm, and the fields that we were getting ready to plant. The boys want to plant pumpkins this season, as they have done well before, and they were good to yield well on this clay and sand dirt. They have made some progress and made a review of the land. We decided that we would get the plow out since the day was fair, and get things going. We would start out by redoing the wheat field that was ruined by the hailstorm. There was little wheat left that was useful. Troy said that he could salvage enough to fill at least a wagon. I did not know if it was worth it. But he could try if he wanted to. The boys helped him and he filled up a wagon by evening, saying that he could work another day to do some more before we burned the field off. Tonight we read from the Bible: LUKE chapter 18, verse 27. "With God, All things are possible."

July 8th. We saw much getting accomplished here. The boys were getting along with Troy. They were practicing their roping skills against a tree stump. There were getting some pointers to enhance their skills. The boys then showed Troy their weekly "slingshot practice." He was in awe of that, and he tried it a few times, and it was too dangerous for him to do. He just needed more practice, perhaps. They then made the smoke signs and waited a few moments, and the signs were returned. They saddled up their horses, and they went riding out to meet with the Kick-a-Poo brave, Young Bull. He needs to know the new helper, and it might teach him something good for his survival here. We let them leave out, and finished our chores. We then followed their trail to the Kick-a-Poo's camp. They were down at the river wrestling up some catfish, and their elders were standing by to keep watch over them. We made the friendly signs, and they waved, and made the signs back. We rode up and gave them a rope of tobacco. The women came and took the fish that they caught. The Kick-a-Poo elders asked about the new fort being built. I told them that it was to keep the settlers off their land, and to keep the Mexican soldiers from taking goods, crops, and horses without offering good trade in return. They seemed to understand that it was for the good of all that live here. The elders got out the pipe bag, and we sat in front of their **smudge** fire in their **wigwam**. The boys dried off, and they were invited to their first Pipe Ceremony. They were due that since they were Braves. Troy was in for a special opportunity to become a smart and peaceful citizen here. They coughed and gagged as they smoked the strong tobacco. The elders smiled, and they continued to talk and pass the pipe. The boys stood up and fell over, as they were strangers to smoking. The elders asked them to sit, and brought them a gourd of water to drink, and some dried jerky to eat. They talked and Young Bull told them what their words meant. He said that they were to have a buffalo hunt soon, and that the smoke signs would invite the evening before them when the day was right. That sounded like fun, and the boys told Troy how it was a serious thing, and a great privilege to be invited. Young Bull told Troy the proper word to say, and the sign for trade, and for blessings. Troy practiced the words, and the elders nodded their approval. So Troy has made some new friends, and they will see him as a friend when they cross paths. We rode home with a few nice sized catfish in a wet burlap sack. We sent some well wishes for the next time that we can go hunting with them.

July 10th. We went out and plowed the field that we had burned off. It was easy going and Troy kept the rows fairly straight, and not too deep. The boys followed behind and planted pumpkin seeds from a seed pot. Phoebe followed behind and covered up the seed with a clod of dirt. She walked along the rows and she found some old broken pottery. She put it in the bed of the wagon to show her mother, and aunt. We went along and brought more seed pots for them to plant from. They got a nice sized acre done, and they went to plow the new plot until it was dark. They did well, and they covered a big piece of ground today. We got home and Phoebe showed the women the pottery she found. They were impressed by it, and they put it on the mantle above the fireplace. Some light rain came and it was good for all the pumpkin seeds that they have planted. We ate a great dinner, and we talked about our plans for all the pumpkins we will get this fall.

July 12th. We went out and saw the smoke signs to go hunting with the Kick-a-Poo. We hugged the wife and she wished us well, and to be safe. We took the lance, and a good rifle. Ben Bird took his best bow, and some nice darts made from some reeds. The boys took their slings, and some iron rock they treasure for ammunition. Troy had a nice army rifle and the will to make a good hunt. The Kick-a-Poo painted their face for battle, so we had to put the clay on our face too, to be proper, and "keep our face hidden from death," the elders said. They have some different practices, but they seem to be well fed, so they must know something, since they have lived to be elders, one over **100 Winters** old! We rode out to the place by Copper Canyon where the buffalo gather. There was a dust cloud coming up, and the buffalo signs were close as we rode by many buffalo wallows. We had Sam Bird climb up a tall tree to scout the best place to attack the herds. He whistled, and pointed to the northwest. Then he shimmied down the tree and jumped on his horse and he lead the way there. It is exciting to see him ride like the wind. Some others followed, and the looked to see which way the wind was blowing, and then they set the prairie on fire to move the herd into the ravine where they could be picked off from both sides. Others were rushed from the other side, and they met head on with nowhere to go. The Kick-a-Poo forced the other, smaller, and less desirable buffalo away from the others, to the open fields, as they would be saved for another time. They did not take anymore than they would need, or be able to use. There were a few cuts and scrapes, but nothing that was life threatening to anyone. It was a good hunt with no one trampled, or hurt too seriously for a change. The women were called and they went down and yelled for joy, as a good hunt deserves praise to the Great Spirit.

We were enjoying a great day hunting, and that we were all going to have 4 bulls, four cows, and a calf that was put down because it had a broken leg. We have got the buffalo butchered, and their women helped put it in the wagon, after some time to eat a few buffalo livers, and hearts. We had to do at least one dance to show gratitude, and made it a good one. Even Troy got into the dance, and he was good as any Kick-a-Poo when it came to "shaking a leg" dancing. Josiah and Sam Bird were doing the Bragging Dance among the young braves. The buffalo horns are raised high in the air, and they shouted loud like it was a thunderclap. They beat the drums with the singers, and made a good song of victory. We get it all home by after dark, and we took the buffalo to the smoke house for they were all divided up well, ready for the meat hooks, and curing barrels. We lit the fires and got it all going well. We then lay down on the floor and went right to sleep. We woke in the night as the women were putting blankets over us to keep us warm. They always are so helpful to us. We would be lost without them.

CHAPTER SEVEN

The Quilt raffle and the Cakewalk.

July 20th, 1847. We go to the monthly church meeting at the Dove settlement. It was a good day to travel and we moved our camp to a good secure spot. Troy rode along with us to the meeting. He said that he hoped to see that young lady named Betty that he has met. I thought that this was the best place for him to meet a wife, and the fact that he was wanted to go to church meant that he was trying to do right, so all was well with that. We heard that a wagon was having trouble by Midway Camp, so we rode on to help out. Ben Bird came along with the boys to help. A wagon has gone off the road after its wheel had fouled against a large stone. We went down and righted the wagon after we have unloaded it well. A man was hurt and his wife was unharmed as she jumped as the wagon fouled. One of their horses was lame so we had to shoot it. It was sad to shoot a horse but it was suffering so. The other horse was just skinned up a bit, but some liniment was good for it. The man seemed to have a broken arm, and his hand was hurt too. Ben Bird had us hold the man still so he could reset his arm. He said to do this quickly before it was too swollen to help him. We took a few scraps of wood and a belt to make a splint. We took a bandana and used it to keep his arm raised up. It all could have been worse, and Troy was a big help. It seems that he has learned that being on the right side of things has been rewarding to his life. We got things back on track and we loaded what we could on our wagon. The others came to help put the couple under a tent that was set up in case it rains. There are many good people here and they had better goods to help them. There were a couple that had a stack of sawmill slats and some linen torn up to better address the man's arm. The wife was crying, so the ladies made her some coffee, and they gave her some comfort with a "wedding ring" quilt they had brought to show

off. It was better suited to be used this way. Ben Bird made some **mesquite tea** from some leaves and tree bark he has in his medicine pouch. The man felt better and Pastor Hodges came to see if all was well. He prayed for them, and the loss of their best horse. There were offers of a new horse from several people. That shows the kind of people that live here. Many would give you their last dime. Troy met up with his new acquaintance, Betty, and they looked nice together. The ladies got a good roasted beef warned up over a fire, and then there was some good meals being served with some vegetables. We got settled in for the night and we have over 60 people here. We got things secured for the night, and it was nice to visit with all the folks that came here. Some people came here saying that we were hard to find. They were just "newbies" to traveling out away from what they consider a town, or a settlement. They were green as green can be. They have learned from this to be more attentive to the road. It was fairly marked well on how to get here, and there were only a few "trapper traces" that the French had used to trap beaver pelts, and those were marked by a pile of stones. We have much to do to educate a few people about the way things are done here. We heard a few people ask about Indians that live here, and we told them about Spotted Tail the Kiowa chief. They laughed at his name, and we told them that he was no person to be laughed at. He saved the settler's lost boy, and he always helps those that are in dire circumstances, no matter what tribe they belonged to. He is a great chief. He even helped those that trespassed on his land, and those that had tried to harm him, he spared. Some Christians could learn a few things from him. We had our usual time to inform people about how to trade with the tribes, and what not to do to avoid trouble, as some had failed to do when they were slain. We told them to pay a toll when they cross their property. They are to give some bacon, an iron tool, a pot, tobacco, or something of value that they would value. We showed them the friendly signs to make the proper introduction, and to promote a good trade. We told them to keep away from their weapons, and not to threaten violence, and it would not set well with them, or make you any safer. People's ignorance was the biggest problem here, and some good information would go a long way to keep people safe, and well in their new home. This may be the early sermon here when we have new members. We also told them of Red Sun, and Young Bull, the Kick-a-Poo that live west by the Clear Fork of the Trinity River. So we have some basic survival instruction here to go along with the Bible study. Most were appreciative of the information we told them, and some needed the Bible study more to open up their eyes to our ways here. I do believe that God does not want us to be stupid all our life, and we should listen well when good instruction is given. That was that. We had a short time to sit along the trail to build a fire, and direct some latecomers here. Ten more came and it made it a good group for our prayer meeting this month. We hope to attend every time we are able.

July 21. We have a good meeting here, and there was a chance to meet many new members. It was nice outside so we have our meeting outside under the large oak tree. We have a good study, and some wonderful music. A man played the fiddle, and another man played a guitar to accompany our signing the favorite hymns. "The Amazing Grace" is our favorite song as it tells me that God found me worthy of saving, in spite of myself. I sang softly as I had been told that my singing is not my talent, and I did not want to offend anyone's ears. At least I can sit a horse, and I can farm, so that was my gift. They have a party planned for the evening after the services. They planned to have a cake and quilt raffle to raise money to buy more tools to build cabins with. The price for iron nails has doubled, and many things cost more because of the great demand for iron for cannons from the Mexican War. We thought it was fine to have it today since the cause was a good one. Also being a good Baptist means that you love to eat good food when the proper time presents itself. We have a good afternoon ahead of us. There was a chance to bid on some pies, and cakes that the ladies brought their special recipes. They were some lovely quilts to buy a ticket for the raffle. The ladies are very talented, and resourceful. There was some music that was church music, and there was old time traditional music that people brought form the places that they came from. We heard some Louisiana music, some German songs, many songs from England, and some songs from Ireland. There were happy Mexican songs, and some really great music, all in all. I just love music and it is a shame that I can't sing, dance, or play any instrument. The pastor Judge Hodges said that he was to be here for a while until the Lord calls him to be elsewhere. He has some lovely children, and their eyes got as big as the full moon when they saw the pies and cakes on the big table. People are like a big kid when they get around all the good cooking. I am no different. Since I could not sing, or dance, I chose to draw their picture to remember our meeting here. What had started off terribly has ended well, after all. They have raised $85.29 for some tools, and iron nails. It could buy a two-man crosscut saw, 3 good hammers, a good double axe, and 2 kegs of nails. People have brought cloth squares for a quilt that is to be made to make another way to raise another twenty dollars for another raffle to buy food to feed the poor. It was good that so much could be done from our church meetings. Our settlement benefits from all the people that have come here with the desire to build something from this wilderness. It is indeed the Promise Land. Moses would have been proud because this is truly the land of milk and honey. It is worth the chance we take here to benefit others from the opportunity we have here.

August 2nd. We went out to Rich Land to make the new settler's home. We did not know this place well as it was off the trail, and well down into the woods. The trees were so thick that a wagon had a tough time getting through the undergrowth. We followed the wagon ruts that were faint. We stopped and cut a few trees, and low limbs to make it more practical not to get swiped in the face by a low branch, or a small tree being in the path to get there. The horses stopped and refused to go until we cleared away the low brush. The boys got out and went in front of us with some machetes that Simon has made. We went close to a stand of cane and we had to remove some of the cane break. We got more people following us, and some rode up to our wagon. They offered to go ahead and help clear the way for us to make some progress. General Sam was always talking about the plans to build new roads here, and we were in the middle of it all just to help build a new cabin. He would be proud to see all this effort. There looked to be a good group coming to help. We got down in our back after swinging an axe so much. We helped survey the place and we put stakes out to make the spot where the rooms would be. The kitchen and front door faced the wrong way. We asked the settler's wife if she wanted it changed, as it was the mirror image on what would be preferred. The little details is what makes a house a home. Josiah and Sam Bird put up their tent as a place to rest. It clouded up and it turned awful in a hurry, and it rained to the point of a flash flood. We had to leave out in a hurry, as we would be stuck here for a week. Some of the logs are cut and laid out. But that is all as it is thundering and lightning now. We will return, as we are able to. We left them Josiah's tent and some blankets we traded from the Kick-a-Poo. This is all that could be done today, as we would be cut off from home when the Trinity floods and the roads are too muddy to go anywhere.

August 15th. We went out to finish the cabin for the new settlers. They wanted it to be more like a barn than a cabin! A person has their own taste about what they like. We went down to the Rich Land community and we came down to a clearing in to what has already been started on another day. The work was halted because of a terrible rainstorm. We just tried to do some of the planning, and let the more able bodies do the lifting. We are making sure that the walls were square and notched properly. We helped choose the proper logs to be placed where they were best suited. Most of the logs were already cut, so it went faster than we thought it would. We had trouble figuring out how to make sense of their plans, as they were not very practical. We helped with the fireplace and it was a nice one. It made up for the other part to being so awkward. Still I am not living there and my own biases do not count here. We helped lay out the pitch of the roof, and it was not steep enough. It would have caved in during a heavy rain. I drew it out on a piece of paper and they do not understand. Then I drew it out on the ground with a stick to show the outline. We argued a bit, and then we agreed that we could make it work with a better slant to it on the front where the rain and storms would not wreck their roof in a short time. We managed to cut and set the gables and have the younger carpenters put up the shingles before it was too dark. We steady helped make shingles, and it was a group effort to make it work. I was very tired and my head hurts from this one. I was just glad to help, and weather one lives in a barn, a tent, a wigwam, a lean-to, or a cabin: you are dry, and warm. You have a safe place to sleep. I just know that I am not always the best carpenter compared to some others, but I am learning. They thanked us, and we hope they will be prosperous in their life here.

September 1st, 1847. We went out and put hay under our pumpkins in the fields to keep them from rotting. All the rain has made us fear that we will lose this crop to the weather as we did the wheat to the hailstorm. Simon's boys, along with Troy, and our boys are out in the hay wagon trying to save what we can from the rot and the mildew. This one field has more sand so it is not as wet as the eastern, mostly clay dirt. The fields used up a great deal of good hay that could be for feed, but it is the lesser of two evils to use it here. We tried to raise it above the wet ground, and the sky has cleared for now. So maybe something could be salvaged from all this mess. Losing a few might make the remaining ones bigger than they would be, since they have less competition for space. The main thing is that all our hard work would not be for nothing. We would hate to write General Sam and tell him that two crops in a row failed in back to back seasons. Farming can be that way sometimes. Still it would be great to have a fine harvest and bring both our wagons to the fort all loaded up, and be the envy of others that wished that they had grown some handsome pumpkins. It seems silly, but still important to have a goal in mind. That is the 'carrot on the stick' that gets you to make some progress. Failure is not part of the plan, so you must also have a plan to deal with that possibility. You must support and feed your family no matter what. Excuses do not make things any better for anyone.

September 14th. The rain has stayed away and it makes us glad that most of the pumpkin crop has survived any more mold and mildew. We found a man asleep in our field. We though him dead, but he was just very drunk. When we checked to see if he was breathing he did breathe on us, and his breath would have woke the dead! We felt he might be another deserter for Rio Norte battles. There seems to be many that have lost their heart for soldiering. The battle has left him behind to die alone. We thought that we would make sure that he had no weapons on him. Then we woke him carefully. He was scared thinking that he was in trouble. We assured him that he was among friends, and we gave him some good water, and then fed him. He slept for a little bit, and then he asked if he could do some chores to return our kindness. It was not necessary, but we did not want to offend him wanting to make things right. He got a hayfork and got to pitching out some hay for us, and he did a good job. Later a horse rode by without a rider, so we figured it to be his horse. We took it to the barn, took off its saddle, and tack. It was a Mexican army issue, along with an **escarpito**, and a muddy pistol hanging on the saddle. The poor horse drank what seemed the whole trough of water. It stopped to eat every green bush it saw. The boys washed down the horse and brushed her down good. Ben Bird rode up and I told him of the visitor. His Spanish speaking ability was much better than mine, so I had him ask the visitor some questions. It seems that many have deserted, and if they were caught, they would be executed on the spot. It seems that he had his fill of being shot at, and he has lost his stomach for killing in battle. It is never easy to see so many die, and for what good reason? Many times it seems some sort of cockfight, a dogfight, or what ever you want to call it. No matter the name: it is most gruesome at best. We just knew that we were no longer in a battle with anyone who tried to be peaceful towards us. We offered him a chance to rest, and then he must move on. The army would not take kindly to have any enemy soldier so close to the new fort, weather he is a deserter or not. We must take his weapons so he cannot do harm to anyone. He will not like that very much. Ben Bird told him that he could not have his weapons back, and he was most disturbed. We have to protect our family from him in case he is a spy, or a thief. A detachment of men came by because they are training out here for their time in battle. They saw the Mexican man resting out by our well when they came by here on maneuvers. They figured it was their time to pounce on some unfortunate man. They took him prisoner, and threatened to take us in too for helping him. We were just being kind to a stranger that needed help, and we would hope for the same good treatment that we were offered when we were in distress. They grumbled under their breath knowing that we were not doing anything wrong. They know who we are. Troy rode up, and he tried to get in the middle of it, and Ben Bird dragged him away from this would be troublesome. He would be back in the stockade, and this time it would be more serious for him since he was still under a probation warrant for his earlier offences. This Mexican soldier has information on recent troop movements, and that is what they want him for, to pick his brain to see what he knows about Santa Anna these days. We are just tired of being on the edge of civilization, and we always seem to get all the castoffs from society on both sides of this trouble. We miss the peaceful times we had in east Texas living with the Cherokee. This war is bigger than all of us put together, and it would take the Wisdom of Solomon to figure it all out. The tired soldier was taken away and he cursed us all the way down the road. We hated that, and we prayed for him. We pray for us too, and all involved to find some real wisdom. This will all get worked out properly in due time. Today we read LUKE Chapter 18,verse 27, "God makes all things possible."

October 28th, 1847. We went out to finish picking pumpkins for the trade day. We have plenty of good help. The weather was cool enough to make the work not too terrible. We made a line to pass the pumpkins along to the wagons. We cut the vine and then it was passed along to the next person in line. We asked for more wagons, and Simon brought some that he has made over this past year. It all worked out well as he has plans to sell them, so why not make them full when they get there? We got six wagons of pumpkins ready for some good trade. We could sell them individually, or by the wagonload. Either way we could sell them in a hurry for the pie makers, and bread vendors. We went to the new fort and made many good trades for some solid money, and barter for goods. We heard that there have been so many terrible battles and that we needed to bring more horses to be broken. We sat with the vendors in the new market area. We have sold half our goods by the early afternoon. I did not count the money in the open market, but my tally sheet looked to be over $100 dollars for our trouble. We offered $10 to each of the people that helped harvest the past week. We still did well with more trade to follow. Troy helped load the pumpkins, and he handed them out and he dropped the money into the seed pot, and he wrote down the barter goods. We gave out a few to the widows, and the poor folks. That was just good and plain advertising, as they would proudly show them off as they went through the fort to their camps. It was worth it to see the look on their faces as many sit at the gate and beg for alms. One woman was singing, and she talked to herself as she left. She needed something to make her happy. One man that saw her not only bought a wagon full of pumpkins, he bought Simon's best wagon too, and Simon was happy about that deal. He made a good profit here. The quartermaster came later and bought the other 3 wagons, and the fort's cook bought a dozen pumpkins for pies and the baked seeds. We felt we should stay another day and made a good weekend of it. We pitched the tent, and the guard asked us to move to a different place because we were too close to the corral. So we asked where we could camp and he told us to move outside the walls. We went to go talk with the Officer of the Day, and he told us that he apologized for the new soldier's ignorance. That was fine with me, as we were a part of this place since we have helped build it up from nothing. We kept our temper in check, and that was the worse thing that happened here. The boys have made some good sales and today they sold $20 and $16 apiece. We have settled in for some rest. It was a little too noisy here to sleep much. It would have been more restful outside the gates with all the early bugle calls, and the changing of the watch, and patrols coming in and out of the gate. Still it was for the sake of selling our goods and being set up in a nice spot. It is a small price to pay to sell our crop today.

October 29th. We sold the rest of the pumpkins and the other wagons too. We made another $92.50, so we did well after all the profits were settled against any debts we owed here. The quartermaster asked us to bring more horses for the war effort for General Zachary Taylor in Northern Mexico. He has held Palo Alto since March. It has kept the Mexican army from staging further attacks of our settlements, and taking our young men, goods, crops, and stock. That means that we need to do our part to make things right by keeping our homes strong, and to keep our trade in horses on a regular basis to keep them available, and ready for their use.

Tonight we read: ROMANS Chapter 6, verse 23. "The wages of sin is death, but the gift of God is eternal life through Jesus Christ."

The Chupracabra

CHAPTER EIGHT

The Chupracabra.

October 31, 1847. We have been having our stock troubled by a prowler the past two nights. Sleep has not been our friend lately. Many of our stock had been run off, and many of our best chickens are long gone or killed. The cows that are left have stopped making good milk, and the chickens we have left have stopped laying decent eggs. We looked for the trouble to get worse before it gets better. We knew that once we have established our farm here that we just might need a big fence around us like we helped build at the new fort. We went out and looked for the troublemaker. It has been preying on us at the nighttime, just before dawn. Ben Bird has a similar problem at his place, and he is not very happy. He said that he followed some animal tracks from his place out towards the west to a grove of persimmon trees, and then they returned back here to my place. He stayed up all night keeping watch and he was working on his weapons to get them ready. He had his knife, his gun, and a bow with a quiver of long arrows. He said that this was not a good animal as it was contrary to what makes sense. He said that the animal took live animals to eat such as a chicken, and it left dead animals such as a crow, and a possum in its place. He would know what makes sense, as he is a great tracker. We walked out and we saw it left tracks walking on all four legs, and then sometimes it stops and walks on its hind legs. So it sometimes it must stand, and it walks like a man, on its hind legs! We found handfuls of feathers from some of our chickens, and then we found a number of slain animals: squirrels, a cat, a skunk, and a coyote just killed for the sake of being killed. They were laid in the forks of a tree, hung up like they are trophies. It was most odd. This was just a spiteful animal that was not just hungry, but just mean and something to be feared. At least the bad bear we killed had stolen from our smokehouse to fill its belly. This just kills just for fun. We scratched our head on this one. We headed back home and we set to make a trap for this animal. We did not know what we were looking for, but it seems that we will know it when we see it. We do not look forward to that. Ben Bird said that he has heard the Elders speak of something like this that is a cursed thing that passes over the country side until it is appeased someway. It walks on all fours until it gets mad and then it walks on two legs like a man does. He called it a **Chupracabra**. I hope that this is just one of those tall tales that is told over the campfire to scare bad children into acting right, like the "old ogre woman." Maybe the Mexican deserter cursed us with this awful thing for not helping him more when the soldiers took him? I do not believe in superstitions, but this looks to be a real thing that has wrecked our livestock, our poultry, milk cows, and peace of mind. We make plans to try to deal with this.

We get back home and we take what chickens and cattle that we have and we put them over to Ben's place. We sent the family to the fort to keep them safe. Captain Patterson will let them stay at their place since we are friends. We set up a trap of one of Ben's scrawny goats in the bear trap we saved. This would be the way to go. We put a tough old hen out on a tether to entice the animal closer to our trap. The sky clouded up and it turned cold and windy. We wait and we watch by the woodpile. Hours passed and nothing. Close to dawn the dogs bark and then they run away, so we know it is coming closer. We hold still and Ben holds an arrow in his teeth, and he notches another arrow in his bow. We see an animal that looks like an ugly coyote, a large one! It raises itself back on its long legs. Its tail is long and thick, so it rests on it. Ben lets an arrow fly and the bowstring makes a twanging sound. The Chupracabra swings around and it knocks the arrow to the ground with its tail. Ben bites through the arrow held in his teeth, and he throws it to the ground. We run for cover and the Chupracabra picks up the hen and it throws it at us. It hisses and it grabs the scrawny goat. It spits at us, gives us an evil look, and it growls terribly. We ran away like frightened children! We retreat as this has long teeth, and claws. It was not afraid of us. I pull out my gun, and Ben Bird pushes it away. He says that a gun will only make it angry, and then we would not have another chance to get it close to us. It walks away with the goat, and we go to inside the barn and bar the door to keep it out. We go up into the hayloft to watch it leave on two legs. I was too scared to try to shoot my gun, and Ben said that it was not to be killed easily as it batted away a good arrow away like it was a mosquito. It would only be meaner if it is only wounded. I would be.

November 1, 1847—Josiah and Sam Bird came up to the barn and knocked on the door. We were asleep because we were tired from not sleeping a few days. Sam Bird has the broken arrow, and the arrow that was batted away. He held them up, and we smiled and we went down and let them in. We told them what has happened, and they said that they would help. Perhaps they knew how to make a good capture of this beastie? We were in need of a solution. We could capture wild horses and fare well, but not this animal. I did a drawing of the animal and the boys could not believe me that this was true. Ben said I made it too handsome, as it was much uglier, and awful! I told him that the animal stinks and was foul acting to go along with his good looks. We took the bear trap away from the barn and we took it close to the place where we found the trophy animals in the tree. We put another scrawny goat in the trap hoping it would entice the animal. I am sure it is watching us from the stand of reeds and cedars, breathing its pathetic breath. We got that awful feeling that it was out there mocking us in our attempt to capture it. I did not like something so evil keeping us from being free to do as we want. The boys went out to pick up some stones like little David getting ready for Goliath. They have a plan too, and we will be patient to see what it is. We all took time to rest during the day know that it does not like the daylight. We will now be ready if we are at least well rested so our aim will be better. It has turned cold and cloudy. It was sunset and it was time for battle. We went out and made a place to attack. We were covered in clay and brush from head to toe, as we did when we went deer hunting. We were well hidden in plain sight. Our weapons are ready, and it is the right time. We waited and after a few hours it came from the reed break. It was holding a dead bird and it carried it like it was a prize. It put it in the trophy tree, and it would be rank if we were not downwind from it. The Chupracabra was walking around on all fours and it sniffed about sensing we were close by. It stood up and it went about sniffing the air to find where the intruder was. I could feel my heartbeat in my throat, as it got closer. It was not a fool and we have leaned up against a tree to keep from moving. Ben Bird had his arrows ready, and the boys had their slings ready to fling a rock or two. I had my pistol ready but my hand was shaking from the cold. Ben notched an arrow and he shot at the bad animal. He hit it through the shoulder, as it was moving as it was shot. It broke the arrow off and it was showing its nasty temper. The boys flung rocks at it, and it was running towards them. They struck it and it just got madder and more determined to advance on us like a rabid animal would. I shot my pistol and it was scared off by the loud noise more than from my aim, which I was not so sure about. The boys kept flinging rocks at it and they hit it good. It fell down hard and curled up like a snake. We took a moment and got closer to it, as it was breathing hard. We got closer to poke it with a stick. As we were a few feet from it the beast jumps up and it takes a swipe at me and it knocks off a great deal of mud and brush I was wearing to help me hide in plain sight. I was bleeding some from this, but it was not too bad, considering. The Chupracabra knocks the boys back as it rushes past them. Ben pulls out another arrow and he lets it fly. It hits its shoulder blade and the animal rolls on the ground into the brush. We light a lantern, and we use it to help find the animal so we can finish it off. We find tracks and blood, and later we find the arrow where it has been pulled out somehow. It has run away to lick its wounds, and if we are fortunate, it will not come back! We feel that we made it clear that it was not welcome as if it were a rabid dog. It was most awful and we did not have time to worry over such things that wrecked our security, and our way of life farming and raising animals. Anything that kills our stock and cost us our safety is bad for us all. We made it more understood by shooting a gun in the air a few more times to scare it off. Since it is so smart it will keep going and leave us alone. If it don't then we will not be so nice next time. Nothing, or no one will push us around without paying a terrible price. We have wasted many days over this and we need to get back to the tasks that need to be done. We get back home. The boys go to the fort to get the women to come home.

Young Bull and a few braves come here with some of our missing cows that they found wandering with some wild cattle. They bring us the wild cattle and they herd them into our corral. We thank them and we gave them some iron tools for a gift. They accepted them and we told them of the strange animal. They said that they have seen a strange animal that laid slain animals into a tree. It did not bother them as it did us. They thought it to be a spirit of some kind, and they were afraid of it as they have heard of such things. We offered to let them stay here today, and they said they would stay tonight and help keep watch as their hunters were back at their camp to protect it. I showed them the picture I drew of it, and they did not like it. One of them wanted to tear it up because it looked so evil. I told him the drawing was to help remember things worth remembering. Just like the animals they drew on their rawhide shields they carry and hang in their wigwams and council house. I showed him other drawings I did and they liked them, so they were fine with us. They helped us sort out the tame cows from the wild cattle. We left one of the lead cattle in with the wild ones so that they would learn to follow the others as we lead them to other fields to graze. We were happy to have some new cattle, and we took the braves to the smokehouse for some food to eat. They are big grown men, and they were hungry. We built a nice fire, and we heated up the meat over a fire to make it better tasting. They would have eaten it cold, but since they were so kind we wanted to give them some consideration. The boys and the women came back home, and they danced around to give thanks that we were all safe. Sarah hugged me and pressed up against my wound, and I flinched in pain. Sarah tended to my wound and she fussed at me for not addressing it sooner. I had put clay on it and she made me clean up by the horse trough and change clothes.

She took a honeycomb out of a gourd and she rubbed it into the wound to seal it up. It smarted, but I was brave and the boys watched her clean the bad wound, and how she made use of the honey as some good medicine. So some good came out of it, and it was done as Ben Bird would do. I told her that we scared off the bad animal, and it would be smart enough to stay away. Hopefully.

The braves went over to Ben's to visit and they like Ben as he teaches them some medicine as he can. They asked if they could take two cows to Ben's and I thought it proper. They cut out two cattle from the corral, and they took them over to Ben's. I felt bad and I had to get some rest. It felt like rain, and my old wounds were bothering me terrible today. I slept for a few hours and it was better after that. It thundered and that was what woke me. The rain came down steady, and it was a welcome sight. It turned colder and it was nice to sleep under our own roof again, as we have become spoiled to sleeping in a nice bed. I sat at the table to read the Bible as I felt like I was at a loss to understand some of the recent events, and some good Wisdom was in order. We read: ISAIAH Chapter 58, Verse 7. "Divide your bread with the hungry, bring the homeless into the house. When you see the naked, cover them, and do not divert your own eyes from your own flesh."

November 3rd. We went to Simon's for the blacksmith instruction for the boys. We sat back and watched how he used the bellows to make the coals glow. He showed the boys how to pile the coals closer together, and how to make the iron hot enough to work into horseshoes, and tools. Simon asked about the strange animal we had tangled with. He rested for a bit, and he drank some long drinks of water while I told him the details. He just blinked hard and he did not say much more.

His boys took out some iron and started shaping some horseshoes. They dipped them into the water and cooled them. Simon took the file and filed off the rough spots off the horse's hooves. It was nice to see him take pride in showing what he knew to others, as my talents are limited to farming, and not much else. He had me shape a horseshoe, and I did not do too terrible. He could have made three in the time I made one, but it takes practice like anything else. I felt like I had made something good, and I will hang this up over my door for decoration. I bought a few more of his knives to replace the ones I traded to the braves for the cattle they brought me. I saw Simon needs more iron, and I offered to bring him some back with my next trip to the fort. He gave me some money to hold for him, and I told him that I would make a fair trade for him since he is too busy to get away. He looked around and he found a voucher for $100 dollars of ironwork he did for the new fort. He said to get as much iron as they could spare and to buy some coal with the other money. I told him those wagons he made were really nice and he is a great carpenter, and **wagoner**. If I stay with these people long enough I might learn a few things.

November 5th. We go to the fort with two wagons. The boys are driving the other wagon to give them the benefit of learning how to drive a team of horses. We will get the iron and coal for Simon's projects he has planned. We arrive to see the fort closed shut. The sentry tells us to leave. We call for the Officer of the Day, and we look for the doors to open. He said that he could not open the doors because some of the soldiers are sick from some illness. A few have died. Their own doctor was stricken, and they did not know what to do for them to be well. I told them that I would get Ben Bird and bring him back as he is the best person here to ask about such things. They agreed, and we went back home to get Ben. We rode over to his place and he got his medicine pouch and we stopped and picked some plants he knew of called "Five Fingers" used for good healing. He also went and picked a bushel of mesquite beans, and some leaves from the trees. We hurried to the crossing, and we made it to the fort by early afternoon. The doors were opened for us, and we went about to check their well, their main source of water. Ben said that their **latrines** were draining into their well, after he smelled their water. They were far apart, but they were still coming into contact with each other. This was fouling the good water. He said that they have the Typhoid fever, and that they must not drink from this well anymore. The bugler played "Assembly" and the ones that weren't on Sick Call came and lined up. There looked to be many people ill from the short lines.

The Officer of the Day asked us to pick out the men that we needed to get things fixed. We asked for the best carpenter and stonemason so we could cover the well up solid, like a cistern. A guard was posted to keep anyone away from using it that could not read, or was a new visitor. Ben Bird said that all visitors were to be kept out for a while to make sure no one else gets sick. We had them to make a sign noting that the well water was not to be drunk until further notice. We went to the barracks were the sick were kept and they also had a tent set up for those that were most ill. The soldiers were turning over all the horse troughs, and their canteens were emptied. A detachment went down to the river to get fresh water in as many new barrels that they could muster together. I sent the boys back home to tell the women that we might be gone a day or two to help out. Ben Bird got the cook from the Mess Hall and he had them make a fire outside using a big pot to cook in. He put half the mesquite beans in a pot of water with no meat added to it. He then said that no pork could be added after he considered it. Pork was bad to some illness, he said. The cook got some beef to put in it to make a broth to keep the ill strong enough to prosper. He then asked for some cloves of garlic, and some onions to be put in there. The cook got another big pot and added the fresh water and they made a tea using the mesquite leaves. Ben said that the ill were to get as much mesquite tea that they could drink since they had lost so much of their water weight, and many could not stand up at all. Ben then got a green limb off a tree and he walked around looking for a source of water. He found one far from the other and it was marked so the men could dig a new well. The sergeant came and he has a detail to start digging. We asked if we could help get it started to make sure this was a good place to dig. We started digging the well and it went quickly. We wished we had the boys here as there dig like gophers. The soldiers took over and they have a good crew working on it, so we could go back to supervising the digging. The water table here is higher here and less prone to be tainted. The ground was sandy here so that was a good sign as the other well was mostly black land that did not filter the water as it passed through it. That would be the difference. So this would be a good source of water if the gate is shut and they are cut off from the river. We have suggested that all burials be outside the gate to prevent the runoff from a grave to contaminate the water. Ben Bird has said that before in the past. Two men have died and that is where we were to help conduct their burials. We got cleaned up and we borrowed some clothes from the quartermaster, as we were too dirty to properly conduct a burial. We went downstream and got cleaned up. We were ready to start the burials and there was another man added to the group. They buried them all in the same grave, as that was their tradition when several died at the same time. They had them each wrapped in a blanket. There was a time for the bugler to play after I said some words over them. I had no idea that this day would turn out this way. Ben Bird said that some of the men were trying to feel better as their color was returning to their face. He used the Five Finger plant and bull nettle was boiled and it was applied as a poultice to relieve their fever. So small miracles happen, and it will take a few more days to see if any more will be helped.

We had the camp chaplain hold a prayer service to pray for the men here, and their families. Many attended, as they were sad to see a soldier die from such a simple fate. We grew tired and we had to rest for a while until the evening comes. The evening watch came and we had two more burials. It was tough to have two burial details in one day. We were hoping to not lose any more to the illness. Ben Bird said that the others looked better, and that these men had waited too long to ask for help, that is why they died, because they were too stubborn. That would be me if I was there, too proud to ask for help. We had a prayer service in the night, and regular duties were suspended, except a man in the watchtower to keep the gate secure from anyone coming in undetected. Candles were lit, and lanterns were hung from the trees. The men spoke of their friendships, and it was a proper wake to deal with their loss of their fellow soldiers. Ben Bird was tired, and we made him rest and I took the first watch over the sick. We kept the men drinking the tea, and one man had some improvement that we thought was great as he was the sickest one that was left of the bunch. We kept watch over them and they showed improvement. Ben would take over the watch at midnight until six in the morning. The commander came to tell us how much he appreciated us, and he offered us anything from the trading post that we wanted. We did not expect anything for helping, as it was our duty to a fellow soldier, and as a Christian. Still we did not want to hurt their feelings. We took 2 bolts of colored cloth for the women, and there were a few new shirts that a soldier gave us. We gladly accepted them and went on, as if we could not use them the boys could, or we could keep them for a trade good. We wondered how long it would take to see that the men were better off. The doctor of the fort was feeling better, and he asked Ben what he did to help the Typhoid better.

Ben was glad to share some of what he knows to someone that is also a healer. He sat in a chair and he took out his medicine pouch, and the doctor asked him to tell him some of his healing methods. I sat with them incase I need to ask Ben in Cherokee words what the doctor has asked him in English. I helped write down the details as the doctor's head still hurt, and he could not stand for long. That freed him to ask questions, and not be hindered by trying to keep up with Ben's answers to his inquiries. The doctor was surprised that I could write, and Ben said that I write all the time, and that I have taught him to write and speak well. I just did what I should do to help my brother, as he did for me, and that is all. We wrote down a number of pages and it was nice to see the doctor perk up as he had learned some things that would help him here, and that he had a new appreciation of Indians he did not have before. I made a copy for myself as I was always learning something new that I needed to know. We were keeping with our promises made at the Great Council, and we are bound to that as long as we are drawing a breath. The doctor grew tired, and we told him that we come to the fort on trade day, and he could visit us at our booth where we trade regularly. The doctor said that the worst of this illness has passed and today was the day that made the difference. We told him that we should stay at least another day, and leave when he was more able to tend to things. The doctor fell asleep, and we went and tended to the others that were looking stronger. We will get them out tomorrow to get some sun, and see that they are not wobbly, and stoved-up from lying down so long. We took the time to help them get better. There was no other way to go.

November 7th, 1847. We went out to leave after our days helping out. We have a great new respect for the new soldiers here, and they have the same for us. We only lost one more soldier to the illness, and that was plenty enough for us to wonder what we could have done to help him. The doctor told us that we did all that could be done, and it was out of our hands what happened next. That was left to a Greater Power than we have. The Officer of the Day asked us to meet with Major Ripley Arnold, and that was a fine time for us. He thanked us, and gave us a civilian accommodation that would be that we would always be welcome, and that if we ever needed help that it was understood that we would get that help, no matter how many days, men, or horses it took. I did not expect that but we got some good friends for life here. It was good for a freed slave, and a Cherokee to be in the good graces of the army after what had happened **seven years ago to the Cherokees in East Texas** and at **the Council House in San Antonio, by Lamar as President.**

We told him of our experiences with General Houston, and our commander, William Goyens. We were asked if we knew of any new horses for the army's needs. I told him there are the places where the Kiowa and Comanches allowed us to hunt and take horses without question, and that we have made councils with them as we are given the chance to make peaceful trade that benefits us all. We told him that they should be given food, or blankets if they were asking for it when the winter comes so terrible like last year when so many of their children, and elders died. Major Arnold wrote down notes and he said that he has heard many good things about us and that a newspaperman was to be here at the next trade day to talk with us. Many newcomers have written letters to the fort and the newspaper wanting to know about many things, and he felt that since we were well established here that we would be the people to talk to. We were nervous speaking to the concerns of so many strangers, but we would give it our best try. He said that we were the kind of citizens that he wished he had more of in this settlement. We are just two of many, and we are not used to so many complements, just criticism, as we are our own biggest critic. We look over our own failings and shortcomings. We promised more horses for them, and we thanked him for all his confidence, as he is someone that we admire from his accomplishments like our General Sam. We saluted him and left for home to take care of our own place. We missed the wife and children and it was time to be back home.

November 16th. We have enjoyed some days at home, and the burdens of life here aren't so bad compared to what we have seen from others at the fort. We promised the wife that we would be at home more and do less wandering about on our crusades here. It would be easier said than done. Major Arnold comes here with a detachment of soldiers to ask me to find them some horses that are needed badly. Many horses have been captured by the enemy soldiers and have been eaten when rations are scarce. Many have been lost, or slain in the terrible battles they have endured. I did not want to know all the details as I have relived my own battles in my dreams many times. I find myself in the midst of battle when I was only trying to get some rest: I dreamed of when I was wounded by the robbers being left for dead. I dreamed of my wife Delephine who fought as well as any man when she was hard pressed the night she died. I missed her sometimes, and I hoped that she was resting well. I miss my life with the Cherokee in east Texas. I was learning from my new life living with them. Then I dream of the battle of San Jacinto when some of our soldiers did not stop killing the prisoners, even after the battle. It was most terrible, and there are times I can't forget some of them. We had to make them under arrest and some were bound with rope and gags in their mouth to make them stop their lust for killing. We did not know whose side they were on. I did not want to be in that place again. Being with these men put me where I did not want to be. I just wanted to farm the dirt and curse the crows and varmints. I just did not know if I could be up to their demands and keep my wife happy. That made me unhappy to come home and she was mad at me for being gone so much. She did not deserve any of that. I did not either, as I was just trying to do what I should do. I did not want to lose this wife from stress and worry, which is as bad as any gunshot. I told my wife that I wanted her to come with me on this journey to see what I deal with to make her know that I did these things for my family, for her and myself. She laughed, and then she got her things and she had the children go over to Ke-Ke's to stay. This was to be for us to do together. She would capture the first colts and use her special gift with animals to help us capture more horses. The soldiers asked, "Why was a woman coming along?" I told them that she was a gifted person, and that she could lure in the colts that would help us to capture the quality mares, and stallions. It took a special person to attract the horses that they needed desperately. We were too rough, and we needed someone who was gentle as the horses could sense trouble close by. I also needed to be with my wife, and this allowed both things to be achieved. They stopped protesting once they saw Sarah jump on a horse and ride like the wind. She was raised on a horse and she was not shy about running circles around them. It made me smile as I loved her for her great spirit and that is what shines about her in the things she does. She rode off to the west and we followed, trying to keep up with her. We ate her dust, and we stopped at the river crossing to water the horses before we went on. She asked us, "What took you so long?" She smiled and she enjoyed that we have included her on our journey. She was happy in the wide-open places.

I was wrong to keep her home so long. We rode on and the soldiers enjoyed that she was so headstrong and she rode point to where we saw the first signs of mustangs. She jumped off her horse and she pointed to where the tracks led. She raised her index finger to her lips to invite the soldiers to be quiet. Sarah squatted down, and she made a kissing sound and out of the brush came a handsome sorrel colt. She sat on a rock and she petted it to make it calm. She said that we have to be calm so it would not be scared. She told the soldiers to start building a corral on this spot and to "not stomp around too much to not scare the baby." The men obliged and they went to find tree limbs and stones to make a nice brush corral. They started building and Sarah said that this is not big enough for what we need. The tracks here say, "many horses!" There was good water and good food about, so that may just be so. The men made the circle bigger for the floor of the corral. Sarah shook her head, "No." So they smiled knowing that a woman can be hard to please, sometimes. She carried the colt as she went out and stepped off a place twice the size of what the men have planned. The men shook their heads in disbelief. I said that it would be better to have too large of a corral, than not. I went out to get wood and we all picked up many logs and we found much wood to use for our cause. Sarah got some nice green buffalo grass and fed it to the pony. She breathed in its face so it would know her scent, and it became calm. She took some water from her canteen and poured it into her hand for the colt to drink from. She then let it go and it followed her like she was its mother. The men stopped and looked up from their work, and then they went back to work trying to finish the larger corral. We then took brush to cover the fence, and we left a small place for the gate area. We used larger stones to help secure the fence at the weak places and Sarah walked around and she approved of what was done. One of the men wanted to start to make a fire and Sarah took the flint and steel out of his hand. I told the man that a fire would scare off any wild horse for miles, and it was plain to see that he has never been out to capture some horses. Sarah took out some ears of corn, and she passed them out to the men. This was for if they got hungry. It would also entice the horses to come near as what horse would not want a nice ear of corn to eat? Sarah was wearing a corn kernel necklace. She opened up her saddlebag and she took out enough for most of the men. She told them to wear one, and they refused. She stood and tapped her foot waiting for them to comply with her wish. They put them on, and then she asked them to put some clay on their faces to help hide themselves. Again that was asking too much, but the men knew how this was to help capture the horses. They did as they were told and she showed them how to cover their face to help lure the horses the best way. Even I learned a few things. I am always humbled by her knowledge. It is like this all the time. We put clay on our faces, and then she asked that we put on some brush on our shoulders, and on our hat. They grumbled a bit, but they did it. She told them to hide down wind from the corral and they did. She put the colt in the corral and it whinnied for its mother. We put a loose lasso around the colt's neck and it fussed more. We have left open a place big enough for a horse to come in, and directly it's mother a lovely pinto came stomping in, and it stood inside the gate and came inside. We blocked its way out, and it was not too happy being penned up. We laid some fresh buffalo grass inside and we had it at our control in no time. Sarah spoke softly to the animal and it calmed down in a short time. It was her gift. Sarah went out for a while and she came back with another colt and she brought it to the corral. Again in a half an hour a mare came to find it. It was a nice paint horse that was most healthy looking. A soldier put his corn necklace on a stick, like it was a fishing pole to entice a pony to follow him and it did. He was calm and he was happy when it came into the corral. Now they were getting the hang of it. It was a matter of having the proper attitude, and some nice corn to offer them. In a short time there were eight horses, and it was not a bad way to spend an afternoon. Towards sunset more horses came on their own sensing the others were close. A soldier was able to get the led animal inside and the others followed. We closed the gate for the night and we lowered some buckets of water with a rope over the fence. The horses drank a great deal and it was quite an ordeal to keep the horses well watered. A stallion came and it tried to nip at a soldier. Several worked together to rope it and it was contrary. Sarah walked over to it, and put out her hand, holding a cob of corn. It came closer, and she fed it. It became calm and she led it inside with the others. It was gentle as gentle could be. One of the soldiers tried to pet it and it tried to nip at him, so it was not to be messed with by just anyone. The other soldier laughed and they kidded him about it. We took turns keeping watch over them.

Dawn came. We got painted up with more clay and covered in tree branches and leaves to help hide us in plain sight. Later on in the day we are visited by some Kiowa and Comanches who are out on a hunting party. At least it wasn't a war party! There was no paint on them, or their horses. A certain Kiowa chief named Lone Wolf came by to check on us. He did not look very happy to see us here. He walked a circle around us to look us over. The soldiers got nervous and I told them to hold their ground, and not draw a weapon, or get close to thinking about it. I made the trade signs. The Kiowa stood and looked us over for a while and they asked for something for a toll to be on their land. I had some salt pork, and some bacon. They accepted it. One asked about the soldiers with paint on his face and the tree limbs about his neck and arms. He laughed and pointed and talked with his friends. He realized that we were getting some horses and he asked for more presents for the Comanches in the group. We have some blankets, and a few iron fire strikers. That seems to pacify them. Sarah made the sign talk to them and they seemed more reasonable after that. I brought out a rope of tobacco and they made the word to get out the pipe bag. They had it all ready to be passed and even Sarah joined in because she was a part of the council by being a sign-talker. They knew she was a Qualls, and they appreciated her council. We sat under a shade tree and they asked us what our business was here? We answered and Sarah signed-out our words to them. They nodded. Then they told us that they remembered us from the **Great Council** at Bird's Fort. They asked about the war in Northern Mexico, and they said that they were stuck in the middle of a battle from both sides. They understood that more horses meant that it would help end the war sooner and that would soon leave them alone. They seemed tired from all the people crossing their land and giving them nothing but grief from all the dead that were left behind that curses hunting on their land. In return of their consideration, we made sure they had plenty of gifts. They seemed pleased with themselves. At least they won't go home to their village empty handed. They left and returned later with 6 horses that they herded close to us. It seems that we will be not looked at as enemies as long as we can maintain a polite trade between us. Sarah was most happy that she came along with us, and we were too as she helped smooth over the talks between us. She is still a good Cherokee, and a fine Christian too. The soldiers praised her and they said that they would tell others about us, and our day rounding up horses. We appreciate some praise from soldiers that would have treated us badly just a few years ago. The evening came and more horses came to join the others in the corral. We secured them and brought more food and water for them. A Kiowa scout came out and he pointed and gestured for us to follow him. There was a big dust cloud ahead, meaning a herd of horses was coming. We split up where we could force them to the corral. Sarah stayed at the corral to be ready to open the gate when we returned. We went out and circled the horses. Some of the Kiowa lit fires to force the horses from cutting back to the open prairie. This forced more horses to the main herd and it looked to be over 60 horses in this remuda! We kept going strong and we did not stop pushing them until we reached the corral. Once they smelled the other horses they rushed to meet them. Sarah opened the gate and they rushed in. The corral was just large enough to accommodate them, so Sarah's judgment was sound indeed as it would have been too small if we had not built it up like we did. We rode up and gave the Kiowa one of Simon's iron knives and he was most happy. He held it up high as he removed it from the sheath and admired it. He rode off most happy and we have thanked him properly for his help to us.

We got the horses fed and watered well and that took a few hours. One stallion tried to jump over the fence and Sarah told us to give him some room and not bother him so he would settle down. We would have to wait until the evening before we would drive the horses to the fort. We rested well and we took turns watching over the horses so they would be calm around people. We walked around the corral so they could see us and not fear us. We kept bringing nice green buffalo grass, and green limbs with nice leaves on them. We put them over the fence and the horses ate well, so they will be content on our journey to the fort. The sun was getting low in the sky so we headed for the fort. The wind was blowing from the west and the horses could smell the fires on the prairie. We got ready to go and Sarah opened the gate. She jumped on the back of a horse and she grabbed a handful of mane and she rode off in a hurry. The others followed, including the stallion that was so troublesome. It rode next to her, and that helped keep the others in line to follow. We made it to a clear stream and we stopped to water them briefly. Sarah stayed on that mare and she kicked the horses in the side and continued the fast pace. The soldiers cleaned of the clay off their faces, and jumped on their horses before they would have to walk back to the fort. They ate dust all the way as they were riding **Drag.** In about an hour we made the gate of the new fort and the sentry ordered the gate open and he shouted for the road to be cleared of anybody who was on the road, or in the way. We rode in and the Officer of the Day came, and he made the call for the quartermaster. They come out and they were overjoyed to see about 100 horses for their new remudas. The soldiers closed the gate and they made room for the horses at their corrals. The bold stallion ran off and tried to run loose. Sarah rode up to a soldier and took a rope lasso off his saddle and she rode to rope the horse. She rode hard and she threw the lasso out and pulled hard. She jumped off the horse and tied the other end to a stout post. The rope pulled tight and made a twang like a bowstring as it reached its limit. The horse reared back and other men came with ropes to put it separate from the others. We were tired and we were welcomed as heroes, as horses have been in short supply around here. We were given a place to rest and plenty of good food to eat. The quartermaster came to make a tally of our horses. His helper came and they both counted to compare their tally. They counted 115 horses! So we had a great many horses for them to break and it will take at least 8 to 10 weeks to break them all. It was a tall order. We wrote General Sam down at Huntsville for his advice.

November 20th, 1847. We are offered some good jobs to help out at the fort. We get paid higher than the going rate. The commander came over and he told us that so many men are gone out to support our General Zachary Taylor to help fight the new battles in northern Mexico. The revenge over

Santa Anna's capture has been great. We knew all about that issue and then some. They told us of the new battles but we did not want to hear any more of it. But their forces are spread too thin here at home. Since we are have been veterans of San Jacinto, and Buena Vista, we are allowed their trust and their hope to have us as citizen-soldiers, to act as the Texas Rangers do. They offered for us all to work at the fort to help in maintaining, breaking them well for dependable horses. It was suggested that we would possibly to help deliver the horses when they are ready for the troops. We refused as we have caused our wife too much grief, and we have done our duty twice over. That is too tall of an order, and we have to pray for the wisdom to do all they expect. We talked it over with the wife to see what she thought. The wife is excited about our new assignment, as she liked being out with us when we caught the horses. Josiah and Sam Bird rode home to tell Ben and Ke-Ke. They will go tell Simon and his boys so they can watch over our farm. I told them that the boys could live at our place to watch over the stock and maintain our fields as we have posted our plans for this season on the back of the barn door. This kept us focused on our duties, so we could be the best help here. This war has put us all in the line of fire and our place has been at the mercy of vagrants, deserters, and varmints of all kinds. We are putting a hedge against all that and it makes my stomach calm down, and I feel that this is the answer that I have been praying for. It is the answer to many prayers.

November 21st. The commander gave us a list of our duties and we are a detail to do those things in the best and most efficient manner possible. We met for the evening meal and we broke down the duty roster into parts to assign who does what. The boys will feed and maintain the horses, and Ben Bird will help me break the horses a few at a time. Ben uses different methods that the men do here at the fort. They ride them into the ground and they ruin what is a great horse by breaking it down to where it tends to be disobedient when time allows it. Ben uses less stress on the horses by using the more gentle methods that allow the horses to gain our trust as we did as we captured them from the prairies. To break their spirit makes them useless in warfare, and even for the plow. The boys are so excited that they are learning a new job at the fort, and they might have found a place to be incase farming is bad. We went on to find a place to stay and Captain Patterson asked us to stay at his dog-trot cabin as our barracks. Our children would enjoy the company of his children, and that would give us some peace of mind with all the meanness about these days. We are settled in and we made ourselves ready for tomorrow. The commander gave us work clothes and the status of being an acting captain as that was our rank when we left the army. So if we command the men they are to do as we command or they will be on Kitchen Patrol, and extra Guard Duty. We are to break the horses and let some of the younger soldiers do the hard work that we cannot do these days. The boys are given the status as privates, and they are getting some of the basic training as part of their duties. They are good boys and they are the same age as most, and they are tall and stout as any of them. So the last few months have been a trial by fire and we will come out better than we planned. We never know what the Lord has in store for us. We just must stay diligent, and ready for what demands must be in front of us. We pray for wisdom, and we hope to do what is right and proper, as our well-being demands it. Tonight we made the duty roster and made the proper assignments to it. We put our boys in there to help them learn to support our efforts here. They are responsible, serious minded and more mature than some of the grown men that are here. We gave them advice and encouragement that we would not let them struggle in our new assignments at the fort. Tonight we sat together and read the Bible. We took turns reading so we could get some wisdom from it all. We read JUDE, Chapter 20: "Difficult Days."

November 24th, 1847. More Peters' Colonists have come to the fort for orientation. We are to give them some advice so that they do not make the mistakes that many others have. We are to tell them about planning their cabins, what is best to plant here, and the proper advice to make trade with the local tribes. All the little details matter as it can cause you loss of life and limb. We have seen how people's ignorance has cost them much. If people listen and try to learn then they might just have a chance to make it on this frontier. We set up times to talk with them and some do not show up. We went on to find the people and bring them over to the meetings. I find several good soldiers and they bring them over to the Mess Hall to be better educated. I imagine that some stubbornness will come in handy here, but not with me, today. The day goes well and we answer their many questions, as well as give them the best advice. We get everyone on the same page. We have some good people coming here for the most part. The bad persons have been weeded out, and they are mostly married couples that have been carefully screened to keep out troublemakers and outlaws.*

December 2, 1847. We given leave to go back to our home to spend this month. We get settled back in to make a good Christmas. We have needed some time to break away from all our duties and the burden that has come from it all. Regular chores are welcome, as they are not set by someone else's clock. We are glad to be a part of the army to help out, as things are tough for many people who live here. Still to hear the birds in the trees and to watch the cows grazing in the unplanted fields was a wonder to behold. We have missed the small things, and we have seen that we are truly blessed with a family, and a nice home to come to. We went out riding horses with the family. We watched a distant storm over west Texas. The clouds billowed, and it looked much like an anvil. We rested the horses and we took time to sit and watch the storm over the desert. The lightning flashed and it was a sight. The sun shown bright through a break in the clouds, and two bright rainbows shown across the sky as other clouds grouped together. It was a handsome sight and we pondered it all, as we sat to eat lunch as a family. Having quality time together was what all our struggles have been about. From now on our focus will be our time like this were burdens were put away, and work was put aside for a time to be together. We watched the distant storm and it changed direction. We saw that it would be upon us in about an hour. We figured that it would be closer to ride to the safety of the Kick-a-Poo village and stay in their corncrib for safety. We rode on to the village and we made some comfort among them. Their dogs barked to greet us, and they wagged their tails as we offered them some scraps from our meal. Their elders came out to meet us and we were welcome to visit and take shelter here. Their women brought us gourds filled with water. They have been watching the storm as many have been out on a hunting party and they are due to return before sunset. We will wait for the storm to pass and hope and pray for their safe return. The storm comes and we head for the corncrib. We run the horses off for them to be safer. Their women and children huddle in to be safe as the wind becomes great. Then it gets very still, and we feel nervous. An elder says that **"E-Oh-La"** is coming! A tornado blows by and we hear the roar of the wind and the trees snap like twigs. We huddle down close to the ground and we hear the roof come off the corncrib. We are down below the ground in the deepest part of the root cellar. There is the rush of wind and then it is gone past. The sun shines through the open roof, and we come out to see that only their council house is mostly in tact, and most of their wigwams on the east side of the village escaped harm. Their children cry and we try to console them. They get quiet and we carry the smallest ones with us to show that all is well. Phoebe carried a toddler about and the camp dogs came back and we were throwing a stick about. The others joined in and it was making them calm again. We went about to look for anyone who might be lost in the storm, and the elders said that only the hunting party was missing from here.

A few hours and they returned safe with some 3 nice deer they have hunted. They took stock of everything, and we were glad that we were here to watch over their elders, women, and children, as we should do as good neighbors. We will stay here tonight and we will help them set back their homes.

December 3rd. We slept well in the council house and we woke early to make good use of the day. We help them gather the water sprouts that have broke off the trees. The elders directed the older children on how to best choose the limbs for the repairs that the men were doing. They helped carry water, and limbs to the workers to help save them steps and it was nice to see how they learned from a terrible event and that they were very positive on their outlook and nothing much set them back for long. The women have cooked a nice deer and there was a dance to celebrate surviving the storm. They called it "the water sprout dance." They held up a green tree limb and they gave thanks for it being used to make their shelter safe. We got up and joined in and the children did too. The drums pounded and then it was time to throw salt into the air to bless the ground again, and the give thanks for the nice deer they are enjoying for the hunt. We helped where we could and we ate of their hunt. They were grateful to be alive, as are we. We parted company and we headed for home to see if the storm had done us any harm. We get home by nightfall and it was good to see that only some treetops were taken off, and a few shingles were loose from our roof. We give thanks for the rain to be gentle on our home, and that all were safe.

December 24th, 1847. We meet at the church to celebrate Christmas together as a church family. We brought many things that we have put back from trade day to give as gifts, and a few extra things for just in case we have some new members to let them feel welcome with a small gift from us as new friends. We had many nice blankets and some trade items that Simon had made: some new iron fire strikers. We had some flint from the Comanche trade that we could spare to give since flint is so scarce in this area. A warm fire always warms a heart to think and rest better after a good meal and to keep the coyotes away when traveling out from home. I had 15 iron strikers here and 5 at home to trade and to use. So there will be some warm **hearths** in our part of Texas! We found some decent iron strikers after the war.

The wagons were placed in a secure spot and there were a good many here this month. We put the horses in the corral outside the churchyard so the boys could meet their friends to catch them up on the latest news and events with the Kiowa and Comanche. Some others stopped and asked us about what they heard from their boys' talking. I told them: "our responsibility as Christians goes to ALL our neighbors, as a good witness to what ever tribe they belonged to!" That is the gospel truth. It is our promise and pledge to do this thing.

Pastor Hodges heard me say that and he said that this would be in his Christmas message that he was to preach on tomorrow. I was proud that my words were well spoken, and not in vain like I do when I hit my finger with the hammer while doing the roof repairs. He laughed at my remark as he said, "we all have been there." I told the pastor how we had met with the Kiowa after finding their lost son. He likes that and he patted me on the back for returning the **prodigal son** back to his father. "He was a good son that was lost and now found again." I told the pastor that I felt being a Christian went beyond the churchyard and went into shoe leather as far as practicing doing what was right in God's sight. I have seen many at trade day that talked so vile for no reason and acted worse. We enjoyed seeing everyone and there were many new faces since we were here last. We talked and visited until we had to rest for a bit and take stock of some things. The women had decorated the wagons closest to the church with cut paper, tin decorations, *and some pies to die for.* I was tempted to look into the **pie keepers**, but I had to let temptation alone for I had to be polite and not sample the cooking until it was the proper time to do so. It is that we work so hard and we find reason to celebrate everyday. Christmas just makes it that much better as we have much to be thankful to God for: our family, our friends, and all of us celebrating our good health together. The ones that could sing sang Christmas songs, and the fiddles and guitars came out, and there was clapping of hands, and making the joyful noise to the Lord. It was wonderful to see so many together for our celebrating. We exchanged names on slips of paper and we drew with whom we would give a gift to tonight. The women helped in so many ways, and they treated Ke-Ke and Sarah well and they were kind to them as they were strangers to the new members. Red Bird has taken the Christian name Ben, but many still called him Red Bird for he is well celebrated for his role in the **Great Council** as a peace maker he is much honored in this area, and honored for his efforts. I had trouble thinking of my brother as "Ben." He was my friend no matter what I called him, and I would not be here if he had not healed me the day he found me on the hunting party years ago. I have so much to be thankful for and I do not know where to start for it is much to consider when I really think about it. Most of all I thank the good Lord for everything pales in His Sacrifice for me. We celebrate His birth, and His great gift to us today, and everyday. We read the Christmas story from LUKE, Chapter 2. We exchanged presents, and we sang and listed to the fine tunes on the instruments. The stars were bright, and it was fair to be outside under the lantern's glow. Thank God for all that He gives us! It is truly a Merry Christmas! It has been a good year for us all.

January 15th, 1848. We went out after a few cold days. It turned very fair for this time of year so it was time to do some hunting to put some fresh meat on the table. This was the boys' first attempt to a real hunt, so we will see how it goes. They took their guns to hunt with, but then they wanted to use their slings and rocks to hunt with. It was good because guns would scare off any worthy game. We held the guns and let them get more experience hunting. We stayed out of the way and watched. Boy, it was something to see them at work! They killed what game they aimed at and there were plenty of swamp rabbits to be had. We took them back home and the women had much to cook for the next few days. They skinned them, and got them ready for the cooking pot. We got the hides ready to be made into something useful. The coyotes were about and we had to use the firearms to scare them off. The boys had the slings, but we wanted to make sure that they stayed away from the boys to keep us safe. We told the women about our day and they always enjoy a good hunting story. Red Bird still likes a good rabbit cooked over the fire and the rest will be stew tomorrow. Sounds good to me.

Someone came knocking on the door disturbed the middle of the night. It was some lost travelers that had bought some land on Comanche land! We told them that their money was thrown to the wind, for the Comanche would not allow anyone to live any farther than our lodges. We are the last lodging on the edge of the frontier. The Comanche would not appreciate strangers moving to their hunting grounds, or cutting down their trees. They had come from Bird's Fort, but they did not listen to Captain Patterson's words, either. They described him from head to toe, and they must be as stubborn as a mule to not listen. We told them that there are many persons calling themselves land promoters who are as crooked as the Caddo's bent tree. The name on the paper was listed as **"Hedgecoxe."** He has a name that I have heard of a while back as a person connected to the **Peters' Colonists.** I understood him to be contrary, but not anything worse than most strangers here who do not know what is customary to do in Texas. They would not listen. We explained that our place is the edge of the settlement and that new settlements west of us would be disastrous to do!

They did eat as much rabbit as they could, and we asked them to please listen to reason. We asked that they keep their boys here to stay with our sons. They can stay until after they could go back to the fort with us in the morning.

Our words fell upon deaf ears. It was so hard to see that they wanted so much to have some land to call their own. Many of the new settlers have contempt for us older settlers thinking that we have no vision on what is best for the future of Texas. They also supported slavery, which is unthinkable! They had two slaves, which looked treated bad. The strangers would not sleep in our house for they thought us to be escaped slaves and "Indian-lovers."

They were rude, but as Christians, we had to show compassion in spite of their ignorance. Beggars can't be choosers. We showed them our San Jacinto Medal, and our letters from General Sam Houston. I called Red Bird by his Christian name "Ben" but they still saw him as an Indian because of his beads and feathers on some of his weapons. My Sarah is a good woman and she no longer interprets dreams for anyone. She is no longer called **Say-te-Qua**. She is now "Sarah." They were in awe of that, but still they thought us to be trouble. They can sleep in the barn if they want, if that is the way that they feel. It is too cold at night to sleep outside and I would not put a dog outside on a winter night. We put them in the barn and they had many blankets to keep them warm. I had trouble sleeping, but I finally slept after the moon set. We heard noise this morning and they were leaving out, and there was no stopping them: they were headed to the Comanche lands and there was no stopping their foolishness! We tried. We had promised our allies the Kiowa, and Comanche that we would do all that we could to stop travelers coming across their lands. We do all that we can, but we cannot be responsible for crazy persons who do not listen and think that they know it all! Our boys went out and jumped on their horses to follow them and ask them to come back. They got rocks thrown at them, and it hurt their feelings to be hit by rocks for their trouble. So we all have tried, and if they risk their lives to be foolish, then so be it!

It was stressful to me and I could not eat anything. I drank coffee and paced back and forth. The wife put me outside because I was in the way of her chores and I was underfoot too much. We did not make the boys to do chores today because they were hurt by the rocks and because it was warm during the day, we took them fishing because a cold front coming in this next week by the feeling of my bones. So this was the better thing to do was to get out and about. We went out and it was off in the distance that we see the big fire. It looked to be bad and we had the boys come with us as they need to know about the real world and not letting them see important things lets them know to be wise in their choices. We went out and found a burning campfire that had caught the woods on fire, and a burned wagon. We found both the man and woman slain in a terrible way. It was saber cuts as the **Texas Ranger** we had found. Their horses were gone and their boys and slaves were taken prisoner. They probably are to be traded to the Mexicans for servants, or worse to be treated as bad as slaves to work in their silver mines. We have to find some traces of a trail, but they knew how to make their trail covered well. We went as far as we could, but without more help we were going against the Mexican army with no arms, or men to help. It was headed towards the Del Rio area and that was keeping our women and children unguarded too long. We buried the dead and tried to find any important papers to take back to the fort. It was a tough day. The boys dug the graves after we started them dug properly. We wrapped the dead in blankets and made them a good funeral by saying some proper words over them. The boys did well and we were proud that they had learned some important lessons from this bad situation. Ben Bird did not like the dead bodies as he is still a healer, and the dead are something that he avoids as much as possible. He helped but he was very quiet the rest of the day. He then burned sage in a small fire to purify the place of death. He got out the drum and sang a blessing song to make the dead rest well. It is his way to do things, and I did what I could do too. I prayed for wisdom to know how to deal with all this.

Today I read from the Bible: MATTHEW, Chapter 18, "Forgiveness."

January 21-23, 1848. I went to the fort and left Ben to tend to the family. He wanted to go, but I asked him to stay and help protect the family in case of trouble. I brought all the papers I had found and I had written out the details of what happened in my journal. I copied it down on some paper and filed it with the Officer of the Day. They know me well at the fort so there was no problem. It was still difficult to think about those deaths and those that were taken captive. I saw Captain Patterson and he said that the **Texas Rangers** would be visiting us when the weather was decent to do a search. I felt like it was too late to do anything useful. I still will help when they arrive to search. It was a quiet ride back home. I stopped to water the horse and let her feed on some nice buffalo grass. We saw a herd of deer. They are healthy looking and that is a good sign to see that the hunting grounds were holding up to all the new settlers about. At the fort they said that close to the Del Rio that the buffalo and larger game had left that area, and headed elsewhere. I hope that that is never the case here, as we want it to be peaceful again and a good place to live. I will make sure that we keep all the **varmints** with four, and two legs, stay clear of where we live. I will do so even if it means giving my life to do just that. My family will inherit a good place to live and I will make sure to do all that I can, if it is God's Will.

CHAPTER NINE

Deaf Smith and the Caddo's Canoe.

January 24th, 1848. I got home late in the evening and the house was empty. There was a note saying that the family was at Red Bird's lodge. I went there and he looked glad to see me. The boys were trying to patch his leaky roof, and it needed a new **gable** to brace it to make it stronger. I saw a proper piece of timber and the boys helped me pry the old piece loose and cut the new timber in its place. I felt good helping him out, as he is not much of a carpenter. I am not much of a healer, so it works out that we all have our own special gifts that we can do best. We were able to reuse a good many shingles, and we made a dozen new ones just in case they were needed. It got late and I had a busy couple of days, so we stayed here to help out my good brother. I told Ben Bird about the turkeys and deer I had seen and he smiles as he enjoys hunting as much as anyone I know. I told him that it went well at the fort and that I hoped that it would be quiet around here for a few days. As soon as I laid down my head, I was gone to dreamland.

    I woke up to hear the hooting of an owl. It was very close by. I went to go outside to shoo it away. Red Bird said in Cherokee, "to stop, and be still. Listen and try to be quiet." It seems that an owl close by your lodge means that, "company is coming." I did not know this, as I have been a Cherokee a shorter time than most. I thought it was just an owl looking for a chicken dinner because his hens like to stay outside their roosts more often than stay in. The hooting owl continued for a good part of the night and I tried to sleep just the same. Red Bird got up and put a piece of wood on the fire and smoked his pipe as he does when he is thinking about important things. We will see how it goes.

    Well it rained this morning and the roof held up very well. I feel like it was well worth the effort to keep your lodge dry and warm. It turned a bit cold early in the morning but later it cleared up and it was nice. That hooting owl was gone, but he did get a few chickens for his visit. Red Bird said that the owl thinned down the poorly birds and let the stronger ones live. So he was all right with the owl's visit and disruption of a good night's sleep. We had some stout coffee and headed for our own lodge to see how it was holding up. We got home and found a visitor was camping there under the **lean-to** of the barn. The visitor looked familiar, but different. It was General Sam's scout, Deaf Smith! He looked well and life away from the regular army had not hurt him any. He said he was glad to see us, and we wished him the same. He was wearing a raccoon cap as the Louisiana and Arkansas tribes do. He had heard about the Kiowa boy that we found, and about the people that were being killed by someone with an army saber west of here. He was working with the Texas Rangers and he was writing a report to follow up to see if we had seen any new signs of trouble lately. Thank goodness, No. There was none that we knew of. I showed the scout around our land and he was most proud to see it because it was so far into the Comanche, and Kiowa lands. I told him that we had warned the strangers about the danger to leave out and we tried to take them to the fort to talk with the commander Ripley Arnold who was back from his duty with the peace details with Mexicans at Buena Vista. Smith said that it is important to keep our Indian neighbors good allies as we are still struggling in the war, and we could not afford to fight a war against Mexico, and any Indians that would side against us. A battle on two fronts would be most tragic for us, for certain. Santa Anna was a handful anyhow, and his commanders are just as ruthless and mean as he is. They have been waiting to jump in and do their worst, as they have had quite an education since Goliad, and then the Alamo battle. The Devil has his demons, and Santa Anna has his helpers.

Red Bird came over to have coffee and he was pleased to see that we had company, and an old friend at that! He elbowed me in the belly, and he reminded me about the owl the other night. Smith smiled at this, as he is most familiar with the Cherokee, and other tribes. Red Bird walked him to the place that the Caddo's canoe was hidden so we could return it when the weather was better. Smith said, "It was quite a piece of carved cottonwood!" Also that he was returning to Jefferson by the spring, and that he would return it to the Caddo tribe at Timber Hill. I thought about our Caddo boys that we had for sons when they lived with us for a Winter Count. The Timber Hill had lots of trade ties with the Red River trade, and the East Fork of the Trinity, so they would be familiar with who might own the canoe. So he will return it for us, and we can stay here to protect our home with trouble staying so close to here. Our old friend was a good sight to see and we had the boys show off their use of a sling and a rock to show him how their aim is so good. He was impressed. I told Smith, "If you see a Kiowa sling a rock, you know where they learned it!" I told them about the feather ceremony, and the chigger bites and the camp at the salt spring to cure them. He laughed and he enjoys a good story over the campfire. We whittled on sticks like General Sam and we talked and visited for most of the day. We have missed our friend and we have some catching up to do. The women put on a great feast and they well remembered the scout named Deaf Smith. He held the new baby and we showed him all the members of our tribe. His raccoon hat scared Phoebe, and he took it off and stuck it on her head to show that it was just a fancy head covering. The boys then teased her, and she chased them around like a proud Cherokee to show that she was not afraid of them, just that hat he wore. Smith said he could stay a few days and rest up and leave out if the weather was fair. We had no complaints to having company and letting him feel that he was still our friend after all this time. It will be a good reunion to have him stay here a number of days. He can rest and visit with us anytime he wants to come this way. He is our friend for life.

Deaf Smith and the Caddo's canoe

February 9th. We were out looking for horses and Young Bull rides up to tell us some news. He said that he heard that La Morris had passed away yesterday while out picking up firewood. He was trying to lift his wagon out of a bog and he died right on the spot! I felt bad for his wife Mina, and his sons David, and Roscoe. We will have to put off rounding up stray horses, and go to **Free City** by the **Cross Timbers.** The boys rode ahead to tell the women so they could pack up the wagons for traveling. We hated to hear that **La Morris** had met his reward so soon. Ben Bird told me that he will miss La Morris too, for he could tell some good stories, and he loved to farm and hunt. I told him that we would help put things right at his house after we give La Morris a good burial and a fitting send-off. We got home and the women had packed some quilts, food and some clothes for the journey. The boys had the horses harnesses up and ready and had secured the cabin for while we would be gone. We put out extra corn and feed for the animals and the pond was full enough to give them all the water they would want. So there was nothing left to chance. I did not look forward to this visit. It was something a friend does for another friend. So we headed down the way past Bird's Fort, east, down Grapevine Springs Road to the place of the cedars, and hills that lead to Free City. People were waiting along the trail looking for visitors. They showed us where their cabin was now located. This was some new settlement! There was nice and neat cabins put up, a good well, and a lake made by a beaver dam that they let go up. It was quite a lovely place in spite of the situation. We put up the horses and wagon in the open place and went to their cabin. We saw Deacon Brown and Belle. They looked well. We saw their son Samson had grown into a grown man worthy of the name. We saw Mina and the boys. They looked tired and they held up well. We brought out the food and a sack of flour and sugar, as was our tradition when seeing old friends after a long while. They enjoyed seeing us, and the **lagniappe** from us was most appreciated. We hugged them and we tried to find the proper words to say. Mina asked me to speak some words from the Bible since I love to read so much. Pastor Hodges from the **Lonesome Dove** could not be here because of an illness in his family. I had my Bible in my pack as always, but a number of verses came to mind as I thought about it. I went outside to pray about what would be proper to say over my friend's funeral. It was an hour past noon by the sun's path and I had about 2 hours to consider my words well to give my friend La Morris a good send-off. I walked among the trees and prayed for wisdom to speak well and not stammer as I can do at times. Much like Moses did, I have my "Aaron" here to help me sort things out. **Ben** Bird came along and found me. He brought my inkwell and a reed pen. I took a piece of scrap paper and wrote down notes with some Bible verses put in the right places. Ben Bird has always kidded me that I was never short on words like General Sam. I guess my mentors have done well to inspire me along the way. I wrote down the words and then they poured out like rain on a spring day. I tried to be brief, but then a friendship deserves to be well remembered, and well respected with some fine words during their wake and funeral. Ben Bird carved on a stick and he handed it to me for a while to give me time to consider my words. He can read well, but mostly the new Cherokee alphabet. I have yet to learn read or write these letters. I took my paper and read it for him and he stopped and listened to my words. He said, "Ahho": "Very Good!" I am now ready. I went to washed my face and put on a nice shirt and a tie, my church-meeting, best clothes to look well. We went to the front room of the cabin where La Morris was laid in a cedar box that the carpenter and blacksmith had made. It was well made and thoughtful. **Ben** Bird stayed outside and waited for me. I went in and had some private time to think about my friend and our times together when he was considered an outlaw and an outcast. We all have been there. Now he was free from the burdens and trials of life. It is time to speak. A friend got out his **fiddle** and played the wonderful song, "Amazing Grace." We all knew all the verses. I tried to take notes from the sermon writing words from the church meetings. It was quite fitting and it inspired me to speak that much better when it was my time to give the words of consolation for La Morris. I spoke and there were many hardy "Amen's" added and I did not stammer once. I tried not to cry, but even a man has feelings sometimes for a lost friend. Friends carried his coffin underneath a shady tree and we lowered it into the ground. His wife placed flowers on the coffin and we threw a clump of clean dirt into the grave and we said a prayer for our good friend. We will miss our good friend and remember him. We walked away, and others filled in the grave after we left as they had that as their duty to La Morris. We were quiet and Mina asked for us to tell about our friendship as some had done at the wake. Many were not there as the word was slow to get around. We stood up and talked and rejoiced over our times together and we celebrated his life. We ate late in the evening and it was a feast to celebrate our friendship.

We turned in early, as we would need to help the boys with their chores as they had much to do and they had been helpless with grief to do much these past days. We work early and tried to be quiet as not to wake the household while we did their chores. Samson, David and Roscoe came outside and started pitching hay into piles into the wheelbarrow. We told them to go back to bed and rest today. This was part of our duty to our friends. They did not want to because they had not slept hardly at all. It was understandable, but we urged them to go back and rest for a few more hours. Ben Bird came with some swamp rabbits for their cooking pot. He handed them to Roscoe to skin it, as it is tradition in the Cherokee tribe to let the young ones skin the kill of the hunt to teach them to clean a kill well before cooking to make it taste better. I handed them my sharp knife and they got busy skinning their food for today. I guess it was better to let them do something since they could not sleep. We will handle the tough chores today like mucking out their horse stalls, and let the boys have an easier day to give them time to ponder their father's loss. Well, it was a full day and we had much to do to get caught up around here. I put up a few fence posts, and worked on a gate that had fallen down. Mina was up and she brought hot coffee and **johnnycakes** made of coarse ground corn. There was milk and honey and all a body could stand and need to survive. I pondered over all they had done here and I realized that we all are building a fine place to live here in this wilderness called Texas. We have tamed this wilderness with the good Lord's Grace, and lots of motivated people working sunup to sundown. We will leave in the morning as the sun is too low to travel home and the coyotes here are too fierce, and plentiful. They would endanger us on the road home. Mina does not need to be alone here, and we need to fix their roof in the morning, as it is to be the rainy time soon. Tonight we read the Bible over the hearth and we pondered the mysteries of God's Word. We read the words of the Apostle Paul. We read FIRST CORINTHIANS, Chapter 9, "Self Control and Discipline."

February 12th, 1848. We came home to an empty house! There was no sign of anyone and the animals were stressed out running in circles. I have just walked around to check on things. I threw some hay and feed out to all the animals. Then I saw tracks all over the place. Ben Bird headed for his place to see if all is well. I asked him to make the smoke signs if he needed me to come. Well directly he made the smoke signs. I loaded up the weapons, the lance, and food, and kept the horses and wagon hitched. I headed full gallop to Red Bird's place. It was a mess and it did not look good. I was beside myself and I did not know what to do.

Simon came there because he saw the smoke signs. I was glad because we would have to head into the **Comancheria**, the lands of the Comanche and Kiowa. Simon brought plenty of knives, so we were in good for some decent trade. A rider came out to inform us that our family has been found, and their captors are now prisoners. They had our wives, our boys and some Mexican deserters as their prisoners. We made the trade signs and the word was passed to their chief to come meet us. We were to meet at noon when the sun was high in the sky. We were relieved that they were safe. Josiah was hurt, but alive, and Sam Bird has a broken arm trying to fight off the Mexican soldiers. The soldiers were bound to a tree with ropes. We were allowed to tend to them, as their **medicine** was not as strong as ours. Josiah had a busted mouth, and a black eye that was swollen shut and it was most fearful to see him that way.

Red Bird got out his medicine bag and burned sage and he beat the drum to let others know that healing was about to commence and that they should give us some room to do what we needed to do to help them. I took a stout piece of cedar and carved it to make a splint for Sam Bird. Red Bird asked some braves to hold Sam Bird still when Red Bird pulled his arm back in place. He threw up from the pain, but he did not cry out like a good Indian. The women brought mud from the salt spring and put on Josiah's swollen eye. It burned like the sun, but then it started helping after a few hours. Their medicine man was watching all we were doing and he danced around like a crazy person as they do to ward off evil spirits. The Mexican soldiers were deserters from Del Norte and the Kiowa and Comanche had them staked out in the sun to punish them. These tribes hate deserters and cowards and they were being punished. One had died from exposure to the elements, and one had been staked to a red ant bed. They were paying well for their crimes. One was left alive. He was badly wounded by the slings and rocks that our boys had sent against them when they attacked our home place. I was proud of the boys that they were all well and they had fought like good Cherokees to protect their home and family! At noon Chief Peta came along with a cousin of Buffalo Hump's called Red Rock. He did not like us at all! We showed our Kiowa necklace and lance. That put him to being quiet. He had no say over us, and we liked it that way.

Chief Peta and young Quanah came and sat with us by the sage bundles and the campfires. They asked us what we should do with the surviving prisoner? We considered what to do. We said that we would take him back to Bird's Fort and let them have him as a prisoner. Young Quanah went with the boys and sat with them. He practiced slinging a rock with Sam Bird's sling. The flying rock leaving at the wrong time made him nervous. Chief Peta laughed. He told us that they have no use for cowards and that we could do with the prisoner as we wished as he has attacked our lodges for no good reason. Simon brought out some of his knives and iron goods. They smiled as he had made some iron goods they needed some stout spear points, knives, and fire strikers. Simon showed them how well the fire strikers work and they looked well pleased. They accepted them in trade for the prisoner, and that they had well treated and protected our women and let no one bother them. They were brought to us and we held them and they cried for joy to see us all well and back together safe, in spite of the circumstances. They had a council and a **pow wow** that will last all night to seal the deal.

The Texas Rangers

CHAPTER TEN

The Mexican deserters and the sick stragglers.

February 21-26, 1848. We went out and got the plows to plow around the cabins to make a firebreak. The grass was so dry from the cold winter wind of the past weeks. The ground was tough but we needed to keep the lodges safe from the threat of fire until the spring rains come. We started out the plowing and directly my back gave out so it was time to let the boys continue to let them get some good practice for spring plowing. They were good on the reigns and did not over burden the horses too much. It seemed that it went by faster with our boys helping us get it done. We went over to **Ben Bird's** and plowed around his place and it was done well before nightfall. We decided to stay at Ben's and plow his new field to get some clay for the women to make pots and clay baskets from. He has some nice red clay in that northern section and it makes better pots than that black gumbo clay does. We got out there and dug up some clay and the women were up in the porch making some fine pots. Phoebe made some nice ones and she like to make pots with animals on the handles. She made a tall bird handle, a frog, and a turtle. They were all quite interesting and useful too. Ben Bird had a shelf put up where the pots could dry before they fire them in a few days over the coals. The boys were kidding Phoebe and called her "turtle" because they liked her turtle pot the best. That was a good name and Sarah liked it for her as a pet name to call her by. So she has got a new name as of today. It turned cold during the evening and we packed up and went back to our lodge to tend to things. We enjoyed the fair days while we could and it looked like it might snow by the way the clouds looked.

Tonight we read from the Bible to show our appreciation for having a good family, a safe home, and good allies. We read ROMANS, Chapter 12, Verse 12, "Faithful in Prayer."

March 8th. We had a week of snow and it was cold as only Texas could be. Ice sickles hung off the trees and some were so large that they broke the tree limbs. It was much as it was at Washington-on the Brazos during the **Consolation.** It is colder than you can stand, for too long. The boys were outside putting out hay for the animals. They were taking too long so I went to check on them. They were using their slingshots knocking off ice sickles off some of the trees. I stood back and watched them for a while before they knew that I was there. They had been hold up in the cabin for a few days so they needed to get out so they would not fight with each other as brothers sometimes do. They are quite good in their aim, and they had impressed the elders of both the Kiowa and Comanche nations. I let them play a while longer for that is how they learn of the world. There will always be chores and plenty to do around here, so some fun is in order when the time presents itself. We went out and picked a few chickens for the cooking pot and the boys had them dressed out in a hurry for they were hungry, as always. I brought in some bigger logs for the fire and some kindling to make a good fire. The women had the same idea for they were well into making a fire when I opened the door to come in. It was fair today, but the cold just creped into my bones. A good fire made it all better. We had a knock at the door and it was Major Patterson who had been out in a scouting party. He was most welcome to come in. He asked if his men could camp on our property. They were tired and needed to camp here. It looked like it was going to be a cold night. The ferry crossing was closed because of the ice and cold of the past days. We had some chickens to spare to feed them, but he said that the men had killed a deer to eat. He said that he had found sight of the man that had killed the settlers west of here. He lost sight of him as the snowstorm broke and he was most frustrated over it. He thought the man to be *another deserter* from the Mexican army from the cut of his coat, his saddle, and tack. Major Patterson had an idea to stay here and let the man think that he had returned to the fort, and then he plans to go back and get sight of him and capture him. I offered to get Chief Red Sun, or Spotted Tail to help track him as only an Indian can. He considered it good since he gets his trade horses from Red Sun, to let him help out in the capture. The army needs all the allies that it can get. I went out and built a fire to make smoke signals to get Red Sun's attention. Ben Bird came by and it was good timing for he is the expert on making smoke signs the best. He took an old blanket and wet it down good and placed it over the smudge fire. He made the signals four times and then he saw a distant fire return the same signs meaning that he understood we wanted some help. "He would be here by the morning," Ben Bird told Major Patterson. Ben Bird was ready to capture this person as well as he has contempt for that deserter who kills women and children who are innocents in battle. I did not know that Ben Bird was the one who found the others that had been slain! He has been quiet, and he does not talk much anyway. He gets things done and talking is "wasting daylight" for him! Today he had something to say and he reported what he had found a few days ago while he was out hunting. It made me angry to think of it, and Ben Bird said for me to save my anger for when I was making battle. We went to sleep early because we were going to have a full day tracking this deserter. The boys wanted to come along and the Major thought it good that they come along too because they were old enough to be helpful. They were over their injuries, and restless to help out, and get the troublemakers who have made us not sleep well at night. They are good and strong braves. They want to be Texas Rangers, Josiah and Sam Bird said. They could be if they wanted to. They would pass the test.

We woke early and the Major's men helped us do our chores. We gave then a bucket of milk and fresh eggs for them to enjoy. We might not get to eat for about a day so we had better eat good while we can. Red Sun rode up about daylight. He had several of his tribe with him. He also had a horse pulling a travois on which his son Young Bull laid. Young Bull was wounded, and next to him was a horse on which a prisoner was tied. It was the Mexican deserter! Young Bull had caught him robbing the Kick-a-Poo's corncrib. Red Bird rushed over to tend to him. Red Sun brought the deserter to the army to tend to him so that it would be fair in the sight of the army and the settlers. A Kick-a-Poo hates a person who deserts in battle, and someone that kills for no reason is most hated and not long for this world. Young Bull is wounded with saber cuts to his arms, and his left shoulder. Red Bird had the women get some linen torn into strips. He got some sinew and the women's sewing needles and stitched up the boy's shoulder and arms. Like a good Indian he did not cry out in pain, or complain when he was being sewn up. Red Bird then wrapped the boy's wounds with linen to keep the air and dirt off it so it would heal better.

The soldiers wanted to hang the deserter on the spot, but Red Sun said, "If I wanted to kill this man I would have already done this!" Red Bird said, "We do not want to shed blood on this land, as enough blood has been shed here. The army will take charge of him and do with him, as they will. This young brave has lost very much blood. He will die if we move him any more today."

Red Sun was silent, and he stood tall and made it clear that he agreed with Ben Bird by staying here a few days. My sons were distressed to see their friend hurt so badly. They stood by the **travois** and tried to make their friend comfortable. We let him rest for a few hours, and then the soldiers carried him carefully into the cabin to be safe. The deserter cried out, and shook uncontrollably. He asked for mercy. Red Sun told him in Spanish, "You have chosen to take the wrong path, so you end up at the wrong end of trouble. You make death, and death is what you deserve!" Red Sun took out his buck knife and cut himself on the arm to draw blood. He then wiped the blood off his knife unto the deserter's shirt, and put it back into the sheath. He then handed the reins of the prisoner's horse to the Major to have him dealt with. The women watched from the window of the cabin and they came out to bring a pot of stew on the porch. We all had lost our appetite. The army saddled up and left with the prisoner in half an hour. It was awful to see Young Bull hurt so badly. The boys brought a young pup to him that our dog had 10 weeks ago. He smiled and held the dog as it licked his face. He fell asleep. It was a relief that another deserter was caught and getting his due reward. We were quiet the rest of the day and let our guest rest and get stronger. He slept the rest of the day and he woke up in pain. I gave him some **mesquite tea** that Red Bird had made and he rested better. He woke about midnight and he wanted to talk and see his new pup. So I felt that he was doing better. He is young and strong so he will heal well. I prayed for the boy to be healed, and for there to be less killing around here. It is bad enough that *life has been lost in battle from both sides*. We just want to farm, live here, and hunt in peace. Just to trade horses was enough to make ends meet. It is a shame that so much energy was being used to kill, and for what good reason? We thought that our battle at San Jacinto would end it all, and we could let the dust settle and live in peace. It seems that it is the first of many battles we will have to fight to just lay claim to our own land. The Lord knows all, and He will tell us in good time. So we must be patient and act wisely in all things, large and small. We look to find wisdom in reading to find some solutions, in solitude. Tonight we read, ROMANS, Chapter 3, Verse 23, "All have sinned."

March 12th, 1848—Red Sun came and took Young Bull home. He brought two slain buffalo as a gift. We took it with gratitude, as turning away a gift is a bad insult. We appreciate the meat for the table just the same. We gave the young brave another pup so it would be stronger with another of its kind. We will go to their camp for **winter count** in a week. By afternoon a big rain came and it poured down in torrents until the West Fork flooded. The Kick-a-Poo are home by now, and safe, so it is good just to rest and consider what to plant this spring. Some blue and yellow corn would be good. The roof is leaking so there is good use for the new clay pots. We gathered together in a dry corner to sleep. The rain was still a welcomed guest, the roof will wait until it gets clear outside again. It will be a good time to teach the boys how to fix the roof better.

March 15th. We got the tools out and fixed the roof. Sam Bird stepped on the wrong place and fell through the roof. He was just stunned, and no real damage was done to our boys, or the roof. So once he gathered his wits back he went back up and fixed the roof better than it was before. I was just glad that he was not hurt badly. This is how you learn, by mistake, as much as anything else. We then went to Ben Bird's cabin and fixed a few places before the spring rains come again. He had been setting out a few clay pots to catch the rain too. So it has been a good day of work, soon to be followed by some rest. Bossing the boys was harder work than doing it myself. How would they learn unless we try to let them do, and sometimes fail, or sometimes to fall?

March 21st, We went to the Kick-a-Poo's and Kiowa's. There was quite a **pow-wow,** and at here was many new children to name from since last spring. We had quite a good visit, and we traded some good horses for barter of blankets and buffalo robes. Simon went with us, and his iron tools, and goods made him very popular to the tribes. They did a dance to honor him, and Simon did not want to join the dance. We drug him out to dance, and then he joined in and enjoyed himself. The tribes held up the tools, knives, and implements and danced the Iron Dance, which showed respect for someone that forges iron. Flint has been hard to find, so some iron spears points, knives, and tools, will help everyone eat better. Simon got a leather vest, and they put a turkey feather in his hatband, to show he is well-favored in their sight as a wise person. We had a good visit, and it was nice to forget our troubles for a while and have a reason to celebrate together in our extended families. Their elders and medicine men burned sage, and threw salt to all four directions to bless everyone.

So we brought a barrel of corn seed to give out between them. It was much useful. The women all lined up and filled their corn pouches. They did the blue corn dance, and they made a happy song that filled the whole valley. The single folks were joined together, and our boys will be among them in a few years. The elders patted us on the back like we were their own family. They asked us to include our boys to marry their maidens. (*"They still have a few more years to learn more, for their mothers' sake," we said to the elders.*) Their elders were ready to marry them off to their fair maidens. They grow up so fast, it seems. I remember when Ben Bird were in those shoes. Being single persons was good, but being married to our wonderful wives is what is best. It has made me know what true happiness is all about. Our sons make us proud, and they will be good stewards to this land, when their time comes to take over. It is as the Lord had intended for people to live.

Tonight we read, SECOND TIMOTHY 1:7, "I have not given you a spirit of Fear."

We headed back, and made a tour of Copper Canyon, after seeing some wild horses there. They were some beauties, so we would be back soon to catch a few of them for the army, and a few for ourselves. It was tempting to catch a few, but the day being so late made the attempt to catch horses, too dangerous for today. Red Bird mentioned this tonight: First things, first: since it is spring, we need to plant more crops first. Squash is what would be best, according to the farmers' almanac. We will check the seed pots to see if we need to trade for some at the next trade day at the fort. We enjoyed our time with the tribes, for we have missed the freedom they have to move about, as the wind blows. We pray for our Cherokee families at **Telaqua.** We have missed our **Chief Bowles**, and **Chief Mush**, since they suffered terribly at the hands of Lamar's forces almost seven years ago. We hope that they would be proud to see how we have maintained the tribe here. We have tried to do as many things as they would have wanted us to. We always pray for wisdom to do what is right in the sight of the Lord, and to make our wives happy that they married us. Red Bird helps me everyday to stay on track, to keep me motivated, and to ask me questions to make me think about things I might have missed. We took a tour of the barn with the boys. They showed me the new kittens that will keep the barn free of mice. They were most handsome, and they will keep the corncrib free of pests too. So our life has many small blessings that we do not always get to see, or enjoy our lives as we should.

Today we read: PHILIPPIANS, Chapter 4, verse 9: God will supply all your needs.

A sky stone on a travois

CHAPTER ELEVEN

The Falling Star.

April 3rd, 1848. It has been a long day working the new fields. Our decent night's sleep is disturbed. Some coyotes are loudly barking by doing some serious howling outside. Our mule Jenny brays like there is trouble close by. I go outside to look around and I try to figure out if we have uninvited guests. The frogs stop croaking and I look up at the night sky. There is a roar like cannon fire and a falling star races low across the sky. It burns bright like Mexican fireworks and it hits west of here making a loud whistling noise. It broke into several pieces and then it was gone. It made me wonder where it came from and then I wondered where it landed. The children and wife come outside to see what was going on. I put out some hay and oats and I tell them about the falling star passing so close and low in the sky. The noise woke them and they barely caught sight of it. None of us have slept well for the longest and the slightest thing keeps us on edge. We pondered on what it was and where it came from. I pointed out the direction where part of it landed past Ben's place to his far fields. The other part landed much farther out to the Kiowa's lands towards the Clear Fork. I told the boys that we could ride out tomorrow to see where it landed. We went to bed and we tried to sleep. The frogs continued to croak and that lulled me to sleep, finally. I woke early and made coffee, and the boys got up and they made use of my old map to see where we might look. After our trips for horses, and their finds of the Caddo's canoe, the metal arrow point, the strange alligator bones, and fossil shells: they were looking for a day of adventure to look for a fallen star. We would probably not find anything, but the boys needed a distraction from their chores. These kinds of things teach them important and unexpected lessons. I learn a good many things and most of all I get to see how my boys act in different situations.

April 4th. We went out looking for some adventure as we have the chores well tended to. The wife came along and we went to Ben's. He was out in a distant field with a shovel digging. Some of the ground is burned. It was a firestorm from the sky! We rode along where a long trench went across an unplowed field and there were broken trees tops like a big storm has passed. Ben said that a big noise passed over his place, and he looked to see a bright light in his distant field. He waited to see what it was and then he saddled up his horse to ride up to see it. Part of the field was burned and the rock has made a trench and a hole where it hit the ground. There were several pieces of iron rock and smaller pieces about on the ground. There were pieces of glass where the hot stone melted the soil as it touched it. It was pretty and awesome! Ben Bird let us have some pieces of it. It looked like tear drops where the hot stone cooled overnight. Sarah was looking at it all and she said that this is something that she has never seen before. She loves to watch the summer nights when the falling stars are abundant. She said that this one was unexpected at this time of year. She did not know what they were and to see one up close was exciting as she did not know that they were so big as this was just part of one.

We saw the smoke signs and we heard the drums across the prairies. The dances must be on for this one requires a special way to remember it. We rode on to the west and we saw where the treetops were torn out like at Ben's. In one spot the whole woods were cleared away and there was a deep ditch with the same glass dewdrops that we saw before. There the Kiowa have made a big dance to celebrate the passing star. They were decked out and painted up well. The majority of the Kiowa wanted it left alone. Their **Qualls** comes out and she said that she wants it moved. They have a negotiations and she wins out. We have a shovel in our gear and we offered it to them to use. They first pick up all the glass dewdrops on the ground. They passed them among the children to keep. Digging out the stone would be a harder task, as it was down fairly deeper than expected. We took turns digging and we uncovered quite an iron rock. I went to raise the shovel and it pointed towards the rock. I held it by the handle and I tried to move it away and it still pointed towards it. I let go of it and the shovel stuck to it! The metal is very much attracted to it. I took out my compass and it was pointing west towards the stone, and not towards the north! So it seems that it is magnetic, so it has an attraction to all iron that gets close to it. So now their **Qualls** wants to move the stone to the north, away from their camp because she thinks it to be evil. Women: what would we do without them? Ben sympathized with the Kiowa and he said that the stone is heavier than it looks, as it is quite dense and heavy for its size. We knew from the small pieces that we picked up that it would be hard to move. They finally got it all uncovered and it was quite a rock! It looked like a strawberry in color and the pits that covered it. We showed them how to make a lever to move it. They were impressed that we could move the big stone with ease, as it would be impossible to move no matter how many tried to move it. They drew a picture of it on their buffalo hide that marks Winter Count, to mark the event for a future time. It is much as when I wrote things down so I can remember them later, Ben said.

Their Qualls walked in a circle around the stone and she had words for it: some that are not so pretty. Their chief, Lone Wolf stops her. He has her to sit down and be quiet. I was glad for all our sakes. I was still hard of hearing these days, and what I could hear was not very pleasant. It was good to have her quiet to return to the peaceful afternoon. We are asked to help move the stone and the broken tree limbs are being used to make a stout travois to move it. We helped pick out a suitable horse to move it along. We offered some rope to use to bind the wood together. We managed to use a lever to move the stone to where it can be taken away to a different place. It seems that they think it is bad luck since it came so close to their village here. We rode along to the north and we made progress to move the stone. The horse pulling the travois tires and we rest by the Clear Fork. We resume the trip and we head towards the Red River. It would take another day to get there. I send the boys back home with the wife to be at the farm as they were getting tired from this, and there was nothing for them to do. We headed on and the trip went smoothly to the north. It seems that they want this rock placed in the Red River where it would be placed along the banks.

The rock has a few crystals hanging off it so I broke one of them off to keep for a souvenir. The Qualls sees me and she asks for it back. She has a fit and she takes it from me and she throws it to the ground. Some people are no fun at all. She has no sense of humor, or a sense of adventure. We rode on and she was giving the evil eye the whole time. The Kiowa braves laugh because they know what a pain she is. I am glad that I do not belong to their tribe and that my wife is a good Qualls, and she is a Christian to boot. We make camp for the night and we settle down. No one slept very well because of all the dances that had to be done. I felt it was not needed since we were moving the stone away from their camp.

April 5th. The morning came sooner than we wanted as this was another day without much sleep. We headed on to make time to the Red River crossing. We stopped to rest and we made better time towards the afternoon. It would be another day before we got there dragging that rock along on a travois. We joked that the trail home would not be hard to see as the travois made such a deep ruts as we went along.

April 6th. We finally made the trail to the Red River. The Qualls, **Waunell**, was happy for a change. We were all glad about that so this day was already off on the right foot. We got up to the river so we pushed the stone into the river without any fanfare. I hated to see all the trouble it was for this to be moved so far. This stone came from a long distance to get here, and now this trip was the longest of any. I know that the horse was glad that it was no longer dragging that big rock around. We are keeping our part of the sky rock and we feel that it is a sign that our good fortune will continue as it did not hit our homes, or their village. We went on and we had time to rest before we headed back. The Kiowa broke out some parfletches of dried buffalo meat and it was time to have a good meal and then we would head back. The Qualls came up to me and she handed me the crystal that she had taken from me and thrown to the ground. I accepted it and she sat besides me and we got along well. She talked with me and she tried to ask me a question about farming and about horses. Ben Bird smiled and he answered for me. He told me the words to say, and the Kiowa laughed at my attempt to speak their language. We understood each other better now. We enjoyed the rest of the day. We camped here and we would travel back tomorrow. Tonight we saw another falling star and it was high up in the sky and distant. We smiled and knew that our troubles were well behind us, for now. We are like this falling star: we have traveled a long way from where we once were. We have moved along and changed for the better.

April 8th. We get back to the Kiowa village, and Chief Lone Wolf says that they are moving to a different spot as their spring camp is farther south. We were told that we are always welcome and that we would go hunting together sometime after they get their new camp settled. The trip home went faster and we made it back in a day since we did not have to rest the horses so often.

We get home and we tell the wife and children what we knew of our trip to the Red River. I gave Sarah the crystal that the Qualls gave me, and she put it on the mantle over the fireplace. We worked hard for that and it was a nice prize to bring home. The best of all it was good to be back home and we hoped for no other stones to fall from the sky anytime soon.

April 14th. We have a serious thunderstorm yesterday. It rained and made a twister out across the prairie. Many of the old oak trees are broken like twigs. It also hailed last night, and it was so deep that it was like it has snowed outside! We measured hailstones three inches across! They are over a foot deep, and even though it was yesterday there still are piles of the ice still intact around the shade of the house. Many of the trees are striped of leaves. We found several wild animals killed by the hails stones pelting them: we found rabbits, squirrels, and a chaparral killed. Our cattle were banged up and restless from being out in the unexpected storm. So what looked like a spring storm was more than we expected.

April 21st. It is the anniversary of the San Jacinto battle. I try to stay busy and not think of it as many die as the armies are still fighting battles in Northern Mexico. We wondered how Santa Anna was surviving as a captive and that the others in his command were more wicked and fierce as they have learned from the best! We still respect him as our enemy, and we pray that he can help negotiate a peace treaty that would end the battles between us, for good. It would be better than the Velasco treaty twelve years ago. This is always a tough day for us to remember the terrible day of battle. Some days need to be forgotten as they were terrible even though something good came out of it. Still many people died fighting for what they believed in as that deserves remembering for their sacrifice on both sides.

Ben Bird said that he saw buffalo west of us and that we might be on a hunting party soon. It sounded good to get out and ride and we got the family out to see it. We rode to see how large a herd it is. It was larger than some we have seen in a while. We saw the smoke signs and we were ready for a good hunt. We left them and we rode towards the new Kiowa camp. The Kiowa have their lines set up to hunt and they offer us some of their best arrows and darts to use. They said that no guns would be used as it scatters the whole herd before they can sort things out. I liked the idea of using the arrows and darts, as that would be a sign of a great hunter. The boys get a chance to show off their skills as young braves. We meet and we draw out our plans in the dirt with a stick so that we all agree on a battle plan. We take several stones and place them to represent a whole herd, and we made our plan to push them towards the river and make them bottled up at the West Fork. We agreed that it was a good plan. We have plans to have their elders start a fire to keep the best part of the herd away from the open prairies. The wind changed so that plan could not be viable any longer. We still planned to drive a great herd towards the ravines of the West Fork. The women and elders stayed clear of the hunt and they watched from a high hill. This made our aim that much more careful as we have a reputation to maintain. The signal is given to start and the drums start on the high hill to startle the buffalo towards the river. They yell and sing and they are very bold in their songs. We ride and make good time to catch up with them and we make a good many kills and the others are slain in a good and quick manner. I looked to see if my wife was watching and a bull came up and startled my horse. I fell down and a young Kiowa rode up with an extra horse for me. This was a lovely sight as being on foot was not something that would be healthy for me. A fine horse was available and I jumped on it. A young Kiowa shot a nice dart at the bull that was so aggressive towards me, and my favorite horse. He was most proud, as I was proud of him for both our sakes. There was a ridge we crossed and there were some nice cows to be taken down. Again a bull ran up and it was my turn to shoot as I had the best chance to taking it down.

So we were even on the saving of each other's bacon. I was glad to be in good company. We rode on and the drums beat loudly from the hilltop meaning that enough buffalo were slain to feed us all from this hunt. We sent to see if everyone was safe. Thankfully no one had anything worse than bruises. I have a few and that isn't so terrible considering what it could have been. My horse was not hurt too bad, and she could be mended with some time. The women and elders came down and we have to eat some hearts and livers, as we are due, as good hunters. The women come down and cut the buffalo along the backbone and they start the careful butchering of the hunt. There is a great beating of the drums, and singing being thankful for the hunt and the safety of the hunters. The young hunter came and he gave me his knife, and I gave him mine in trade. It was one of Simon's best, and his was made from a black stone with a horn handle. The blade was like glass, and sharper than iron. It was most handsome and we made a great trade. The main thing is that we are unlikely allies. We have a common mission: to survive here and prosper. The butchering is done and the meat is put into parfletches to keep it clean. The hides of the buffalo are used to wrap up the meat and we head towards the Kiowa camp and there is a big celebration. Ben makes the drum ring loud and others join in as singers.

We bring in wood and the fires start up well and the buffalo roasts up good. It smells great and there is much joy here. We see their Qualls and she is talking with my wife Sara. They whisper among themselves, and they are telling secrets from the look on their faces. She then speaks with sign talking which I can understand better these days. I enjoy that they are good friends now and that we will have allies on a day that would normally be a tough day for me to remember. I now have new memories to add to this day and now I can make it a day of celebration, and not a day of sadness as it has been in the past. Things are better and we have allies and friends that support us as well as we do them. The goal of the Great Council has been met, and five years later we can still believe in the peace treaty made by General Sam Houston and the Red River tribes.

May 3rd. We go to the old fort for trade day. The new Worth's fort is getting more finished and Bird's fort will soon be closed to regular trading and army affairs. We got the notice when we went there today. Several people were setting up their booths, and it was always wise to get there early to get the best spots to sell. They have some nice rugs that Sarah liked. She has some money from our trading horses. She wanted a number of them to make the house nicer. I thought it a good deal and she was happy to get something she wanted. She is always so good and she seldom asks for anything. A man has some nice mirrors and we got a few for the house. There were some lanterns and we needed a few of those. So we needed to sell some of Sarah's pottery and baskets. They offered to barter for some of them, and she was happy with that deal. I smiled and nodded my approval. She was most pleased that we both got a good deal. A lady has made some clothes and they were the right size for the children, so she traded baskets and pots for those too. Sarah is quite the trader, and she would have made her father proud. The people that are food vendors set up and they have barbeque, and some nice vegetables, so all we have spent is one dollar today. We were most happy that there was a good day of trade, and others came and they have bought up all her baskets and pots she has made with Ke-Ke. So today we have made twenty dollars profit, all in all. Ben has sold some of his goats, and he made a deal for some tack that he wanted. He likes the silver work and this looks like something from Santa Fe. So he will be the envy of many when he rides by in such style. He got some new clothes, and he encouraged me to brush up on some new clothes too. The wife agreed, so we all will be nice looking when we go to church services, and have something better to wear when we go visiting the neighbors to invite them to church. We were still ahead ten dollars, and we were pleased with ourselves. We will give half of this as a tithe to the church.

We are asked by the quartermaster to get more horses, the first thing we can. He brought us some letters from General Sam. We were glad that we have written him three letters to send out to the postmaster. We agreed that we could go this month and thin out some of the herds, as they will be stressed from the warmer weather coming soon. We got to read the letters and General Houston said that he was coming down to visit with us soon to see how the settlements are doing. He spoke about many things and he always writes wonderful letters. I told the wife and she was happy as she looks at him as part of our family. We headed home and it was a good day.

We passed a wagon with a broken wheel and we offered to help them. They had an extra wheel, so we helped remove the old one. We told them about Simon, and we took them over to his place to get a spare wheel. His wagon was in sad shape and they needed to trade it for a sturdy one. They did not have any money and they needed ten dollars to make the trade for their old one proper. I offered my ten dollars to them if they would make the trade so they would not be stuck out somewhere with an old fouled wagon. They were excited, and Simon enjoyed that we remembered him when it was word-of-mouth advertising.

We told then about the church and we offered to take them if they wanted to go this season.

We finally got home and my wife hugged me for being a good man by helping the strangers. We offered to let them stay at our place for the night so they could head out in the morning refreshed. They accepted and we made them comfortable in our home. The man was named Bryant and his wife was due to have a child in six months. He has fought in the Mexican War and he had just got out of the army. We did not talk about battles, as it is not proper to talk about such things around the ladies. We told him that we were going soon to capture some mustangs, and he was interested in helping us to make some money to help build a cabin for his growing family. He seemed mature enough to help out and he was a decent person that did not drink, or curse. We set them up to sleep in our bed, and we slept in the boy's room. They pitched their tent and they stayed outside so they were fine with that. We settled in for the night, and it was good to be home.

May 4th. We woke and showed the couple our place. They enjoyed walking across the fields to see what they could aim for as a newcomer. We gave them some advice, and they asked what crops are best to grow? I told them to first grow wheat. Then growing corn brings the best return. I told Mr. Bryant that this puts nitrogen back into the ground. I told him that every seven years you must let the ground rest and plant other fields. I told him that he should belong to the farmer's co-operative, and that are welcome to come to our church. I did not pressure them at all, but I needed to say my peace to make sure I did my part as a citizen. I stayed away from politics as that can make a sore subject as I have seen at church socials sometimes. I stayed off my soapbox preaching and I got my point across to them. They agreed to come to the next church service the twenty-first of this month. They left out for the fort to talk with a person from the Peters' Colony about the land grants. I told them about the man that tried to sell lands out in the Comanche lands, and we told him not to fall for that foolishness. Anything west of here is out of bounds and off limits to strangers. They got a first rate education at a cheap price. Perhaps it would save them some grief their first year out here. We asked them to travel with us to the church meeting if they wished, so we could introduce them to the congregation. Sarah gave them some of our new gourds for water bottles, and we filled them up before they left out. We wanted to go with them, but we had to let them go themselves.

May 21st. The Bryant's come to visit the church together. We left out and made good time going down Grapevine Springs Road. We met up with other churchgoers. We met down the road from the church at the watering hole. We introduced each other and we secured the horses and wagons. More people came and we talked about our plans to build more cabins for newcomers. Mr. Bryant told us that the land grant was set to be close to the Clear Fork. We informed him that those lands belong to the Kick-a-Poo tribe and that he would put them on the warpath to settle there without their permission. I knew that I should have went with them to the fort as that land manager was either stupid, or crooked as the day is long! We told him that we would go with him to renegotiate his land deal since he was a veteran and he served in the Mexican War. He is a bright young man. The Bryant family is being led astray: some unscrupulous person is working at the new land office!

It was the same name as we have seen before. It was this "Hedgecoxe" person. He is an Englishman who is a stranger here. He seems not to be familiar with how things work around here. A person just does not set at a desk writing out land certificates and not know whose land they are selling off with no consideration, or payment to the owner. The last people he did that way we found dead on the prairie because they were ill informed, and unprepared. I talked with the pastor and he agreed that we needed to talk this over after the service and make some sort of plan to fix this. I was stressed out over this and I wondered how we could fix this. We put our concerns away for a while so we could have church, but my anger burned over this nice couple being wronged. They were only given a half section of land 320 acres. As a veteran he deserved a full section of 640 acres of choice land, and a land bonus of 320 acres also. So this man is cutting back into what was their reward, and reselling their land to others. So it just became more complicated than it had to be. I was red in the face and my wife told me to take off my "warrior face" and be calm and relax. I just have to talk with this land speculator and straighten him out on a few things. I have a responsibility not to let this pass unnoticed or uncontested. I asked the pastor to pray for me not to make a fool out of myself dealing with this person. He understood where I was speaking from as an elder, and a deacon of the church.

Troy came with Regina and they were married recently at the fort. It was nice to see them so happy, so some good things were going on too. We have some new blankets and a nice rug that we could give them as a proper present. We went to the wagon and we gave it to them as a wedding gift. We looked at their horses and we fixed a problem that Troy's horse has with a sore tendon. We doctored it and wrapped it with linen to keep it from being stone bruised. We went back and we settled in to talk and get a place to rest from the trip. Everyone introduced themselves to the congregation. The evening came and the sermon started after the singing service. Pastor Hodges preached about being fair, and we enjoyed that he always speaks so well and makes his point in a concise and timely manner. We built a fire and we sat along side and we talked and visited. It was nice to be social and talk over things like farming and hunting stories. We were asked a number of questions and I tried to speak well and not stutter in front of the group. I tried to be informative, and not sound too boastful about my past, and my accomplishments. Since I am older than many of these people some of them look up to me, and I must mentor them, as I was when I was a "newbie." So we have a time to talk about the Bible, and I tried to speak about the sermon and how it related to my own life and times. Some asked about General Houston, and we spoke highly of him and his accomplishments on our behalf. We spoke of building more cabins, and we make plans to go out and help the newcomers. There was a growing list of homes to build so we signed up to help as much as we could. We settled in with the family and we tended to them and spent some time with them. The ladies have quilting squares that they are working on to make something to raffle to help make money for building homes. Today we read: SECOND CORINTHIANS, Chapter 11, verse 26: "False Brethren."

CHAPTER TWELVE

The Kiowa, Comanche, and Kick-a-poo capture horses for the army.

June 14th, 1848. We go out to find some horses for the army. We have spoken with the Kiowa and Kick-a-poo allies and they said that they would help us so they can get winter supplies early this year. The army promised blankets, iron goods, and implements like cooking pots and such. They agreed for 100 blankets, 150 cooking pots, and some 80 Mexican saddles and tack that were captured at Buena Vista and the Siege of Vera Cruz.

    For some reason they take great pride in having those things since the Mexican army has taken so much of their livelihood from them. They want something from them to help steal their "thunder" back. We went out and they have the brush corrals and a good many horses already. They were some handsome ones and this will make the others healthier that are left. This is the first day and I counted over sixty-seven horses and this was the best yet as we have their wonderful help. Even some Comanche brought 8 horses donated from Chief Peta's people. They are tired of the wars scaring off their trade partners from the Mexican tribes and from the Rio Grande valley of south Texas. So we have a unique chance to have a peaceful assembly and councils that would be the envy of General Sam. They might not like the Texan army but they hate the war with Mexico worse, as it has upset their way of life. It has upset many of us and we are all ready for a change. It makes us put our difference aside for a common goal: peace. Even warriors grow tired of battle and they want to see a decent life for their families. This has united us and made us greater than we once were, all alone.

They have brought twenty-eight more horses for the corrals, and six buffalo on two travois. They make a big fire and it is time for a pow-wow. The usual Rain Dance is done a week early because everyone is together for this special occasion. They dress up and they are painted up from head to toe. The drums go strong and the singers get their songs going.

I do not know many of their songs but they sound very positive over some I have heard before. We counted one hundred-fifteen good horses and six colts that are most handsome. No one can say that Lone Wolf and Spotted Tail aren't good Kiowa's: as they have teamed up to help the army with the capture of our new horses. This time we are able to enjoy ourselves more as we aren't stressed over capturing horses and having to keep watch over everything. The tribes have horse races and games of skill throwing darts. We took turns at a target like it was a turkey shoot. I got close enough to hit the mark, but it was a matter of luck than skill. We have brought six of Simon's good knives for prizes to those that win the contests. I was out matched as these were real hunters, and I am a novice by comparison.

Our boys use the sling to throw rocks where it threw sparks off a bolder that they have drawn on a buffalo with some charcoal. That impressed the Kiowa, and their elders as some have heard of their skill and thought it was just bragging or a tall tale. No one was too shabby on their skills, or their dancing. The maidens and the women showed off their best outfits and the single braves are joined together with the Jimson Weed Dance. Our boys have five or six years before we would let them marry, even though they are very mature in their size, and their way of thinking. We watch the dances and we settle up with all the goods that the tribes expected. We part company on good terms. We have made some good councils here. We all do well in our plans to capture horses off the prairie.

June 18th. We have made our way back to the fort with some fine horses for their remudas. We go to the quartermaster and he counted one hundred-twenty horses and six colts.

We wanted to go to talk with the person from the land office who was trying to fool the new settlers from the Peters' Colony. We talked with the commander and he said that he has no jurisdiction on that matter. I told him that I was informing him so that when settlers are killed for being on land that is not theirs, that the army would not retaliate against any tribe protecting their land from confiscation. We just have seen enough death, no matter who it is, we did not want to stand back and do nothing when it could be avoided. The land speculator was out doing survey work out west of here, on land that is not theirs. I had to get on my soapbox and make my point that we have allies that we are going to alienate if we did not think and plan things better. Captain Patterson asked for a detachment of men to go to find the foolish surveyor who has just missed my complaint by one hour. I offered to go with them as a civilian to make sure that we educated the land speculator. We rode on and we found that he was slain and his gear broke over a tree trunk. Even his horse was shot. We could not figure who did it as the ground was hard and it would not do any good to blame anyone over this, but ignorance. There was enough of that to go around. We had a burial detail, and we made it our point to make sure that it did not happen to anyone else. I wrote a report to the commander and he filed it with the Peters' Colony Company. We wrote General Sam a letter and we filed our report with him also as he has more wisdom of all of us put together. I hated to trouble him with such things, but I knew that it needed to be fully addressed. I prayed for us all and that was all that I could do for the time being.

July 1st, 1848. The boys have took Troy as their new big brother as he teaches them about horsemanship, and how to rope better. He has taught them to saddle a horse in a hurry. He can also quickly draw and throw a knife at a target and hit it safely. They were showing him to use a sling like little David, and he was slowly getting the hang of it. The boys had an idea to have a horse race across the prairie. I told them that I would have to be there for it to happen. I worried that they might be hurt, but I can't baby them too much or it will seem like I had no confidence in them. We rode out with Ben Bird and he saw a good place for a good run. The boys took turns racing and it was good to see a fine race. Some soldiers out on patrol saw them racing, and asked if Troy would ride along with the boys in their next trials to show off the cavalry's skills. They have a longstanding argument that the settlers would be better in a horse race than a cavalryman, and vice-versa. I do not bet good money, but the chance to see some of our horses run in a race might be good to see. I told them we could when they set a date to see them. It was something interesting to do and the boys like to idea of competing against some fine horses. There is a July 4th celebration for the new Federal Independence Day. We agreed to be there if we did not have to pay any fees to enter the race. We parted company and the boys are excited about a good contest to test their skills. Troy insisted that they train themselves more to give the soldiers a good trial in the saddle. I told them that their chores would be put off for this week if they would give them a good test of their skill. They are excited, and they deserve a chance to prove themselves as young men.

July Fourth. The boys have practiced and honed their skills these past days. We are ready for some real excitement. We rode into Bird's fort to see that no one was there. We then rode to the new fort west of here, and there were hundreds of people, and there were banners flying, and the new Federal flags all over. We knew that the excitement of the new fort was about to be opened and fully operational by January. It was good to see so many new faces and people clapped to the band playing, and the soldiers did their drills to impress the crowd. There were games and exhibits. There will be a turkey shoot for the men, and a quilt show for the ladies. There was a good chili cook-contest, and a cakewalk, so there would be plenty to do. We walked around to soak it all up. We gave the boys a silver dollar and they went to all the food booths to get cotton candy, popcorn and peanuts. They shared with their sisters, and we got a few goods for ourselves. One exhibit was one of the Twin Sisters' cannon, and a display of Santa Anna's saddle, boots, and bridle when he was captured at San Jacinto. We wondered where he was now since he has been recaptured? Was he going to finally sign a real treaty and back it up with his word of honor? The man running the display asked me if I knew anything about Santa Anna? I knew all too well, and I hoped to never cross his path again. I was wearing my San Jacinto medal, and I brought it to the man's attention. We told him how Santa Anna was found hiding among the dead wearing the borrowed uniform of a wounded soldier, hoping to escape when night fell. We told him that at the Buena Vista battle he was wearing the disguise of a peasant farmer after hiding his fancy uniform under a woodpile. He was just a sly old fox. The man stood there with his mouth open, and that was that. We knew all that we needed to know, and then some.

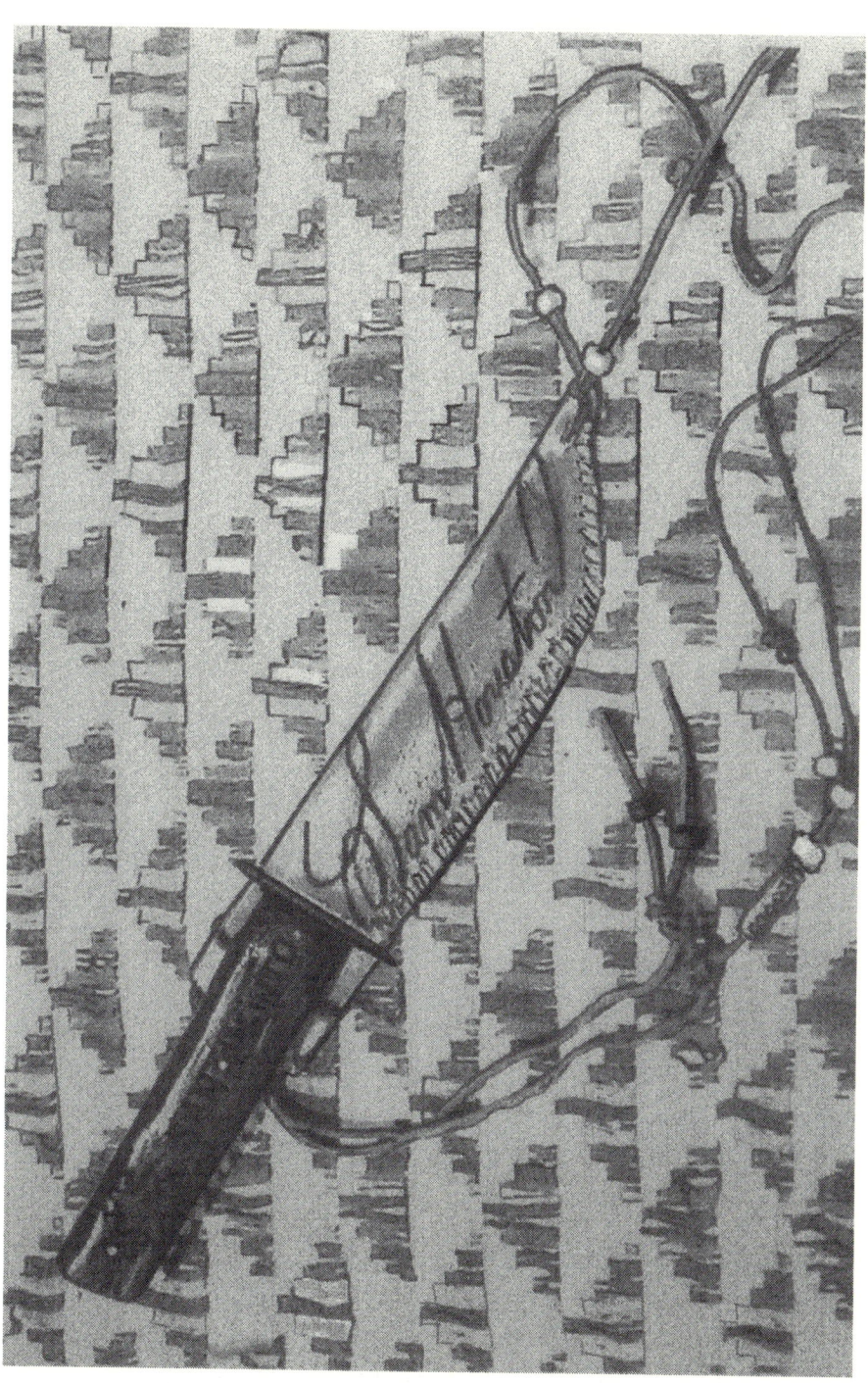

The Sam Houston Knife.

We then went to get the boys signed up for all their events, and to sign up for the turkey shoot. We went to the knife and gun show and we looked at all the things that we wish we had. There were some real beauties, and one prize of the turkey shoot was a new rifle, or an **escarpito**. We were called to the west wall and the turkey shoot began. There were some soldiers from the 1812 War, and some Kentucky riflemen that were most colorful persons. Ben Bird was dressed well, and he has his favorite rifle ready. We were lined up in groups to represent our time as soldiers. We were surprised to see **General Sam** here! He came out of a wall tent, and he made his usual colorful entrance. He spoke a great speech, and he told of the great opportunity that we have here to grow, and make our country better for all that live here. He was very upbeat, and he looked great. He is a head and shoulders taller than everyone else, so he always stands out in a crowd. We lined up for the turkey shoot and we each had our turn to hit the targets and the winner got a small Texas flag as a token. Josiah and Sam Bird took their turns and they hit most their targets when they shot a rifle. Some of their friends shouted, and they were asked to show off their slingshot skill. They hit the same target, just as well with a stone as they did a rifle ball. People applauded and they were given a flag. Troy took out his knife and he hit the target from quite a distance. People applauded, so they will rank somewhere near the top. A Kentucky rifleman took the top prize, a fine new rifle, and the boys each got a fine Bowie knife. Troy won a fine new pistol. The captain said, "the many fine items were donated by different vendors that Sam Houston knew from his trips to New Orleans."

There was some fine music, and food to celebrate the Federal July Fourth holiday. The evening came and the horse races began. They called it a "rodeo." The children had a chance to capture a calf set loose in a corral. It was funny as some had jumped hard to reach one and landed in the dirt. I would be so graceful. The riders were to choose lots to draw which horses they would ride. They were all fine horses: the thing was to ride a horse that was new to you, to see how you would handle it. We settled up to ride against the older riders, and the younger riders went next. I came in dead last, and I ate much dust. Ben Bird rode hard and he came in second on a tan pinto mare. He was just a natural horseman, and I was just a plowman, and that was that. He patted me on the back and offered me some consolation on my poor ride. I laughed and we went to the food booths and had some interesting desserts from the German settlers. It was all very friendly, and fun. We had some nice distractions, and the wives were happy to learn about quilting, and they made some new friends to visit with. We have the cakewalk and the boys have some girls after them to dance. Sam Bird was not shy at all, and he got Josiah to get out there to dance with some really sweet girls. They had tickets to dance, and they made a good show if it. I danced with Sarah, and she enjoyed the nice music. Ben Bird got out there and he was impressive to see that he has so many talents. Troy danced with his new young lady, and they won "Best Stepper." Another nice couple won "High Stepper", and Sarah won "Most Stepped On." So they have a choice which cake that they want. "The only bad cake is no cake" is my anthem! The boys came back and showed us their prize knives, and Troy was in good spirits as he danced with Regina. He has impressed her by not having two left feet and not stepping on her toes. People just need a chance to make their lives better if you let them. So coming in here to ride wasn't too much of a waste of time.

We needed to get around people and catch up on the latest news that we needed to know more about the outside world. General Sam came around and he talked to us all. He is a joy to see, and he made us feel like old times when we were under his command. We have learned a lot from him, and he has made us grow in our knowledge in ways that has kept us alive here. He spoke awhile, and he gave us a knife that he treasured from San Jacinto. He said that his heart was tired from battle, and that each day has become a great battle being reminded of it. I understood that notion. Some days the burden of that battle was too much to deal with, but not great as General Sam's burden must be as a commander. I was still limping about on my left leg as I still use a cane some days. He said he thought I was impersonating him well. I laughed out loud, as I could not begin to fill his shoes. I told him that I was mostly deaf now because of the powder magazine exploding. I was walking with a cane today as it felt like rain and my leg was hurting. General Sam kidded me that I was becoming like him, having a tough time getting around after all his battles. I thought that this knife should belong to Ben Bird, and General Sam agreed that it was "alright" since Ben Bird has done so much to help the wounded in battle, and that he did much at the Red River treaty. He still called him "the Red Bird" because he did not know he became a Christian, and he has taken a Christian name. I told General Sam, and he was most happy for him. He said from now on he would call the Red River treaty "the **Red Bird treaty**," and that he would call him by "Ben" after the tribe of Benjamin from the Old Testament.

He was a sight for sore eyes, and we made our friend welcome to our tent that we pitched. He held little Jacy, and Phoebe sat on his knee and she was a pest. He loved it as she asked him so many great questions. She told him about "Mister Goings" coming and "Mister Smith, the Scout" taking the

Caddo's canoe back. He told her of his new son called "Houston" that was now three years old. He said that his wife Margaret could not come because she had a brief illness that had kept her down for a while. We told him that we would pray for her. He grew tired and a soldier brought him an army cot and a blanket. He took some time to rest among his friends where he felt safe from the crowd. He is sometimes overwhelmed by the demands placed on him, and the many roles he has played here. I sat down and rested. I smoked my pipe to relax. I sat and read the Bible by the lamp in front of the doorway. A few hours later we heard a loud bang and crackle like cannon fire. We all ran outside to see the Mexican fireworks. They made many colors, and looked like some colorful dandelions that bloom as they burst open. It was all very exciting and we enjoyed our day together.

July 5th, 1848. We packed up and went home. General Sam came with us to see the farm and stay a few days since the Trinity River was too low to float a ship. We made room for him and he was most happy to be on the open prairie again. We rode in and showed him the fields of pumpkins that were coming up strong, and the cattle that have become such good stock. Phoebe took him by the hand and walked him to show the chickens she was most proud of. She picked out some nice eggs and cooked them for him and he sat on the porch to drink some coffee. The birds were full in the trees chirping, and he seems most happy sitting there. We let him have some time alone, and he sat and wrote his wife some letters that he has been meaning to finish. It was good to see our old friend enjoy himself, and make room for him. We had the children go over to Ben Bird's for a while to give him some rest. Troy took them out to give them some air, and let them get out and have some fun. He was good with the children, and he said that his wife Regina was expecting her first baby. She was at the fort staying with a soldier's wife. I told him how it was to be a Cherokee with the mean old Ogre Woman after you with a tree stump if you did not do right. I asked him if she was a Cherokee? He said she wasn't of any tribe that he knew of. I laughed that he gave up his status as a single man after meeting this young woman. It does turn your head a bit when you meet the right person. I told him just to take his time, and to be a gentleman to her, so she will know that you are a good husband and a patient father. He seemed most happy with his holiday at the new fort and he has come a long way since his time in the stockade. They rode out together and they were gone all afternoon. They will spend the night there at Ben and Ke-Ke's place. They enjoy having company and he is proud of his place.

We gave General Sam a good-natured horse and he wore his plain clothes to be comfortable. He rode out for some time alone. He was gone for several hours and we worried about him. He went to the west so we knew where he might be. I made the smoke signals and they were returned in a short time. He was at the Kick-a-Poo camp visiting with Red Sun's people. I sent the good signs up and they were returned, so all was well. Later, It rained tonight and it was a real "frog floater." We know that General Sam would have to go when the water was high enough for his ship to leave. We rode out in the muddy prairie, and we went to the Kick-a-Poo camp. General Sam was there, and he was in good spirits. We had enough people to have a full council, so we had a pipe ceremony with General Sam. We have time together to make a good ceremony, and this makes our friendship stronger between us all. General Sam asked us to go with him to the ship to see him off. I said that Ben would come with us, and he said that it would make a nice detail to have him along for the trip. We will have to ride to the Elm Fork, south of the Rich Land settlement for him to catch the ship. It would be a day before the river crossing will go down enough for the raft crossing to be viable to cross. We went home and packed the needed supplies and took out for the crossing. We hoped to find a place to cross, and Ben Bird said that he thought that he know of a good place to get across during the high water. We went there, and it was very muddy, and not a very good idea to cross.

We went farther down and saw that the new raft crossing was set up in a better place. We paid a dollar a piece, which was high, but better than taking a chance drowning. It saved a day, and we were anxious to get there safe above all. We rode until the evening and made it to the ship called the **CAYUGA**. General Sam said it was the ship that was used for the temporary government when things were too awful between Austin and Houston City. He said it looked to be updated with another set of rooms to the top section. It was nicer than he remembered it. It was all painted up and fancy to me. We carried General Sam's goods on board, and he was happy to be heading back to his family. We told him he is our friend that we look at him as part of our family. We told him that we always pray for him, and for him to come visit anytime. He said to write more letters, and keep him informed on what the settlers are doing, and on the progress at the **Dove** Settlement. He said that he would not mind living up this way sometimes so we all could be neighbors, when we were old. That was a nice thought. We sat and waited and directly the ship fired up a big fire inside the top room, and smoke come out the chimneys. The big paddle wheels turned, and we watched as a boat rowed up with another passenger before it left out. The ship's bell rang a number of times, and a big whistle blew for a bit. It was scary to see the big boat move, and no person paddles it off. Ben Bird said that he would rather ride in a canoe, anytime over this thing. I was sure it was all and good, just something that is just new to us. We are just set in our ways. We were not that fancy, and a good day on a covered boat would be nice in case it rains, and the river floods. There was a change in the air. I did not know if it was the weather, or if it meant something else was happening here that I did not understand yet. One day we might ride on one of these and see what it is like.

Tonight we read: MATTHEW Chapter 11, verses 28-30.
"God will give you rest from your troubles."

July 11th, 1848. We thought about our friend, Sam Houston, and I hoped that he was home safe and sound. We have written him two letters since he left here. He always makes me think about things, and the words that come out of his mouth is like reading the words of the Apostle Paul from the Bible. He is very wise and he has taught me so much. It just makes me realize that many things that I think I know, I do not know as well as I should. I look at my family and I see them as so wonderful, and that I do not know what I did to deserve so much. I have just tried to survive each day, and make sense of things that I do not always understand. Today it will be better I am sure. I am sure that what ever is put in front of me will be a challenge, and that I will rise to the occasion. I just never feel adequate.

I see this young man named Troy turn it around from being a thief to being a fine young man on the right road for a change. I was wondering where he might be if I had not intervened and helped him out of the pit he was in? Where would any of these people be if the Cherokee had not helped me when the robbers left me, and **Delephine** for dead? Where would I be if Ben, and General Sam and so many others have not helped me along? It seems that I am just the instrument to be one of the many tools of God's Will. I hope that my children will continue to prosper well, and that if I were gone tomorrow that they would continue as I would want them to go. I worry about the local tribes with all the new settlers coming in with plans for the land farther west of here. I fear for their safety of their tribes with leaders who do not know or understand the delicate balance of our lives. I fear for the war in Mexico that continues to eat up our resources here. I could not sleep last night pondering all these things. It was my hope that writing them down might make it easier to deal with. It has not, but there will be times that I will open this book up and read these words and wonder if I was doing was right and proper in the sight of the Lord. It is always a terrible burden to know what is best to do. We are not just a farmer, but also a good steward of this land. We have a great responsibility that goes beyond the boundaries of our property. Seeing General Sam made me realize that I can never do enough to live up to what I should be doing. I should be doing more. I am not good enough. I pray for the wisdom to make better choices. Today I read: FIRST CORINTHIANS, Chapter 1, Verse 30. "God will give you Wisdom."

The Cayuga Steamship

William Wallace, on a longhorn

CHAPTER THIRTEEN

William Wallace: Texas Ranger, Contrary, and Missionary.

July 20th, 1848. We met William Wallace out towards Red Top mesa. He was having some young Kiowa and Comanche round up some wild cattle to push into a box canyon for use as food during the coming winter. He has them block off the entrance to the canyon so that the cattle will prosper there. He is a **contrary** if there ever was one! He was riding a longhorn bull like it was a horse. It was a sight to see and it made you wonder how he came to be there among them. It seems that he was a captive as a youth, and that he was traded between the tribes to do their hard labor and the tracking of the buffalo and deer herds. He also spoke for the tribes to the army, and to strangers to see what their business was on their lands. He has come in to rescue captives and ransomed them safely. He also went to capture Mexican bandits, renegades, and deserters from the Mexican, and Texan army as most join together and raid settlements to take and burn villages. So he is a one-man army that does not look dangerous, or like a threat, yet he is someone to be dealt with if he makes up his mind that he is coming after you. We are impressed by his character, as are most of his allies. Some people just stand out in the way they dress and act.

He is very eccentric, funny, and quite a longwinded talker. He would out talk General Sam, as we waited for him to come up for air in between his sentences. He could swim with the alligators, and wrestle with one if he chose to. He was a big man. He was a likable person and we could see why he was so popular with the youth here. We stopped to water the horses and Wallace sat on the ground and read the Bible. He was sitting close to a red ant bed and he did not care if he got bit or not. He seemed to know many scriptures, and he was not shy about talking about God to us or the Comanche and Kiowa. He has converted many Comanche to being Christian. It seems that many have suffered from disease after their exposure to some of the new settlers. Many of their children have died from mumps, chicken pox, smallpox, and influenza. Some do not live past the age of five. Many of their elders have suffered the same fate as their children. We saw a number of Comanche with crosses around their neck, some quite large and heavy looking. He has them all stirred up, looking for a way to please God, as many have turned away from their Rain Bird Spirit, and their other worship of natural events to new traditions in hopes of finding a new way to solve their problems.

Wallace has been working with the Texas Rangers to help stop the Mexican supply lines to choke them off in battle to make them short of needed supplies. They call him "Big Foot" because he has bigger foot than anyone else. He has special made boots that are bigger than two boots put together! It only goes that someone larger than life would be so contrary. He has me beat in that area. The Kiowa and Comanche have looked to find a way to fix their problems with people who are not **"washitas."** We have offered them our friendship, and they have tolerated us, and become great allies as we are different, but share similar interests and concerns. We want peace to come to our land so we can take care what we need to do.

We rode out and we talked about our life in Texas and how so many changes are taking place with all the new settlers coming here. We share the same fears that the new settlers won't respect the Old Ways, and try to go against the tribes by having settlements west of the new Worth's fort. I told him that I was trying to catch up to the land surveyors for the Peters' Colony, and one man in charge of them was an Englishman who was 'slippery as a wet rope' trying to talk with him to get him straightened out. He said that we have a long ways to go to make things right here, and that he is worried over what may come next when more newcomers come and out number us here. I fear more warfare against people that are our good allies, as they will lose their trust in us. He agreed and he made some interesting predictions that were not too far fetched for the near future. He predicted a war with the Great Indian Nations of the Comanche and Kiowa. He also predicted a war among the settlers that has brother against brother. He predicted slavery spreading to the new territories. I shuddered to think over such things happening, but

I knew it to have a great ring of truth to it. It seemed terrible and I hope to be long dead before such a thing happens.

We rode along and I told him of the Dove settlement and he encouraged me to continue to mentor the newcomers by helping them fit in by building decent cabins and communities around a solid church. I told him that I was a deacon and an elder in my church and he liked that I was so involved. I have no choice in the matter, as it has been my duty to return what has been given to me by so many people since I crossed over into Texas. I invited him to come sometimes and he said that he would visit when he has a chance. He liked Ben Bird and he talked with him some to get his advice on a remedy for an illness he has. Ben gave him some flowers of Sulphur and some salt. That would fix him up. They talked in Kiowa to discuss his problems. He seemed happy to find some relief, as it is hard to find good medicine, or decent doctoring these days with the war going on. He was pleased to meet "the Red Bird," someone that he had heard so much about over the years. He thought that he would dress more colorful than he was, as some medicine men you can pick them out from a mile away from the way they are dressed out. Ben is more low-key and he makes himself useful, and he is quieter than most unless he has something important to say.

It got to be the hot part of the day and we rode to a nice watering hole and rested our animals. We set under some mesquite trees and we took a siesta. We slept for a few hours. Some Kiowa came and they told of a buffalo hunt that we were invited to, so we went on and joined him. He used a bow and arrow as good as any Indian that I have seen. He has made some long darts that reached their target well. He also used a dart-thrower, which was quite a sight throwing a big arrow made from a reed stalk with a metal point. He did not miss and he made an effort to kill the weaker members of the herd so that the rest would prosper. Most of the time we do the opposite, but that is what makes him a contrary from others, sometimes. He is quite an interesting person. He has taught me a few things from his insight into life. I enjoyed that we had a chance to meet and talk about the settlements with someone who has his unique perspective. The women came and butchered the animals. We went on to make our camp for the evening. They divided up the meat and gave us some in a nice **parfletch**. It was mixed with some wild berries to keep it fresh until we could get back home. We rode along and we stopped to let the horses feed on some green bushes. Wallace showed us a huge boulder that has drawings of warriors, and a rendering of a hunt from a long time ago. So we were on the 'old hunting grounds' that so many elders often speak of. It felt good to walk in the same path that so many others have taken. We offered Wallace the welcome to come visit our church, and to stay and rest at our place anytime he was in the area. He agreed, and we did the friendly signs and we parted company on good terms.

July 21st. We get back home and we bring home the parfletches of fresh meat. Our wife is happy and we tell her of our experiences with the contrary, William Wallace. She laughed when I told her that he rode a longhorn instead of a horse. The Indians called him, "Sha-Stasha-ha:" "Longhorn." I showed the wife the drawing of him, and she laughed and she poked me in the ribs in a playful way. I think she really missed me. The children are so wonderful to be around. It felt good to be home back under my own roof again. We sat under the front porch and we watched the sky as the moon rose. We always wonder what the new day will bring. Tonight we read: PSALMS, Chapter 37—Verse 11. "Abundant peace from God."

July 24th, 1848. We went to church services. There were many new visitors. One of them was the Bryant's who said that they were joining the church. We told them that we have written General Sam a letter concerning the person over the surveyors, and the land grants of the Peters' Colony. They are staying at Worth's fort in the newcomer's barracks.

We saw a golden eagle in a tree and Ben said that rain was coming tonight. I did not know how that seeing an eagle warranted rain, but I figured that he would know. Sure as the world it was pouring down rain before midnight. That golden eagle was pushed south of the Red River ahead of the storms that were coming. We have several tents in our wagon that we bring with us on hunting parties. We broke them out and made a comfortable place for many of the women and children to stay together safe and dry. It poured down hard and it was a steady rain most of the night. We wanted to make a chance to have a safe meeting most of all since so many have traveled so far to be here.

The next morning the rain broke and everything greened up well. The mockingbirds were in the treetops giving us welcome. The doves cooed back from the bushes, so they were giving us a good morning to drink coffee and talk together. The children went out to pick berries and we went along to keep an eye on them. We showed them how to use a stick to run along to make the snakes clear out before they stick their hands in there to grab up the berries into a pail. We showed them the poison ivy and sumac plants so they would avoid them. I think that they ate more than got into the pails, but the blackberries were so sweet after the rainfall. They brought back many pails of good berries and one was passed among us. They were so good this year! Most of all we enjoyed each other's company.

Later, Mister Wallace came. He was dressed very well. He has put away the buckskins and he made a good appearance. He put his longhorn to graze away from the horses so that he would not make the horses so nervous. Some of the older children got to ride the longhorn after he has gone about to introduce himself. He has a chance to speak in front of the crowd and he talked about making good allies with the local tribes as a way to keep us from fighting a battle on two fronts. He answered questions, and he made it clear that the tribes hate the war with Mexico as much as we do. He said that we have a common goal to do all that we can to make the war over with fewer problems as possible. Some did not agree and they asked the difficult questions many times over. The bottom line is that we have a responsibility to be fair towards each other to maintain the peace, and make friendships that show that we are true Christians in our words, works and deeds. Pastor Hodges came and he made references to Mister Wallace, and the things he has accomplished towards the Comanche and Kiowa tribes. Judge Hodges then spoke about Chief Spotted Tail Hawk going out into the terrible storm to save the settler's lost little son. He was using that as a way to say that our concern goes beyond our own settlement, and our own concerns: to others that live here too. Any of those that disagree with that issue were now quieted as they have become better informed from this meeting.

Mister Wallace went on to talk to the new settlers to educate them about a few things about living in Texas. He did not try to preach, he just tried to educate them so that it won't cost them what little money they have. Some have invested with unscrupulous land speculators that have traveled about posing as representatives from the Peters' Colony, or Texas Land and Emigration Company. A few of the real land speculators have been selling half sections of land for what a whole section of land costs. They also sell land that already belongs to someone else, so it takes going down to Austin at the land office to get a new land grant after September. The Bryant's are going to Austin to complain about the land they were sold in Apache country. Another couple suffered the same fate so they are taking a steamship with the Bryant's to complain about some of the practices used in determining where the grants are directed. We will be watchful of people crossing past our land to claim land that already belongs to someone else.

August 1st, 1848. Mister Wallace came and stayed with us for a few days. He has been enjoying getting so much attention from the new settlers. He told us that he would be watchful of any prisoners that the Apache, Kiowa, and Comanche take from unfortunate, uninformed settlers that have been led astray from land speculators selling land in the Comancheria. It was fortunate that he was with us today, as we spotted some surveyors out close to our property looking to cut into our own property lines! They said that 'the boss told them that our property lines were incorrect and that we might have to move.' I felt the blood leave my face. I looked for a way to pull them off their horses and make them listen to reason. Mister Wallace beat me to the punch and he pulled the man off his horse and broke his surveying instruments against a big rock. He held him down with one arm, and tied him with a rope with the other. He told him, "Andrew served at San Jacinto, and at Buena Vista, and if anything he was owed even more land for military service, and for capturing horses! He was there both times Santa Anna was captured. Taking his land would be cause for some serious problems, here. Ben Bird also." He told the man: "this property was the boundary of the Indians' land, and that anyone trying to live farther west would be killed for not being very bright, for going sore against what proper treaties say! That is a threat to them and they aren't as nice as I am if they are angry because they are slighted." He saved me the trouble of making a fool out of myself, and since he was a **contrary**, people are afraid of him, because he looks fierce because he is a bit crazy. My head hurt and I felt sick that someone could be so stupid to sell land that was mine, and that of our close allies. Mister Wallace went on took the man tied over the saddle of his horse. By the time the man reaches the fort his side will be very sore from being hog-tied. He asked me to stay here so that he could deal with him as he could tell the story just fine to the commanding officer at the fort. We let him go and we stayed out of his way. That was just fine with me, and our reputation remains intact. My head still hurt, and I could not see well enough to read, or write anymore today.

Two days have passed and Mister Wallace returned. He said that he talked to the commander of the fort and that this head of the land grants has sawdust for brains. I laughed thinking that I had some terrible anger the past few days thinking about someone trying to make me move, again. I lost my home in

Louisiana to smugglers, and lost my wife in the process. I was going to fight to my last breath to keep my land and I have plenty of people to back me up this time. Including the army that would support me anytime I asked. I prayed for patience to know what to do as I was sore from anger, and I have not spoken since the threat was made. Sarah was very understanding, as she understood about losing her home in east Texas to threats. She supported going on the warpath if need be. I felt that we did not have to go that far, but we had to maintain a clear head to not act out in anger to those who were so ignorant, and foolish to try to suggest we give up what we have fought so hard to have here. I washed my face in the horse trough, and I took some time to be alone to consider my options if the head of the land grants tries to grab my land from under me, or any of my Indian allies. I feared for them as they would deal with them much more harsher than I would, and I pray for them to act more wise than to provoke their wrath. I know them to be fair people and I love them as my own family. These people have fought for this land from ages unknown, and they are not foolish enough to let some silly person mosey unto their land without a fight. I would not blame them, for I would join them in a moment, without batting an eye. I wish the army and Texas Rangers to be on good terms with the tribes that choose to be peaceful, as most want to live and hunt in peace, as do I. I just get tired of fighting battles so often trying to make peace here has been very difficult as some want to kick an ant bed and keep us tied to it. No thank you!

August 6th-8th, 1848. My brother, Ben came along and he wanted to take me out among the Kiowa for a hunting party. He got the smoke signs as a form of a kind invite to go. I was ready to get out and the wife was happy for us to go as we have been carrying around a long face for a few days. The boys wanted to go and we said to get their weapons and some gourds full of water. The women went to stay at our place and that was good. Simon was close enough if trouble comes here. We went out and we met the Kiowa at the Clear Fork. The Kick-a-Poo have moved to a different camp farther south and we felt bad that we had not spoken to them before they moved. Mister Wallace was there and he was riding that longhorn into the middle of the hunt. He was without any fear.

We went on and we made a good council. It gave us a chance to make a good council. They have heard about the surveyors coming and we asked that they capture the culprits over harming them. I can understand being mad when your home is threatened, but we have to maintain our treaty to keep us from looking like the person in the wrong and justify their attempts to take lands protected by the **Great Council**. I still hobble around from my broken leg and our friends among the Kiowa wanted to have a sweat lodge. We have the pipe ceremony to show that we are all among friends. We do and they talk in low tones in words that I can now understand better since they talk slowed for my benefit. I agreed so we will have to fast for a day and only drink water. I have become so spoiled that I have forgotten to fast more often. I was fat enough that missing a few meals would make me have better aim, and be sharper in battle and the hunt. They got out the drums and them made a dance to make a great hunt. The sweat lodge is ready and we get inside. We talk and the sage and mesquite burns bright. The elder pours water over the hot stones and it turns very hot and I feel like I am going to pass out. I hang in there, and it becomes time to run into the river and cool off. We did run down to the river and cooled off. It felt great, and I felt happy to be among friends that were trying to help me.

We did sit by the bank and we were given blankets and buffalo robes to warm up after the chill of the spring fed river. The frogs croaked, and we heard the coyotes calling out to each other. It reminded me of the days that I was with the Cherokee and that made me happy. I told Ben and he agreed that it was nice to be among friends on a hunting party. It was like the old days when we were free to be warriors and hunters. We could move about as we pleased. I now feel even stronger to protect their way of life as I am on both sides of this issue. They are depending on me, and I am ready to protect them with my dying breath.

We go out towards Red Top mesa and we see their best tracker was reading the tracks to see how far away the herd is. There is a good sign of some buffalo, and some wild cows. Then they find deer tracks. So their chief calls for a buffalo hunt as that feeds more people per kill. We are hungry as we all have fasted and we are wearing the painted shirts they gave us. We felt that our aim will be good and that this would be a good hunt. A young man climbs into a tall tree and he spots the dust clouds and he points and blows a bone whistle loudly. He climbs down and he makes a beeline to the southwest. We broke into three groups and the herd is divided up and pushed along the ravines where the best ones are cut out and butchered. There are many on horseback and they ride interference to keep a wounded animal from doubling back to cause trouble. They have clean kills, and they make some nice buffalo to bring home. They make the smoke sign that the hunt was over as plenty has been killed and the hunt is to stop when the whistle is blown again from another tall tree. The horses and travois are brought out and the women come out to make a good finish to the hunt. The livers are removed after the animal has been butchered along the backbone. Some hearts are removed and we are obliged to eat parts of some, and they smile from ear to ear as it is bad fortune not to have a bite of a few to make the hunter's heart strong. The boy helped run interference to the hunters, and they got a buffalo for their help. They get their horse and they learn about making a travois properly. Several men help put the butchered buffalo on the travois and they secure the parfletches of good meat so they do not fall of, or get fouled in the dirt on the way home. No one is seriously hurt, and there are no broken bones, and no one has more than a few bruises and a knot on the head from falling from their horse. We are thankful for that.

On the way back to the Kiowa camp there are some fine songs and we tried to keep up. They smile at our effort to remember their hunting song. They take turns singing the songs and when it was my turn I stop and they laugh when I continue my effort to sing along. I get through it and my melancholy has left me as my spirits are renewed from being out on a good hunt. I am no longer angry over the land speculators and surveyors trying to take my land to give to others. The buffalo hunt released me from my anger and my stomach will not suffer pain any longer. Now there will be something more positive for me to focus on: living my life better. Today I prayed for a better attitude to be a better friend, and make a better father and brother to others. We get home and the women dance around to give thanks for our safe return, and for a good hunt. They have the smokehouse ready, and the barrels set to cure out some good meat to cure. The boys tell of their hunt and we bring the women the livers that are packed away in a cool spot, just for them. It feels good to be home and feel appreciated. We have much to be thankful for, and we always thank God for all his wonderful blessings. There are many more than I can say, here.

Tonight we read: ACTS, Chapter One: "Empowered."

August 21st. The late summer rains came and the bottom dropped out of the bucket the way it poured down. The flood came to quickly so the rivers were too swift to consider crossing the Trinity at the normal crossings. We felt that it would not be safe to go to church services. We stood in the hayloft and looked out across to where the river was swollen up to high on the banks.

We were resigned that we will go next month and hopefully it would be good weather to safely travel. We went to the smokehouse and emptied the barrels of the water and fat so we could smoke the buffalo meat that is well cured out by today. We had a good bunch of mesquite and pecan wood so it would be nice and tasty when it was complete. Simon came by and we told him to come by in a few days so he can benefit from our good hunt. We gave him some meat to put in the cooking pot, and he was most happy as his job keeps him too busy to hunt, as he would want. His boys loaded a good shoulder roast to put in the wagon, and we told him to come before Wednesday to follow up on some good grub. A good hunt warrants some celebration, as it is not always so good.

Simon has some trade goods to impart on the locals, and it was nice to see so many nice implements, tools, and knives for trade. His boys have become quite good knife makers.

One of them made a sword like General Sam brought the Kiowa. It reminded me of the sword that Chief Bowles carried in battle on his last days. We got to hold the sword and it has a nice balance to it like their knives. Mister Bowie would be proud to own any of these. Simon gave us one to carry on our person as a form of advertising their skill in ironwork. We were happy with that, and we were glad that we have a shoulder roast to give in trade. We parted company, and I gave Simon a receipt for him to better remember the knife and tool tally when we settled up on the next trade day, weather permitting. The boys came along and they followed Simon's boys to their place. Phoebe came out and I could not get over how tall she has become lately. She is still daddy's baby. I went to pick her up and I was not sure if my back would hold up. It did, and I took her around like I was her horse. She laughed, and she is the image of her mother. Thank goodness she does not look like me. I am happy for her sake. She took me and showed me her horse. She has taught it to back up when she makes a signal by whistling. She also whistles a different way and it come running to meet her. She got on its back and it reared up on its back legs. I was impressed how well she has it as groomed and trained as well as any cavalry soldier. She is the pride of the Cherokee, and she always has her daddy's heart no matter how much she has grown. She is my little girl who can ride circles around any grown man. She is so much like her mother, and she will make some fortunate man very happy one day. In the mean time I will enjoy having my family close to me. I will be more grateful for what I have, and I will have more faith in God, and not try to do things under my own means.

Today we read: DANIEL, Chapter Five, "The Handwriting on the wall."

The Bent tree

CHAPTER FOURTEEN

The Meeting at the Caddo's Bent Tree.

September 8th, 1848. We were asked by the army to negotiate a peace between the settlers at the Mack Camy settlement at **Tejas** Trail where Chief **Bintah**'s people live, the **Yoiuane** Caddo. It seems that the settlers have taken much corn from the Caddo's **milpas.** The settlers have taken their **cistern** and blocked them from their own water in an effort to make them leave the village they kept for over one hundred years. The Caddo had fought the Cherokee for that same land, and now they are fighting the settlers over their land, the only source of decent water for ten miles. So taking the Caddo's corn was more fuel for the fire to make a battle against them. The **Xensi** warriors have held back fighting the settlers because their **Qualls** has been on good terms with them until last month when she went to them to ask for payment for the corn that was taken without benefit of a good barter, or a decent trade. She was pushed out away from the Mack Camy's village when they set their dogs to chase her away. She cursed them and she spit on the ground. She promised to return for some sort of payment. She made a group of braves to sneak in the middle of the night and take their horses in return for payment. That did not go over too well as these settlers have little sense of proper trade practices. After all this the fire went out in the Caddo's fire temple as it was not being tended to, and that was a sign of bad fortune, too.

Worse of all was the fact that some elders and maidens were taken hostage until the horses are returned. The army wanted to help but the presence of the military would force the hostages to be hurt, or the **Xensi** to attack the settlers before anything could be done in council. An army would be a challenge to them and that would get everybody involved killed. We looked outside and one of their eastern **milpas** was still on fire. A cottonwood tree was chopped down blocking the road to the Tejas' village. Ben Bird said that it could be made into a nice canoe, later on. He always looks on the bright side of things.

We came to make council with the Caddo, and they do the **"Crying Greeting." They circle around us to get the upper hand on us. We stay calm and we keep our hands away from our weapons.** They see that we are not enemies, so they hold out their hands for gifts. We have ropes of tobacco, an iron fire striker, and some nice flints that we retrieved from the canoe we found a while back. We make a council and Ben Bird makes the signs to make us understood. He lights a fire in the center of their council house with the new fire striker, and the **Qualls** took a piece of burning wood to the fire temple where the traditional fire was relit again. She was happy that someone was trying to help and she kept the warriors in line. She brought the letter that Sam Houston wrote to Chief **Bintah** five years ago promising peace if they stayed peaceful. We try to hurry to get past ceremony to try to quickly get to the solution to the hostages being held. We passed the pipe and we made more talk over the problem with the settlers. The Qualls then wants Ben to sit in the Caddo's bent tree to talk, as a sign to the others that things are turning back around, as they should be again. We were obliged to do some things to suit them, as their ways are very different from ours. We have a good talk as Ben explains what would be best to do to make things right again. We tell them that we would act on the Caddo's behalf to make sure that the captives would be released safely. We said that we would return the settler's horses and figure out some way to get the elders and maidens released by sunset. Something had to be done and soon.

We rode out and the Caddo stayed back to watch us. We came to the Mack Camy's village and we heard noise from a barn where the captives were held. Out came a farmer and he looked mad that we were on his property. We told him that we were there to negotiate, and that he could put his guns away so we could talk. We said that we would return their horses if they would free the hostages. They were to give the Caddo something for their corn, and then they were to give back their cistern, or share it, as it was big enough for the village and the settlers. The settler said, "They only took twelve bushels of corn!" I told him that even if it was one bushel they were to at least ask first! The Caddo would have given you the corn for the asking, without a single horse in trade. They are called the "Tejas" because they are friendly, as they always have been to reasonable people. Their word for "friend" is "Tey-Sha." They got their name from the early Spaniards who passed through here who called them "Tejas." The Tejas always feed the hungry strangers, no questions asked. They did not like that their field of corn was burned, and that their elders and maidens were captured when they went to put it out.

Another man came out as he was listening. He was full of vinegar, as he wanted to fight us. We just stood still and gave him a serious look. He backed off and waited for our response. We told him that twenty Caddo warriors were watching and that they could throw a dozen arrows quickly and kill us all if he did not calm down. He reconsidered, and then he asked, "What did they want him to do?" We told him to make no sudden movements, lower his weapon and place it against the wall of the cabin. So he does this. I feel sweat going down my face, as my heart was still beating loudly in my ears. No darts, or arrows come flying so we are fine. Some horses race past us as the Caddo have released them back. The farmer goes and opens up the barn door and the elders and maidens are released safely. Other settlers come out and they put down their rifles and pistols. The Caddo accept the captives as payment for the corn because they are unharmed. So a gift has now been given: the lives of their elders and maidens. That is enough to have their family back again. You don't know what you have until it is taken from you. You just don't know, until you do.

We went among the settlers to give them something for their trouble. We asked them what they needed. They said that they needed their own source of water. We told the settlers that we would help them dig a well so they would leave the Caddo's cistern alone. That way they could stay clear of each other. Ben Bird broke off a green tree limb. He walked around for a while and the limb pointed down to the ground. He pointed to the ground and dug in his heel to mark it. We go out some shovels and gave it to them to start digging. They have so much energy and so much time on their hands we gave them something to do to keep them out of trouble. In half an hour water was bubbling up out of the ground. We helped them pick up some slabs of white rock for some stones to put around the side of the well. Ben walked around and he put down a stake to mark the place where a good pond could be dug for the cattle to drink from. Ben also walked farther down to show where another well could be dug if this one goes dry. So the settlers will have something to keep them busy. The Caddo have left for home and peace would now be restored. We told the settlers to be a lot more understanding about proper trade practices because they were fortunate that their village was not burned down and everyone becoming the loser because of their foolishness. A small thing such as selfishness can cost a person their life. I was tired and ready to head for home so I rested for a few hours. I laid in the shade of the Caddo's cistern. It was shady and cool and restful there. The Caddo brought us some baskets of corn for helping out. We took them, and it was a nice present considering so much of their corn was ruined. We left out about sunset. We headed down to Spring Valley and the old buffalo trails that lead west to home. Home will be a welcome sight.

September 12th. We get back home and we are ready to rest for a few days. The chores need some attention. We needed to build a new hen house, as the old one became a haven for snakes. We will get a fair one built. We set it to be burned down the old one to rid it of snakes, mites, and what ever else sets up in there. Well, before we were to set the fire we found that a man was sleeping there! Thank goodness that we looked to check it out first. This man has been here before. He was one of those slaves that we had visiting with us with the settlers that we found dead on the Comancheria. It seems that he was looking for sanctuary here. We are glad to give it to him. He said that he was forced to work in a large silver mine in Mexico. We got him doctored up and fed him well. We gave him some better clothes as his were mere rags. We told him to rest as he was among friends here. His said his name is **Duellos Penne.** He said that there were others that escaped but he feared that they did not survive to get here. He traveled two days and saw no signs of others. We told him that we would go look at daylight. He said that the Kick-a-Poo helped him by giving him a horse and a gourd full of water. **Penne** said that the others were captured, or killed and that it would be fruitless to look for anyone else. He said that after he left here the first time, they headed west, then north.

He was with settlers that were later met by a raiding party of deserters looking for supplies and horses. The people had little supplies to take, so they were taken captive to be sold to work in a silver mine as laborers. The settler's children were used to carry firewood and tend to horses. They managed to ride away one night and they hide in the brush, so he did not know where they were now. So he was on his own and he was alone and afraid. We told him that he could live here with us, as long as he wants. He was relieved to find a place where he could rest, and not be afraid. That was the right thing to do. The wife was glad to have the new visitor and a helper. Ben came by and doctored him better to mend what looked to be a broken right hand. The boys made room for him in their room. They slept in their tent to "camp out" as they called it. They did not mind and they are good boys. Penne could not believe that he had a roof over his head, and a nice corn shuck mattress to sleep on. The things that we took for granted, are like a dream come true for him. We are very humbled by his tears, and his gratitude. We must do what we can to help him prosper as others have done for us.

September 13th. Penne slept for almost a day! He was startled when he woke and found that almost a whole day has passed. We told him not to worry, but to rest up and mend well first of all. He was anxious to go do some work. We told him that his hand would not mend well if he was using it too much for a few weeks. He was embarrassed, but he had nothing to be embarrassed about. He had been through a harrowing experience, and he was fortunate to be alive. The wife made some good stew from some rabbits the boys caught in some snares. He enjoyed that very much. She made some bread that he enjoyed. We then read to him from the Bible, and he cried as we read some verses. He said that he wished he could read, and write. We told him that we all learned, and that it was never too late to learn some things. We said that we would teach him the way that we learned by reading the Bible by copying letters and words in the dirt with a stick. He liked that and he said that this past year has taught him to appreciate prayer, and he felt closer to God because of all his trials. He is a good man, and we told him that people helped us when we needed it, and we are just returning the favor. He deserves being treated well, if anyone does.

Tonight we read, ACTS Chapter One, Verse Eight, "Missions."

We took Penne out and showed him the fields. He was impressed that we were able to work so much land. He liked our windmill as it pumped water to the fields. He said that he would stay to help if he could have a place of his own. We agreed. He was free to come and go as he pleased, as he was a helper here, and not our slave. He was most happy about that as he looked to be a hard worker from the look of him. We burned down the old chicken house to rid it of snakes. We saw a number of them and a hawk took good care of them. We got some posts lined up and Penne used his left arm to work. We did not want him to but he insisted to help set the poles in the ground. We have some cedar boards from the sawmill and Penne laid up the best ones. He took a stick and he drew out the plans for a good design for the chicken house. He draws really well. It was better than what I had in mind and it allowed for fresh air to enter by opening up some vents and windows. It faced the south versus the east and he made it taller and longer by making an overhang of the roof to guard against bad weather. We looked over the lumber and there was plenty to build it that way. He got to steady swinging a hammer, left handed, and he then used a saw. We have him sit to rest after a few hours and he would not have it. We asked him to please not kill himself the first day, to pace himself as we appreciated his help. He was under no pressure to try to do it all in one day. We got the roof set with a good pitch to the gables, and we got the walls up in a short time. We broke at the hot time of day and we set down to eat. I could have went to sleep, but I felt that eating a good meal was more important to keep me strong as I was in good company. Penne sat in the shade of the well and he made some shingles from a piece of cedar with a wooden mallet and a spoke's shave. The wife brought him a pail of food and that got him to eat. He is happy and we are glad because in a day's time the color has returned to his face as he has hope for the future now.

September 14th. We asked him to pick out a place where we would build him a place of his own. He blinked hard like he could not believe it. He said that he would sleep in the barn, as it was nicer than most places that he has lived. We said that if that is what he wanted, he could stay there. We have a small stove in there and he could have a place of his own. He is welcome to stay in the house any time the weather is inclement, as he is part of the family now and we would consider what he wants. He asked me 'how I came to be here in Texas since I was a freed slave?' I told him that when I was a small boy that a man named Mister Jeremy stole me away from slave traders at Baton Rogue to make me his own son, as his died at birth, along with his wife. He also took a girl named Delephine that became my first wife. He asked, "What happened to her?" I told him, "She was killed by robbers on the trail by someone thinking that we were gunrunners involved with the smuggling along the Sabine trade. We had some money that we got when smugglers took our farm in Louisiana as a hideout. They bribed us with both some money, and then with threats of death because we weren't leaving fast enough! Some men from a trading post saw that we had silver coins and thought us too rich to be farmers from the looks of us. They followed us into Texas and robbed us in the middle of the night." I told him that the Cherokee found me and took me in, as I was almost dead. We then scouted for Sam Houston and the Texas army. He swallowed hard and he understood that we all have a story to tell. I asked him about himself as he said that he has no history to tell, but from now on he will have something to tell. We left it at that, as we understood that he has suffered much in his life, and we know that he would prosper now.

We finished the roof. We took him into the barn and the boys have made a good dry spot for him and he was most happy. The women have made him a good bed from cotton linen and corn shucks. He liked that better than sleeping on the ground. So now we know each other better and we can get some things accomplished together. Simon came by with some hinges, and iron roof brackets he has made. We introduced him to Simon, and Penne liked the idea of working iron. We told him that Simon shows others how to work iron so that when the army gives him a big order of iron goods that he would not be so overwhelmed to meet a tough deadline. Penne asked us if he could learn. We told him to, "ask Simon."

Simon agreed. He told Penne that he needed to let his right hand heal better, first. Penne agreed. He is most anxious to do, and work as much as any two men. The boys came and they brought some fish that they have caught. Penne offered to clean them. We gave him one of Simon's knives, and he went downwind from the house and he did it quickly. The wife enjoyed that the fish were cleaned, and that they were nice fillets. They were then fried, nicely done. She got some cornmeal and she cooked them up good like we did in Louisiana, as I have showed her. Boy, it smelled good and we hurried to finish the roof. It was worth the wait and the boys enjoyed that they can put food on the table. They caught us four croppies apiece, and we had corndodgers too. So we have a good day of work and some good food to keep us going strong. Simon has some work to do so he goes home and he asks Penne to come by sometimes. He asked for him to heal up good as blacksmith work is trying on the body. We rested by the shade of the well, and we made time to rest so we can work late into the afternoon. We went inside the henhouse and added some green tree limbs to have as a roost to keep them off the ground. We have made places for water and feed troughs. We brought in corn and the chickens took to their new house. It will keep out snakes, and varmints looking for a free meal. It was nice and we made a good day today.

We sat together and we read the Bible. It made everything in focus as we have moved to being more positive in our lives these days. I wrote General Sam a letter and I told him about our trial with the Tejas, and the Mack

Camy's village. We also told of our new friend, Penne. We are thankful for his friendship, and his generous help to us.

Tonight we read: Matthew, Chapter 5, "The Sermon on the Mount."

September 22nd. We went again to church services, as the weather is fair. Penne wanted to go, so we get him ready. Simon's wife cut his long hair, and she gave him a new straight razor. He did not know how to use it, so she cut his beard shorter, and then gave him a good shave to shape it up under his chin. He said that he felt like a new man, and he was most positive having so much attention. There was a good day to travel, and we made progress getting to the river crossings. We met other people coming to church services, and it made a nice caravan getting there safely, as no one would be stuck if their wagon fouled along the way. We get to the Dove church, and Penne was afraid to go inside fearing that he would not be welcome. We told him that he was welcome as anyone else who was interested in attending here. He went in and he was most humbled by being allowed to go in to worship. He joined the church, and he wanted to be baptized, today. That is good and we are happy for his life to be better. Penne was welcomed and he fitted in better than he could hope. We were glad because in a short time his life has changed for the better, as he well deserves. We took him down to the river and baptized him with the others that have come from the past two months. Penne cried. He is comforted well by all his new friends at church. He is happy, and now he has a new home to come to: the Dove church. He was surprised at their stand against slavery, and that we supported Free City, a town made up of some escaped and free slaves. He heard about the meetings of **TABOR** and he said that he never knew of any such group of **abolitionists** until now. He wished to meet with them sometimes. We offered to let him go when he wanted to go, and the meeting would be set in different places to be safe from harm from others that are against them. We made him know that the push was against allowing slavery into the new Oregon territory, and New Mexico too. California was taking a vote to see what their fate would be. We just knew that Texas was no place for slavery, and that we have to set the standard that would show to others that slavery was wrong, and has no place here, or anywhere that calls itself a Christian, or a Godly place. This was called the **Cross Timbers** for good reason. It is the new Promise Land.

September 24th. We get back home and get settled in. Our cow has had her calf and it was a healthy one. We tended to chores and we addressed Penne's hand. It was mending, but he needed to give it more time. We could not keep up with him and he has taught us a few things about life and being grateful for small things everyday. I will not complain about too much for a long time. Troy came to visit with Regina and their new baby. We were happy to see the fine young man turn it around. He has matured and he has become a great father. Phoebe made a fuss over the baby, and Sarah loves children and they took turns spoiling the new baby. Sarah has a nice basket that was a good size for the baby. She has made it for them and they enjoyed that it looked like little Moses in a basket. Sarah told them that the baby would sleep longer if it feels safe and secure. We introduced them to Penne and they hit it off well. Ben and Ke-Ke came along and we had a good visit together. Their little Jacy is over a year old and she is walking all over the place, and talking up a storm. She knows many of the Cherokee words and she was a sweet girl. This place is a good place for families, and we are proud that we have a great place to live. We are grateful for our family and friends, as they have made our difficult days better by their encouragement, and their friendships.

October 1st. We went out and checked the wheat fields. They were getting full and the heads were getting heavier. It will be just a week or so before we would be reaping a good harvest. Penne was ready to get out there to harvest it all. I thought that the week of October 14th would be best because the farmer's almanac said that it would be windy that week, and that makes it easier to separate the wheat from the chaff. I admired that Penne was so anxious to help and we will need him when the day comes. We went and got the wagons ready to make sure that they would hold up to the burden of the harvest. Penne had some suggestions on greasing the axles with bear grease. We had some from the bad bear and it was fitting that it continued to benefit us as we struggled with that one. We put the wagon up on wood blocks and removed the wheels. He would have it ready to go in a few hours. He wanted to paint it green with red wheels. I did not know about that, but then it would stand out from the others when we were looking for our wagon. We would be the envy of anyone at the gristmill. So the boys helped him paint and he encouraged them to be neat with the paint and not waste any by being sloppy. It dried and later on they put it all back together, and it looked outstanding. So they plan to paint the other wagon too. Simon came by and he was impressed at the look of the painted wagon. He said that Penne might have a job painting wagons, and learning the blacksmith trade. He was delighted to get praise, and he was most happy. The boys like him too, so everyone gets along well. Troy came along with Regina, and little Theda. He liked the painted wagon and Regina wanted theirs painted blue on the body, with plain wheels. So Penne has started something here, and I know he will be very busy for some time keeping up with the orders. He laughed and he was pleased that he was doing something that other people appreciated.

That is all anyone wants to be respected and known for being accomplished somewhere.

October 14th. We went out and we threshed the wheat. Some drag an old wagon wheel behind a horse to thresh it. Penne said that he would do this the old fashioned way by cutting it with a sickle. The women got the string ready to tie the bundles of cut wheat. The boys laid down a tent canvas for a threshing floor. Penne liked that idea as it keeps the wheat clean, and the wind has less of a chance to blow away the wheat kernels. We stack wheat and Penne throws it up into the air to thresh it. The boys take turns and they pick up the threshing canvas and pour it into the wagon bed. It all goes well and we tell Penne about the brooms that we make from the wheat straw. He liked that and we think alike in many ways. The wind continues to blow and we continue to work into the late evening when the wind dies down. The women have a fine meal made and we rest and enjoy our time together. After one more day we will have the wheat fields completed.

October 16th. We make it to the gristmill. We have been given a number on a piece of wooden shingle to make sure we do not lose our place in line. There have been fights in line before and they want to make sure that people are served properly without someone trying to push into line. I have no problem with that. I felt that the pushy people were just tired and afraid of rain coming to spoil everything. I have a canvas over all ours, so come rain, or shine I was ready when ever. The mill was short a man to help so Penne jumped in there to help to keep things moving along. I think that he might have another job lined up, if he isn't careful. It seems that he got hired to work during the milling season, so we are proud of that, for our new friend to prosper, by being given a decent chance to work, and have opportunities. I could not keep up with him and he works circles around any two men. Maybe three. I just know that when he lays down to sleep he is gone, and I could not blame him. He is offered twenty dollars and a share of wheat for his work this season. He asked us if it was "alright." We said that you are your own man, and that if you want you can do as you please. He smiled a big smile and it was the right thing to do. He is a good member of our community, and we need more good people like him. We thank the good Lord for him.

Mesquite Beans and Prickly Pear fruit.

CHAPTER FIFTEEN

The Peace Treaty and the Gold Rush.

November 1st, 1848. The weather is about to turn bad according to my rheumatism. This I know as my left leg feels like inside the bone is being scraped with a dull knife. That is hard to ignore when the weather is changing. I told the family that we have to get ready for some serous weather coming in the next few days. The farmer's almanac says the same, so I know it to be true, between the two simple warnings. We went out to pick mesquite beans and prickly pear fruits. These are the basic staples of life according to the Kick-a-Poo elders that I have spoken to. Simon, his wife and his boys will join us by bringing wagons to load up with the good vittles that the prairie provides. Troy also came with his wagon. Penne comes with a deep wagon and we get ready for a special gathering. The Kick-a-poo have asked us to go with them to their best patches of mesquite and vast prickly pear cactus. They offered us an invitation by their smoke signs yesterday. This month Sarah, and Ke-Ke have made many fine cane baskets for holding the goods. We also have many burlap tote sacks to hold the mesquite beans that can be made into a nice meal like good corn. We are preparing for an early winter and we have time to get situated, today. We have a good turn out so no one will be hungry when the cold comes again. We are 'well armed' which means the coming cold will not catch us ill prepared, or wanting.

The Kick-a-poo show how to remove the prickly pear fruit by using a stick, to remove them to avoid the awful stickers from the hands. The rains have made many good blooms and these have become big rich purple fruits just full of black seeds. We peeled one and cut it open. We showed the boys how good they are. They spit seeds at each other and they made me laugh. We all liked learning about something good to eat. Also the leaves of the pear can be cooked over a fire to make them more edible, as it burns off the terrible stickers. They can be used for cow and horse feed too as it is very filling and it quickly fills an empty stomach. I tried to make them informed on some things without preaching to them too much. The boys ask 'why is this so important?' I tell them that little things like this can help you survive in tough times, as some do not know these things. This is what makes you survive where others do not. Unfortunately some do not know these things and they will suffer. We are responsible to teach others about survival here, as our allies have for uncounted generations. That makes it proven, and worth knowing. We go out and pick mesquite beans, as the trees bend, as they are heavy with them. They are nice and orange and tan. We break one open and give it to them. The beans are sweet and good. They taste like a Mexican peanut. It makes good feed too, if need be for people and for our animals.

Josiah gets a thorn from a mesquite tree all the way through his finger. I pull it out before it swells up like a mule butt. He does not cry out or flinch, like a good Indian. Sam Bird gives him some mesquite sap to chew on while I address the thorn from his right hand. We have several hundred pounds of beans between us, and about fifty-five pounds of pears, or more. And at least fifty-nine pounds of good cactus leaves. We place it all out and we divide it up equally so that the wise elders will get a good share each. We are happy for the opportunity to meet one more time before the cold snap hits and the skies turn cold and the wind grows unfriendly. We do a dance to celebrate a good gathering, and they allow us to say a prayer to give thanks for a bountiful harvest today. Ben signs the words and they are all moved at our address, and thanks to God. They respond with their victory yell, "Ah—hoe!" We thank each of the participants and we give each other words of encouragement until we can meet again in the spring. Young Bull takes his people to their winter camp to keep them safe. We agree to meet when spring comes, or good weather permits, which ever comes first.

November 4th. The wind has come with brute force from the north and the cedar is blowing over the Red River. My eyes are almost closed from the cedar dust it brings. The rain comes and it helps me breathe better, and I take a cold spell with a fever. Ben rides over because the boys went to fetch him. I have a terrible fever and Ben gets out the medicine bag of cures. I felt terrible like 'I was sent for and could not go!' He makes a tea with the marshmallow plant. Then he has Sarah make a big pot of potato soup with lots of garlic and wild onions. He puts **skunk oil** on my chest and it is strong enough to chase off a bad bear, and anything else with a sense of smell, for miles. I think I will survive, but I fear for those around me that have to stand the stink of a skunk for me to get better. At least they won't get close enough to catch it from me. Ben makes some **willow bark tea** and that seemed to make me sleep for about 10 hours. I woke up and I felt better. I drank a whole bucket of water, and my mind seemed clear again. I stayed away from others and no one else gets sick.

I am glad that the boys and Phoebe went over to Ben's to stay so that they would be away from me. I told Sarah to go until I got better, and she cried. I was not putting her away, I just hated for her to be around me when I was so terrible sick. I am hard enough to deal with on good days. She agreed to stay for a day and come back to check on me. I was fine with that and I was feeling like I was less of a burden that way.

November 10th. I am finally better and the family has come back home. I have cleaned up and aired out the house. I think that the 'evil spirits will stay away,' as Ben says in Cherokee.

It turned sunny today and I went outside. The sun felt good on my face. I was happy to be alive and I am renewed in my strength, and my faith held me strong these past days.

We went out to ride horses together as a family. We have no real chores today but to be together as that is a chore that we do not enjoy enough. We need to have some fun and see some of the land that we love. The wind has died down and we enjoyed some time just riding out to see the land. We saw some deer grazing and they were not afraid of us. The children enjoyed that there were young ones among the herd. They wanted to pet one that came close, as I asked them not to as that might get them in trouble with a wild animal. It still was exciting to see the animals so close with no fear of us. We were not on a hunting party, but just wandering about to see all the sights. We went along and saw a **chaparral** chasing down some dinner of a snake that was out sunning itself on a warm day. We then saw a golden eagle up in a tree swoop down and grab a rabbit without breaking a sweat. I wish that hunting would be so easy for me.

November 25th. We went to visit the church for a fall celebration. Many new members were there and the congregation grows by leaps and bounds. Some members from **Free City** are here, asking for farm implements and some basic goods. We offered to get some wagons loaded up with supplies for winter. They offered up a list and there was a collection made and fifty-three dollars was collected. Simon offered up a new plow he has made, and some sickles, and a hoe. So this was a start. We have a few new blankets and we offered them up, and a few supplies that we have. Others donated some things that they brought to show for the "bragging time" where people say what they are thankful for. I am thankful for my health returning, and that was good incentive for me to try to do more for others as it has been done for me. The talk was that 'the fugitive slave laws were being ignored.' Soon the fugitive slave laws might be enforced again. The army might come in and take over areas where groups of slaves congregate. Some bad laws are being made in the new government. It should be a local issue, decided by the local officials and by local vote. Free City has been law-abiding, and that makes them a threat to no one.

Today we studied ROMANS, Chapter 8. "Do unto others."

December 15. We have supplies for Free City. We have the list that was offered to us and many people at the fort have donated goods for a good cause. We brought three wagons of goods with some offers of help with farm implements, books, and seed. This is a good thing for these people who want to start over here with a new life. Many of these people are free persons like Mister Goyens and myself. Some have run away from a bad situation to have half a chance at a decent life. The **abolitionist** movement at church has been strong and the members of **TABOR** have made a good stand here. **The Knights and Daughters of TABOR** have made donations of money and goods to buy clothes for the women, girls, men and boys. Wagon one was just children's goods. Wagon two was all women's goods, and wagon three was men's goods. So they all lined up and they were matched with things that are proper for them. Some cows, calves, and a good bull are brought for them to have a good start of cattle. We brought some of the seed corn from the Caddo to give then a new source of good, decent food. We brought iron goods from Simon to give out to make their life better. Some people from the **Dove** came with food prepared and ready for them. It was a real feast with some turkeys and dressing, potato salad, and desserts that all the ladies worked for days to do. A man played the guitar and another on a cornstalk fiddle. The singers came out and made a great celebration even better. Christmas came early this year and many now have things that they sorely need. It is a relief to think that they will sleep better now. They have a chance to succeed and prosper in a new society that works with them, and not against them. Decent people deserve a decent chance to live. This is a good start for them to have the basic staples of life. It is the least we can do.

Today we read JUDE Chapter 20, "Difficult Days."

December 25th, 1848. We have a nice Christmas at Ben's place. It was windy and cold. A light snow fell last night. We made a quiet Christmas together. We kept our family close and we gave thanks for the many blessings that we have. The boys read the Christmas story, and the little ones had special gifts of hard candy and wooden toys. The boys got a rifle, and some arrows and a bow that the Kiowa made for them last fall. We got the women a new coat, nice dresses and shoes that fit good. I got Ben a new hat, and a nice pistol from the gunsmith at the fort. Penne got a nice tie, shirt, jacket and pants to wear to church. Ben got him some nice Mexican made boots that fit properly. We burned the fireplace bright, and we stayed warm among family and friends. We have a good time to talk and make quality time to visit together. That was the best gift of all.

Today we read LUKE, Chapter Two, "The Christmas Story."

January 1st, 1849. The New Year starts with all the hopes and dreams that make things possible. We have made our resolutions to be more patient, and to make things done better. It starts off cold and windy. I read the farmer's almanac to see what might be good to plant this year. I looked at my map of the fields and tried to plan out what fields to plant this year, and which to leave fallow so they can grow better next season. Corn looks good so corn it will be. Some of that Caddo corn will grow next to some of that blue Cherokee corn we have in the seed pots. I go to the barn and I put out extra hay for the animals, and feed for the chickens. I got some good eggs and the wife will boil some to have with the mesquite beans. I went to the smokehouse and I secured the door from animals getting in to spoil everything. A hungry coyote comes and gives me a hard time. I take the wooden slat used to bar the door and I chased the animal away. Let him hunt for his own food like everybody else! Penne came to see what the ruckus was all about. I told him it was a coyote looking for a free meal. He laughed and he went back into the barn to sleep in his room. I go back into the cabin and put wood on the fire and I went back to sleep finally. Some nights it is just like that: you hear some kind of noise, and you worry too much over nothing. The wind blows hard that the stovepipe whistles. We try to go back to sleep. We are too sleepy to write any more, or to read anything tonight.

February 28th-March 1st, 1849. We get passage to go to San Antonio to celebrate the victory over Mexico. So the San Jacinto celebration will be even more meaningful. General Sam sent us a letter with passage tickets donated to those that also fought at Buena Vista and their family. Our travel on a steamboat up the Trinity River to San Antonio will be an adventure all by itself. Ben Bird was not sure about a boat that spews fire and makes so much noise. He saw it before when General Sam left us for home. He felt that if General Sam suggested for us to ride on it, it should be safe enough for the family too. Since our family is coming they wanted to see those people that we fought with in battle. It was worth the effort to get there as it was not so hard on the body getting there, and the rooms were as nice as any cabin you could stay in. We got there in three days and it was nice to have a few days to rest up from the trip and visit the places in San Antonio. We went along the river and we saw the Alamo mission, which was being completed with a new roof and it was cleaned up nice as it should be. We went to little family restaurants and we saw many of the **tejanos** that we served with in the army. They fed us with fine meals, music and dancing. Anywhere we went we got well wishes, and pats on the back from someone that we have served with, or known in some capacity when we were either training them, or making efforts to help save Texas from being plowed under by the Mexican army. The family loved the sights and sounds of the lovely San Antonio. It was nice and shady and it was different than when we were fighting so much. It was a place of peace, and it was very pleasant as everywhere was a festival to celebrate our victory. A little tejano boy was playing a guitar by the river and people were sitting close by. He took off his hat and laid it on the ground. People came by and put coins in his hat to show that he was a great musician. He played up a storm and he was good as any grown man when he played. I drew his picture so I would remember him well. We love the change of pace and this is a wonderful time to be alive!

The little tejano guitarist

Sarah's Shaw dance

March Second. Texan Independence Day. We celebrate "The Victory Days" as they call it today. There are many more people at a ballroom, and this large hotel that is unbelievable. We are treated like the good King of France and we are among royalty here. We get cleaned up and wear our best clothes. There is a parade where we ride in decorated wagons, and then was some riders with fancy Mexican saddles and silver bridles of the tejanos. They were dressed in their best outfits. We went later for the Dress Ball. General Sam is here and he is going around visiting everyone. There is music, and food and entertainment of a short play that recognizes the efforts of the Tejanos and the Texan army. There are dancers and wonderful music. Ben is happy to see all the people that we knew. Mister Goyens and Deaf Smith were here. Even Mr. Lamar was decent to us for a change. The children meet the soldier's children and they have special rooms just for them with entertainment to keep them happy. The soldiers have a special dance where we dance with our wives and it is a special song written just for us. They played the song on the fiddles called "the Amazing Grace" which paid respect for those that died in battle. We then danced a German dance called a "Waltz." It was one big step, and one little step. Then you follow everybody else in a circle going clock-wise. I can do that! There was a dance called a "Shod-dish" where people danced like they were all drunk. Some people danced that way anyhow!

I was a good dancer for a change and I did not step on my poor wife's feet. I did well for someone with a bad left leg. That was funny and all the people laughed. It all is wonderful and it makes us feel well appreciated for all that we have been through. The **tejanos** did a "Fandango" which was an old dramatic dance from Spain that had a great guitar player. Then there was a "Tango" which the women loved the best. We tried to do that and we were fair, but not real good for the first try. There were "reels" where the fiddler played like a clucking chicken and then a barking dog, and a woodpecker. It was something like "Granny does your dog, Bite," and then "Piney Woods," "Carve the Possum," "Sally Gooden," and "Leather Breeches." There was a song called "the Wildwood Flowers" which was sad and it reminded me of my home in Louisiana. Then, there was a sing-a-long where we sang the songs we sang into battle. It was something about: "We are going to the Bower." (What ever that was!) Still it got us there and we went through the battle less scared because our spirit was strong back then and we were too young and dumb to be really scared.

There is a toast for Sam Houston's birthday, and he makes a short speech thanking everyone for our great efforts to make peace possible. Sarah looked so wonderful and I was so proud of her tonight. The children had fun and they had many stories to tell of their friendships. They exchanged names and addresses so they can write letters to their new friends. They get to go to a place tomorrow that has animals from all over the world. It is something like the circus that came to Louisiana when we visited New Orleans, twenty years ago. It has tigers, lions, and elephants. We heard all about it. There were Mexican fireworks and sights and sounds of the wonderful night here. We did not want it to end and we stayed up all night to celebrate our victory.

My wife held me close and kissed me like it was when we met, and we first married. She told me she loved me and that she is happy with me. That was nice to know, as sometimes she gets lost in the shuffle of things. I vow to do better to try to keep her better involved in things from now on. She deserves better, and seeing her tonight made me so proud of her.

March Fifth, and Sixth, 1849. We travel back home and the trip home was wonderful. We have many good memories to keep over what was a difficult time in our lives. I have a greater appreciation of what happened to us to make us become more mature, and responsible to our family. We stopped several places to get new supplies, and fuel for the boat. We got to get out and see the sights at the boat dock and the towns around it. We had several hours to walk around and see everything of interest. Most of all people were so nice to us and they would not let us pay for anything we ate, or for anything like flowers that were given to our wives as presents. We have some many things to think about and it was nice to have some time to get away from it all and celebrate our life together. This made all the effort worth it to be honored and shown such great respect this past week.

March 15th. We go to the fort and we read a copy of **The Red Lander**. It was a well-worn copy, but still worth reading. General Zachary Taylor has now assumed the role of President of the Federal States. He has come a long way from the battlefields in northern Mexico wearing a flannel shirt. He will make us a fine leader. He was very bold and outstanding so he is in a better role as our leader. General Sam spoke well of him and he asked us to pray for our new president. The past February a good solid peace treaty has been made! **The Treaty of Guadalupe-Hidalgo** was signed giving peace the possibility of being a reality. It was printed out so we could read the details well and try to understand what it all means.

This will make up for the **Velasco** treaty that failed so miserable, last time. Now, California and New Mexico are being considered for admission as a territory, then as a state. Nevada, Colorado, and part of Arizona are added. The Rio Grande River is the southern boundary.

California is already there. It is hoped that slavery will not be extended to either place. The debate at the fort was for admission of New Mexico and Utah, without slavery being spread into a slave-free place. The spread of slavery has been a plague upon our nation. The war debt of the Texas republic is about to be paid so that the trade dollar will bring us better prices for our crops in the trade markets. Prices at the trading post will go down and they will stay reasonable to keep our trade and barter stronger. We try to be informed so we can plan things better to provide for the family. We do not always do as well as we would hope.

It was all worth it if they can sort things out so we can get back to farming and complaining about the rain, or the lack of it. Complaining gives me something to do while I consider what to do about it, to fix it. At least with this peace treaty we have half a chance to get things right.

The Lord is smiling on us since we won the Buena Vista battle and we were greatly out numbered. Santa Anna's army had the upper hand when he went south to address problems of revolt within his own government. That thorn in his side was all that stood in the way of his victory against us. He folded up and went away as we were getting the tar whipped out of us, and that was the cause of our victory. That and our cannon fire that was double loaded with grapeshot against him. I still wonder about all the confusion of battle and the terrible thunderstorms that followed. I wonder if it was all worth all the terrible indiscretions that happened to both sides in February. We will see how the plan for peace goes.

March 17th. We take some goods out to our allies to see how they are doing. They have lost a few of their elders to illness and old age. We break out some of the **ristas** of garlic and hand them out among our friends. They smile and they give us the friendly trade signs. They hug us and pat us on the back. We greet them warmly and offer them kind words and gestures. They bring out the pipe bag and we bring out many ropes of braided tobacco. We go to the council house and we have gifts and blessings on those that survived and the new babies born during the winter. It is a week before **Winter Count,** but we go ahead and take advantage of the good weather today. We go outside and the children are passed among us for us to get a good look at them. It is almost like a military inspection where they are passed and comments are made over each one saying that: "this boy will be a fine hunter, as his father is," or "this girl baby will be a good mother, as her mother is a good mother."

The chief holds them up and he calls them by the name that they will be know by. Their mothers quietly line up next to the chief and they tell the name of the child as he announces it loudly as he holds them up high. The people clap and whistle. After all the names are told they yell loudly to show their approval of the new tribe members. We spend the night and there is a big feast and a dance that goes into the night. The moon comes up and the dances stop as the moon reaches high in the sky over Red Top mesa. There is a ring around the moon so rain is coming in a day or so. It is good that we celebrate early, as Winter Count will certainly be a rainy one. We part company and we plan to go hunting in the next month. They will make the smoke signs and we will meet the next day that the weather is good.

March 21st, 1849. We go to the fort and find that two weeks ago many soldiers have been dismissed from duty as their time as a soldier is finished. Now they look to be short handed as many soldiers have deserted their posts! Even the cook and the jailer have left! The quartermaster said that the farrier left, and the hired hands too. He has to pitch the hay for himself. He asked if the boys were available to work for him? I asked what has happened? He handed me a copy of the **Red Lander**. I am surprised that the word is that Gold has been discovered in California! It is hard to believe that people are finding lumps of gold like they are digging new potatoes! It is on the American River by a place called Sutter's Mill. Gold was discovered in early January and the population there has doubled in some places overnight. The newspaper was passed around and we thought it was a bad joke. It seems that people believe it, as it is making many leave in droves from a place they know for a place that they do not know. It is crazy, but people were crazy to come here to this frontier just over ten years ago. Now it is the place to be, and it is a fight to get a good land grant without a wait of two years. Many others want to come here and take what you have sweated hard to make. This is our gold discovery, a solid place on the prairie that is black land and red, sandy dirt in some places. The gold we have is the sweat and toil to plant a good crop of wheat, corn, squash, cantaloupe, and melons. That is the gold that we dig, here: something good to eat!

March 25th. A heavy spring rain comes with hail and a tornado. It hails for over half an hour and it is as big as persimmons and larger! The ground is white like it has snowed here. We took a ruler from the carpenter's square and it said it was three inches deep in some places! Some hailstones were as big as a horse apple! Our corn and good yellow squash takes a bad pounding. All our hard work is for nothing. Our cabin's roof blew off and the barn broke in half from the wind. Two of our good cows died in the storm. Penne has knots on his head trying to save the animals, and his left eye is swollen shut from being hit in the eye by a hailstone. We tended to our friend by taking a new handkerchief and placing a hailstone over his eye to make the swelling go down. I am afraid that he might lose the sight in his eye, as it looks most gruesome. We tried not to cry seeing all the damage and the hurt to our friends and property. This is terrible and even **JOB** would be teary eyed over this storm. We found chickens, squirrels, coyotes, and some possums dead. The wife came out and she was very angry. It was not at me, but at the situation here. I told her that at the fort there were offers of a job if we wanted it. It might mean soon eating those prickly pears, and mesquite beans that we have in the corncrib. We hoped that this event was limited to just here and not to any of our allies. Ben rode by and he said that his place was just as bad and worse. He just looked at the ground and he was quiet the rest of the day. The boys were fine just scared and sick over the way things were so tore up. There was some consolation that they were safe. It could have been worse. I keep telling myself that. I should be more grateful that no people were killed this day. We went to the fort to see about the job offers. We took Penne to the company doctor and he looked over his eye. He said it was most terrible, but that we put a hailstone on a handkerchief to make it better was helpful to keep the swelling from doing more damage to his eye. The jobs are ours for the taking, as we will do everything from guard duty and mucking out the stalls. Civilians have more job offers than someone part of the army these days. Sarah took the job as a cook and she has the temporary cook as her assistant. He may leave too from the looks of things. The commander said that he appreciated our help and that the deserters, if found would be put to death as the war rules have not been lifted yet. That is a tough choice but the dust has not settled from battle and orders are orders. We have served and continue to serve even though our time of duty is over. We have no choice, as this fort is all that stands guard against the frontier and all the problems that it brings with strangers trying to settle here.

Penne came back and he said that the doctor said his eye might have to be removed later on because of the harm done to it in the storm. I asked him to wait until the swelling goes away to find how his vision goes. He is not to fret about not being able to work, or labor in the heat with this bad injury. I hope not to see him suffer more from this storm. He is still welcome here for as long as he wants and he is not to fear over his injuries keep him from working hard, or driving a team for a while. Penne says that he wants to go to the gold fields and try his hand at mining for gold. That would be crazy to leave and jump into an unknown area to dig for a dream. There was a banner posted, noting that, "settlers won't be supported by the army any longer." Whose order is this? When they leave for the open frontier they will be under their own authority. I fear for them leaving out as I saw when I was attacked when I rode into Texas from Louisiana. 'Green horns' are fair prey for the outlaws and robbers on the trail. I look back now and I wonder that I survived at all. Anyone by them self are not long to keep a good horse, or being robbed these days.

I got my orders to report tomorrow to muck out stalls and tend to the horses at the quartermaster's barn. I am not happy with this job, but at least we will get lodging, food, and a safe place to sleep. Still I wonder about California and those people picking up gold like it was gravel on a gravel road. When I was younger I was always looking over the next hill wondering what was there. Now I am still wandering looking for a place to put my head. I do not know if I am doing enough to help my family since my attempt at farming has been hurt for this season. With the war over the need for many horses for the army has ended. My contract with the army has ended. I was told today Captain Patterson told me. He was nice about it but it made me realize that if I can't be a farmer, I am not much of a man anymore. It is all I know to do and not much else. I was put on this earth to work it and to grow good things from it. I am torn over what might be best to do to support my family. My wife and boys look to me and I do not know what might be best to do.

Tonight we read **JOB**, Chapter One, "JOB is tempted by the Devil, and tested by God."

April 1st, 1849. A new group of soldiers have come to the fort to take the place of those that have retired and deserted. We are given our walking papers from the new commander! He told us that our services are no longer needed. We are given two month's pay for a 'severance package' and we are asked to leave by the end of the day. I am hurt and my anger is plain to see. I do not know what to do, so I leave out and take the wife as she has been treated the same. The boys still have jobs, as they are young and strong. So there is some consolation to this. Still I would not wish to embarrass them by showing my anger over being dismissed for no real cause other than being old and tired. I leave and try to be hospitable and not hostile. So I am an "April Fool" with no hope of a job. I feel like an old shoe thrown out for the goats to eat. I do not know what to do as I am without a clue this time. Ben comes and he gives me a similar story. He is sad and not sure what to think of the new commander. He is young and strong with his opinions as he shouted orders at us like we were under his command. What would General Sam think of this? He would like to know and I will write him a letter to Washington City. This is how veterans are treated after their duty is finished? He does not know who we are and what we have done for the settlements. It seems that he does not care, or wants to know us. It rains and we ride home before it floods. The boys stay here in the barracks as the river will flood and be dangerous to cross tomorrow. We tell them not to fret about us and we put on our "brave face" to show them that we are proud of them. We tell them to do their job well, as they always do; and that we will find something to do to support the family. It is good that we have the mesquite beans and prickly pear fruits in the corn crib as these are manna from Heaven. We have come a long way since our visit to San Antonio. I do not know what has happened to us all in a month's time!

We went out to check on the allies. We made the smoke signs and no one replied. They must be far away or over out west too far to see us. We hoped that all was fine with our friends the Kiowa and Kick-a-Poo. We went to see Ben's place and he was out trying to make his place back in order. It was bad, but not as bad as my place. We both were quiet and we worked hard to try to clean up the mess. We burned a few animal carcasses, and some wood that was not useful for anything. We sat by his well and we carved on sticks to ponder what we should do next. Ben said that he thought about going to **Telaqua** to be with the other Cherokee. I know it is hard to be away from your tribe, and then try to fit in with the other tribes that are our allies. They are good people, but we are still **"washitas."** The Cherokee would welcome us back, but what about what we have carved out of this wilderness? Who would protect our allies that we protect from new settlers? They protect us from trouble, and welcomed us to hunt buffalo with them, and they trade with us. It was a tough one to consider. I even mentioned going to California. Ben threw his knife into the ground, and the stick he was carving on and he walked away. I have crossed the line and I have to give him some time to think on his own. Our nerves are raw and what ever we say or do seems troubling, as none of it would be easy for us. Ben came back later and he tried to talk about what his concerns are if we stay here. He said that at the San Jacinto celebration that a soldier that was a captain of the cavalry told him that "his days roaming Texas will soon be over." He was at a loss to see that one coming after all he has done to help make peace with the tribes so that the settlements could continue with the Peters' Colonists. He did not say anything about it until today, and he has been boiling on the inside all this time. He is as bad as me mulling things over until his insides ache.

He said this he has dreamed of the old days when he was living with the Cherokee and people spoke and thought like Cherokees. He wants to move to **Telaqua** to live and forget all that we have worked for here. He said that people owning a piece of land is crazy and that you don't own the land, it owns you—until they bury you in it. He said, "we can't sell our land as it states on the land certificate. We can just leave it and move on where we can be ourselves again." He shows me a Cherokee newspaper that General Sam gave him at the San Jacinto celebration. He said, "The Cherokee need to band together as they did in the past and remember the old ways that respected the elders, and protected the young people." His spirit is broken and he needs to be back like we were in East Texas when Chief Bowls and Mush were alive. I told him that I support him in what ever he feels is proper to do. He said that the Kiowa and Kick-a-Poo suffered many deaths in the tornado and that they finally sent smoke signs after they were through mourning their losses. He said that Young Bull died in the hailstorm, and that most all their elders were lost. It seems that Young Bull was coming to their aid when he lost his life. I could not feel my legs and I felt like I lost my own son. I got violently ill and I lay on the ground like I was wounded through in through. I did not know how to tell the boys, and Ben said that he had already told them and they have rode out to pay their respects. I washed my face in the horse trough then I rode out and followed their trail to show the proper respect to them. It was terrible to see the devastation to their village with all the broken trees leading there. I acted brave to try to help. I brought some smoked beef tack for the mourners to have after they fast. It was hard jerky, and something that they would eat at a time like this. I had to cover my face with ashes and remove my shirt and shoes for their mourning rituals. They banged a drum suddenly and often. Then they burned sage and threw salt into the different directions. I helped since so many of their elders were gone and they are the ones that do these things.

The burials were finished and we each went down to the river to get stone to put over the graves. We brought a fossil sea urchin that was heart-shaped. They seemed to like that, as it reminded them of the time we were out there picking up the strange stones for the man that was a rock collector. They watched us from the high bluff and thought we were crazy to collect so many of the odd stones that are common in that place. Today, many made several trips to bring various stones to cover the graves. Some have found nice, thick clamshells and brought them too. It looked very nice and it made me feel better to mourn with them as they have treated me like I was a member of their tribe, and part of their family. They asked me to read from the Bible, as they knew much about it from Mister Wallace, the **contrary** and missionary. Ben made the sign language for my words to them and they cried terribly. They then took off their headdresses, and fine ornaments. They then took a knife to cut off their long hair and threw it into the fire. They fired arrows and darts towards the broken trees. They took their weapons and they laid them among the graves. They lit what was left of the village on fire. They laid facedown on the ground and humbled themselves to God.

Today I read ISAIAH Chapter Forty, Verse Thirty-one, "But they that wait upon the Lord shall renew their strength; they shall mount up with the wings as eagles; they shall run, and not be weary; and they shall walk, and not faint."

April 21-22, 1849. We took Penne back to the fort to see the company doctor. The old doctor has been reassigned elsewhere. The new doctor went to look at him and he says that his eye has to be removed today, or he will surely lose sight in his good eye. It seems terrible but Penne accepts it better than I would. We took him there and the doctor said that he should not wait any longer to do this. He was ready, as he has suffered a great deal. The doctor had him drink much strong drink to ease his pain. He then had him held down and his eye was plucked out to save the other from infection. It was quite terrible but Penne was quiet and still like he was relieved to be done with it. He was now all bandaged up. He will have to stay a few days until he can travel anywhere. We offered to stay with him and we did sit in a chair by his bed. We sat by his right side and we woke to find that he has died in his sleep! It was like our adopted father, Mister Jeremy when we were back in Louisiana. He went to sleep and he did not wake back up. I called an orderly and he called the doctor from his bunk. The doctor said that the infection from Penne's wound had spread to his heart and that he passed quietly in his sleep. I could not believe that such a good man left us so suddenly. The orderly called the Chaplain and he was most helpful to talk with me for a while. We prayed over Penne and I offered to take him back home and give him a decent burial. It seems that this place has been a good place to live and a good place to die, also.

We could hardly believe that our friend was gone and now with the Lord. We prayed the Lord's Prayer over him and we got things ready to take him home to be buried. The man from the livery stable donated a pine box for his funeral, as he liked Penne when we brought horses in the past. We thanked him for his thoughtfulness towards him and he helped load him into the wagon. The doctor brought a death certificate and we will put it in our Bible for safekeeping in case Penne had any family. We wrote General Sam and we told him of our plans to go to Telaqua, and about the tornado that destroyed our place, and the death of Penne. We told him of our allies and how they burned their village and left to join their allies, the Comanche and Kiowa. The postmaster gave us some letters from General Sam and we gave him the letter to Huntsville to post to him.

We get home and the wife sees that we have a coffin in the wagon. She took a knife and cut off the end of her hair and threw the knife and hair to the ground. The boys came and helped me find a nice shady spot for Penne to rest. They were most helpful and they were most supportive of us. Ben came and he watched as we were filling in the grave and he stopped me. He took the shovel and filled in the dirt the rest of the way. The women and girls picked flowers and laid them around the grave as we placed stones to mark the corners of the grave. We all cried and tried to be brave for him.

May first, 1849. We tell the family that we are going to Telaqua to live. I told them what Ben thought of it and they were willing to go because they are ready for a change. In three months we have went to feeling like a king from our visit in San Antonio, to being terribly sad finding so much death here. It was like east Texas when Lamar's army made us—Cherokee leave by force. We went to the Arkansas River to meet General Sam with supplies. We had hid in the stands of reeds and covered our faces with mud to hide from trouble. Well trouble still found us and now it is time to go! **We were told "the new governor, Runnels has made a law asking freed slaves, or 'any man of color' to take a master!"** There are too many indentured servants about, already. It was most terrible to consider such a thing happening to anyone, of any origin! Now, Penne's death, and the death of our Kiowa, and Kick-a-Poo allies were all that we needed to make up our mind to leave here. It is like touching a match to gunpowder. It is a flash, and now we are gone. We need to go again and be with the ones that need us, and speak the same language that we speak, and remember the old ways that respect the lives of old and young people. People have changed here. Sarah was happy to go, and so are Ke-Ke, Phoebe and Jacy. The boys helped load the wagons and we had to narrow down what we could bring in the form of supplies. They did not talk, quarrel or complain. They just acted like grown men and did what they have to do. We will miss all the good church folks. We have to leave before the weather gets too bad to cross the Red River at Waurika. Indian Territory will welcome us. There, we will be part of the Cherokee tribe again.

We will leave first thing in the morning. I will go by the fort with a letter of occupancy, to transfer this place for Troy and his family. They are to own this farm in my place. I can't sell it, but he can have it. He is young and strong. I have had enough of my life here! I feel like I am going to pass away if we stay here any longer! **Indian Territory** will welcome us with open arms. We can make our new home there among the Cherokee nation at Telaqua. They will take me in as they did before, and I can find a place to get my life back. I owe that to myself and my family.

Today we read: PSALM 37, "Do not fret over evildoers."

The End of *After the Republic*.

The Kiowa village

GLOSSARY FOR AFTER THE REPUBLIC

Unfamiliar Texan Terms of the 19th century.

abolitionist: A person that was against slavery, and the spread of slavery, or human bondage. In Texas it was members of an organization called, "TABOR." Many churches were against slavery. Only 1 in 5 white settlers owned slaves. These were mostly "newcomers" who arrived later in the process of settlement. Many original, early settlers abhorred slavery, and it was when California, and Oregon, Kansas, and Nebraska were added to the Union of Federal States that the question of Slave Free States was an issue. Churches such as the Lonesome Dove, (that the author's family belonged to) allowed people of other races to belong. Andrew was a free slave, his wife and brother, and sister-in-laws were Cherokee. This was the plan to make a more viable settlement that allowed good Christians of all races to belong. (And all God fearing Christians. of those days hated slavery.) Also it was not "needed" as most families were quite large in those days, and there were plenty of helping hands to do all the chores. One in Five whites owned slaves in the United States by 1860.

Antonio Lopez de Santa Anna: General Santa Anna. He was dictator and ruler over Mexico during the years of the Texas republic, and the time of the Mexican wars. He was known as the "Napoleon of the West." He was the head of the Mexican army. He was released after he made the Treaty of Velasco in 1836. He said, "Since he was a prisoner of war that he was under duress, and that this treaty was not viable." He was sent to Cuba to keep him out of Mexico's affairs. He returns to power and he builds up a great army to continue the fight to reclaim Texas since she joined the Federal States against his wishes. His intent was to keep a hold on California, which has followed the example of Texas and became a republic. New Mexico becomes independent also so Santa Anna holds on for dear life as he wages all out war against the Federal (United) States.

B
beau coups- (boo-COOS) French term: very much, a quantity, a great deal of something.

Ben Bird- Red Bird: the Cherokee medicine man's Christian name. Many Indians put away their Indian names when they became a Christian. It made them more accepted into "regular society."

blacksmith: a man that works and forges iron into horseshoes, tools, and farming implements.

branch: Here it means the fork of a creek, stream, or river.
brave—a young, male American Indian warrior, or Native American warrior.
breeches, (or "britches.")—slang word for "pants."
bull nettle—A green stinging plant, or weed. It was used before battle to be rubbed over the arms and legs of an Indian warrior to get him fighting ready. This plant was also dried and used in boiling water to make an astringent for wounds, used much like "witch hazel." The seeds taste like vanilla.

C

Californio's—settlers to California that rebelled against Mexico's rule much as Texas did. California was a republic that struggled as Texas did as a province of Mexico. The discovery of gold made a rush of settlers in 1849. California followed the example of Texas and became a republic, and it too became a bane to Mexico.

chaparral: Spanish word for a "road-runner." A bird that chases down its prey of lizards, snakes, and insects. A sign of good luck for fine hunting for some Texas' Indian tribes.
chiggers—deer fleas. Black land, and mesquite trees often has deer fleas that bite, and cause painful red sores, sometimes so bad that people die from shock, or infection, if they do not treat it well.
coal oil—oil from coal used as lamp fuel, and for soaking bad wounds.
Collin McKinney: A land surveyor. The architect, and important signer of the Texas constitution. It was Collin's idea to make majority of counties in Texas, "a 50 Miles Square with the county seat in the very center." (April 1846.) This was in case of Indian troubles, or if the army was needed to act in a hurry. Collin County was named after him, with the county seat named McKinney. Collin McKinney often disagreed with Sam Houston's ideas and actions. He often spoke out when he did.
Comanche: A great Indian nation composed of the Nacona, Wanderers, and Honey Gatherers.
This tribe numbered greater than any other Texas tribe. They covered an area of West Texas called the Comancheria. Notable historical chiefs are Peta Nacona, and Quanah Parker, father, and son. (The son, Quanah, was born to a captured farm girl, Cynthia Ann Parker, captured after a Comanche raid on Parker's Fort in 1845. Quanah was a great, and wise peacemaker.)

Comancheria: The land belonging to the Comanche nations. It went north and west of Bird's Fort. It continued south all the way to the Rio Grande River. It was bigger and contained more people than all the settlements combined, and doubled.

Consultation: The 1836 meetings of the infant Texas Congress to make a valid Texas constitution.

contrary, or contraries: a group of people that live within a tribe that think, act, and dress opposite of what is considered normal. They served as an example to others on what not to do. They were tolerated because they had a different vision of the world, as they were crazy, or they were thought to have some sort of supernatural power.

corral: a fenced in area used to hold horses, or cattle.

council stick: a ceremonial stick wrapped in rawhide, and decorated with rabbit fur, beads, and **charms.** This stick was passed around in Indian councils to allow the speaker to talk without being interrupted. It would then be passed to the next person. If any one interrupted the speaker, the stick would be used on the offender. This was a way to cut down on the internal strife by allowing the person to say their peace, and get it off their chest, keeping turmoil within the tribe to a minimum.

coup: (coo) the touching, or hitting of an enemy by a warrior, with a stick, or by a bow, or a horse hair quirt. Sometimes the enemy was left unconscious, and their weapons, horses, and self esteem would be taken. It was a big deal to brag about over the evening fire that you had crept up close enough to an enemy, and lived to talk about it to others.

coyote: Spanish word meaning "prairie wolf."

Cross Timbers—The northern part of the Trinity River forms three forks of the river: the Elm Fork, the Clear Fork, and the East Fork. The settlers called the river the Cross Timbers, as they resembled the shape of the Cross of Jesus. It was originally named this by the early Spanish explorers. This place had the best land for farming, and most had come here for that purpose: to own farmland of their very own with out paying half their profits to the landowner. The Indians of this area called it "the old hunting grounds."

D

Deaf Smith—General Sam Houston's main scout. (Erasthmus Smith) He looked for a river route between the Sulphur, the Red, and Mississippi rivers, as the Mexican navy has many times blocked the boat routes in the Gulf of Mexico, between New Orleans, and Galveston.

Delephine—Andrew's first wife that was killed in an attack by robbers when they first came to Texas in 1836. Andrew was severely wounded, and he was almost dead when the Cherokee found him. She fought fiercely against the robbers, so much so that the Cherokee gave her a burial worthy of a brave warrior. She was uncommon, and she knew Andrew all her life. (Mr. Jeremy, their adopted father, stole them away from slave traders at Baton Rouge. His wife and child died in childbirth, and he could not stand to see children abused, or sold in bondage.) Many families of different races were sold into bondage as many people were in debt, in terrible Debtor's Prisons, unable to pay taxes, and debts, after the failed markets, and depression in the Federal States after the 1812 War. In those days whole families were in prison, or loaned out to work off their debts for 10 to 20 years and longer! So please understand that many people were sold in bondage which included blacks, whites (English, Germans, French, Scots, Irish, and the like) whom were paying for their passage to America. Some Indians tribes, and individuals, were trying to buy back their traditional homelands as individual farms to re-establish their communities. This was common practice in those days, and it was a tragic fact of life. In the first book, "The Texas Republic," all the details are spelled out, and this is the second story of the series. It is a great deal more than you learned about in school, or textbooks.

Duellos—Greek word for "Slave." Also means "hard-working." A person with good skills.

dew cloths: curtains for the windows of a cabin. Also, the hides lining the inside a tee-pee to keep it insulated, and to draw the rain out of the sleeping/living area.

Dove Settlement—the settlement at Dove Branch, and the Lonesome Dove church/ settlement. (Close to modern day Southlake, Texas.) This settlement allowed blacks, and Indians to live there, as it was their settlement, also. All were welcome that were law abiding, and peaceful persons. A real and historical place that was the ideal place to farm and raise your family.

Dr. Jones—Doctor Anson Jones, a doctor that served at the San Jacinto battle. He was the last president of the Texas republic.

E

East Fork: The East Fork of the Trinity River was used to bring goods from the Red River (and Mississippi) before there were roads that were passable in Texas. The Caddo and Cherokee used this river route for over 100 years before the settlers came. They fought each other for control of the river in 1804-1806, as iron, flint, furs, pelts, guns, and silver moved down this route since there were not many passable roads or trails in those days.

Empresarrio: Leader of legal land grants made in Texas by permission of the Mexican government. Moses Austin, Stephen F. Austin, Juan Seguin, Henri DeZavala, and later Henri Castro were Empresarrios. This was during the time that Texas was a Mexican state, and later a republic. (1824-1836.) These great men planned and settled Texas with their great vision.

E-OH-La: Cherokee word for "great wind." A cyclone, or tornado. A great windstorm.

escarpito: The French provided Mexico with the prototype of the modern shotgun. It fired brass rifle balls used to kill birds. This was the type of gun used on Sam Houston when he was wounded in the LEFT (tibia) ankle at San Jacinto. (April 21,1836.) *According to Sam Houston IV, Sam Houston's great-grandson, grandson of Temple Houston. He said, "it was Sam Houston's left ankle wounded, NOT the right leg as most paintings and references show." He then added the fact about the shotgun that fired brass rifle balls, which was a new type of gun for those days! He also added, "Sam Houston might have suffered from Diabetes which is the reason why he suffered with his battle wounds for years. His wounds never healed well and he suffered terribly much all his life."

F

farrier: a person that tends to horses by grooming them and filing down their hooves. This keeps a horse healthy and fit, and reduces the possibility that a good horse will go lame.

Federal States—the early name of the United States. In the days this book happened it was called the "Federal States."

feather ceremony—a ceremony where young braves get a feather as a sign of achievement, and merit. It is much as when a soldier gets a merit stripe, or a raise in rank, or a medal for bravery. Young men between

15 and 22 "winters" old were taught hunting skills, fire making skills, making a shelter, and the use and making of weapons.

Federal States: The United States. This is the name that the United States of America was known by in the early days of its settlement. (The "United States" was more of a term more often used after the Civil War and Reconstruction when it was reunited after the internal strife.)

Fort Texas: March 27, 1846. American General Zachary Taylor took a prominent northern bank of the Red River to build an earthen, star-shaped fortress to keep the Mexican forces in check at the safe river crossing. Mexican General Mariano Arista started on May 3rd. This week long siege was to wreck the advances of Texan reinforcements towards Mexico. The Mexican artillery from Matamoros fired cannon volleys to try to destroy the fort. Only two Texans died during the attack, which was surprising considering the length, and fierceness of the Mexican army's attack. It was also called "Fort Brown," by some people to honor one of the soldiers that died in that battle. He is all the same man that the town Brownsville is named after.

Free City: a settlement of free, and escaped slaves that was close to Grapevine Springs and the Lonesome Dove settlement, in north Texas. The army, and the Indians left them alone as they were peaceful, and farmed, and captured horses for the army, and they did not allow outlaws, or vagrants. The settlement was hidden in some hills among some cedars. The original settlement was in a limestone cave, north west of Grapevine, Texas. It is now called "Sam Bass Cave," where that outlaw hid out, over 30 years later. Over 184 free slaves lived in Texas. Over 600 run-away slaves lived in early Texas. The local tribes hid them, and adopted many slaves. (As Andrew was adopted by the Cherokee.)

freedmen, or freemen: freed African slaves. Over 184 freedmen had come to Texas as a republic with the hopes of starting over, as Andrew had done. The army largely ignored Lamar's 1840 law that made freedmen forced to leave Texas if they had no legal reason to be here. Andrew had a legal letter that said he was a freeman, and he had served honorably in the Texan army. Some freedmen lived among the Indians to trade and married among them, as the tribes could relate to their struggles.

G

gable—the forked part of the roof. A wooden rafter.

Grants, Land Grants: Second Class Head Rights, 1,280 acres for families, and 640 acres for single Men after March 2,1836. 640 additional acres went to men who fought in Texas battles.

Land titles stopped for a brief period in November 1835 when it was feared settlers were coming undocumented, and unregulated buying land at fifty cents per acre. This alarmed the army who had feared the newcomers would take all the good land. (Land that was to be their land.)

Grapevine Springs: Grapevine, Texas. The site of the 1843 Great Council in which Sam Houston united the Red River Tribes allowing the new Peters' colonists to come here to settle. The author's hometown where his family lived for generations, some living there before it was a town, and before Texas was a state, or a republic. The Torian log cabin is a Texas Historical place, moved from its original site along Dove Creek to Grapevine Town Square on the Main Street.

Great Council: Council made up of the Red River Tribes: The Arapaho, the Delaware, the Biloxi, the Kick-a-Poo, the Ez-e-Nye, the Kiowa. The Wichita bands: the Tao-Va-Ya, Tawakoni, Tonkawa's, (and the main Wichita Band.) The Caddo: the Yoiuane, the Timber Hill, the Honey Grove, and related groups.) The Nadarka. The Great Council met September 28, 1843, at Bird's Fort, the point farthest west that Texas was settled at that time. The land west of Bird's Fort belonged to the Comanche. To the north, to the Red River, were the Kiowa, and Wichita nations. These tribes first met at Grapevine Springs close to present day Grapevine, Texas

gauchos—Spanish word for "cowboys." These are the "real deal" as far as cowboys are concerned. Their horsemanship, skill, and ability to train and break horses are unequalled.

gourd—a hollow fruit with a tough case, it grows on a vine. It was used for water, and food storage.

Goyens, William: A freed Black man that farmed, and traded horses with the east Texas Cherokee. He was the first to try to make a binding peace treaty between the Texans, and the Cherokee. Lamar made this effort impossible since he had control of the Texas Senate.

William Goyens was an officer in the Texas' Army, a first for a freed Black man in Texas.

grist—wheat, or corn is ground at a gristmill to make flour, or meal. The grist is the courser part of the grinding that is often used for animal feed.

H

hand jack—a pump jack—used to pump ground water by hand. Indoor plumbing was unknown in those days and all water had to be hauled in buckets from a well or a stream. A hand jack would be a real timesaver and a wonderful help.

Hardin Runnels: the only person to run against Sam Houston, and beat him in his run for governor of Texas in 1848. Hardin Runnels made an 1848 law that "required freed slaves to take masters." This was a bad move for the governor as he caused a great deal of strife between blacks, whites, Indians, and Hispanics, as most fought to protect the rights of all people in Texas that were law abiding, and hard-working: as most were, or they would not be here long, or be tolerated in any settlement. In spite of what you may have read from other fictional sources: people coming to, and living in settlements were carefully regulated and protected by the army and the Texas Rangers.

harrow: A plowing platform on which a person stood while a team of horses pulled it across unbroken land. The platform had knife-like spikes that tore up the ground to make plowing easier.

hearth—a place where fire was made, and food was cooked there.

Houston, Sam: Twice the president of Texas, governor, head of the Texas army, and a representative of Texas to Congress. He gave much advice to President Polk over the Mexican War. A great Texan in the true sense of the word.

I

Indians: "Native Americans" * At this time the term "Indians" meant any native peoples living here in Texas and the Federal States. This book is written in terms used in the early days of Texas and the Federal States. (Andrew spoke in these terms.) So this book is written in Andrew's words, as he saw things in the **19th century perspective** of a settler coming to Texas. "The term "Native American" was an unknown term in those days, so this reference does not apply here, between these book covers as it would be awkward to speak this way in this particular forum. "Native American" is proper for today, to be totally "politically correct" . . . but most Indians the author has know in his lifetime, want to be called by the tribe they belong to, or be referred to as "Indian" or "Indians." *This author refers to them as "Indians" with all the great respect they richly deserve since they are the first Americans. So please do not write the author letters telling him: "he *is wrong in the way he addresses the earliest American cultures, referring to times in the Nineteenth century."*

J
Jefferson: A town from which the steamboat brought important goods from the Red and Mississippi Rivers. All goods to the settlements came from here, and most modern roads in Texas owe their origins to Jefferson as the paths were cleared of trees to allow wagons to pass through. Indian trails were secured to travel there to get goods. Highway 380 is a good example of that going east and west. It was the old buffalo trail used by the Red River tribes. Many major highways were well-worn Indian trails, wagon trails, and traces.

johnny cakes: a pancakes cooked in lard. Cornbread. Sometime a pancake made of corn, or ground mesquite beans.

K
Kiowa: an ally of the Comanche. This tribe had its origins in the Rocky Mountains. It was pushed south to the Plains by the Cheyenne nation. The Kiowa moved about a great deal. (So much so that they did not make pottery.) Some Kiowa were war-like, but most were peaceable hunters and traders. The best-known chief of the Kiowa is Spotted Tail who watched over the settlers, and scared off hostile Indians. (And some bad settlers.) Chief Spotted Tail (Hawk) went out to find the settler's lost 3 year-old son in the middle of a fierce thunderstorm. He knew that if he waited too long that the boy's trail would be washed away and that the boy would perish all alone in the woods where bears and wolves were frequent inhabitants. Chief Spotted Tail lived close to Fort Buckner and McKinney. He watched over these areas like it was his own village. He died protecting these people from harm when smallpox hit the North Texas area after the Civil War. He tended to the sick, and became sick himself. He is one of many notable "Native Americans" that lived in Texas.

L
lagniappe—(pronounced "lag-Nap.") An unexpected gift. A nice present. A pleasant surprise.

lance—a highly decorated, ceremonial spear with a flint, or iron tip.

la trine: also latrine. A rest room, or out house as it was in those days. The latrine was a wooden shed built over a dug pit. Indoor plumbing was unknown in the 19th century.

La Crosse: (lacrosse) a sacred ballgame played by the Native American tribes before hunting and warfare. Often players suffered serious injury, such as broken bones, as it was an intense game that was often played on a field that was miles across between the goals. The elders would keep score, and maintained fairness, and tend to the injured players.

lean-to: (lean-two) A simple shelter put up in a hurry. You basically "leaned two boards (or planks) together." It was covered with a tarp that was tied down with rope to keep it from blowing away.

Louisiana Coffee: a stout coffee made three times stronger than regular coffee. Most farmers are so short on time that instead of drinking three cups of coffee they would drink one cup of exceptionally strong coffee. They used chicory to enhance the coffee that was so strong it would give you "goose bumps" if you were not use to drinking it.

M

ma`chu- an American Indian—fried corn dish made with onions, bell peppers, and tomatoes, (a Mexican discovery.)

mano: An Indian grindstone, oval and flat on both sides. Some have finger pits put into them by careful flaking, and hammering. Some of these grindstones were passed down from mother to daughter, making most of them quite old, and worn from use. It is one of the most common Indian artifacts to find. It marks the place of a good campsite.

March 27th in Texas history: 1814—Sam Houston under the command of Andrew Jackson fights the British in Alabama, in the Battle of Horseshoe Bend, the decisive battle of the 1812 War. In 1836—The Goliad Massacre of the Texans that surrendered to Mexican troops. In 1846-the siege of Ft. Texas by Mexican forces along the Rio Grande.

mesquite tea—a pain reliever made from the boiled leaves of the mesquite tree.

me-te: The base from which grinding corn or mesquite beans takes place. It is a large flat rock, or, it is sometimes a wooden log, or tree stump.

Midway Camp—a campsite located between the Lonesome Dove Settlement, and Grapevine Springs. It was also the halfway point between Dallas, and Ft. Worth. (Then Bird's Fort, a smaller fort, a few miles east of present day Ft. Worth.)

milpas—Spanish for "cornfields." A large field of corn that can go for miles.

N
Nacogdoches—Sam Houston's home during the time of the early Texas settlement, and land grants. An ancient home of the Caddo nation in Texas.

O
Old Texians: The original early settlers of Texas. Some were Anglos, and some Mexican born.

P
Palo Alto—The location of the first battle of the Mexican War. It is close to Brownsville, the southern point of Texas. American General, (and future president of the United States) Zachary Taylor defeated Mexican General Mariano Arista. The fight was now on with war declared.

parfletch: A leather pouch used for storage. A leather container that unfolds flat to place an object in the center. The sides fold down, and it is tied secure keeping the contents dry, and secure. Meat tamales wrapped in corn shucks are an example of a Parfletch. Also "Parfletche."

par-lay—French "to speak." A chance to be understood, and to speak freely, without fear of harm, or death to the speaker. A chance to make council and be heard in a group of people. A forum for free speech.

Penne—Greek for "Poor Working" class. A person that works hard doing odd jobs to make ends meet. They are still living in poverty, but they are working two or more jobs. Also: a person with a serious work ethic.

Peters' Colonists—settlers from Englishman W.S. Peters' colony. An article written by the author concerning the Peters' colony follows this glossary.

Phoebe—Andrew's daughter with his wife Sarah. (Say-te-Qua) Morning Star.

pied—"spotted." A spotted cow (sook pied), a spotted horse, also: a person with freckles. (pied piper) Here it is used as a spotted buffalo, and its hide that was being fought over because it was a rare item. A survivor of Smallpox was also called "pied."

pie keeper—a cabinet used for pie storage, to keep insects, heat, rain, and nosey people away.

Polk, James: President of the Federal States when Texas became the 28th state. Polk did more during his term as president than his predecessors as far as making life better. (He added the territories of Oregon/Washington state, New Mexico, and California.) He waged a continuing war with Mexico over the addition of Texas as a state. These other states were added after a peace treaty and a sum of ten million dollars. (It was much like the 1803 Louisiana Purchase was done with France's Napoleon.) This helped Mexico with their terrible war debts, and helped give them some compensation for their land losses. The additional states added to the Federal States, and Polk's manifest destiny to control the whole continent. It brought the slavery issue to the forefront as the slave states were fighting for control and power to push their authority to the newly acquired territories. The balance of power shifted each time a new state was added. This brought on the American Civil War in 1859.

potlatch: a meeting and trade time usually in the Spring and Summer seasons.

Pow-Wow: A big ceremonial dance held by American Indians. It usually occurs during the June 21st Summer Solstice celebration. The Rain Dance is held to bring the late summer rains.

The Jimson Weed Dance, called the "Crazy Dance", where the single adults are matched up for future marriage. The Eagle Dance was held for blessing the earth, and the hunt.

puma—a mountain lion, or cougar. Andrew's Indian name given to him by the Cherokees.

Q

Qual-Li: or Qualls—The female leader of the Xensi warrior society. In the Caddo form of government women held high places in their councils. Some women were head of the councils concerning matters of the hunt, also on the matters of warfare. Only the chief could challenge the outcome of their councils. Women sponsored great earthworks where terraces were built for fire temple structures, and ceremonial structures. Men moved hundreds of baskets of earth to build these terraces. Some men were designated hunters; some were farmers, some hunters, and some warriors. The Caddo have an ancient, ordered society. It worked well for them for thousands of years. Anyone with a

"Qual, Quall" name, or "Qua" is a person of high stature and ranking in the tribe. The elder men of the tribe consulted the younger men of the tribe on the fine points on hunting, and dealing with the women of the tribe.

Quanah Parker: The son of Comanche chief Peta ("Bear") Nacona and the captured farm girl, (Naduah) Cynthia Ann Parker of Parker's Fort. **Quanah** means "quiet one." Quanah became a great peacemaker in his lifetime. (1845-1911.)

R

rasp: a file used for wood finishing, or filing down horses' hooves so a blacksmith can put iron shoes on them.

Red Lander—A popular newspaper that was printed in the early days of Texas. It was the main source of real news as the Internet, a radio and television was not known of in those days. So all that you knew was from a great newspaper that gave you a view of the outside world.

remuda: A nice sized group of horses ready to be traded.

ristas—a hundred or so peppers, onions, or garlic's are strung together on long strings where they hang from a peg, or nail in kitchens and doorways, and on doors. They are also "a sign of good fortune," and they were thought to help ward off bad feelings and evil spirits. These are given as gifts many times to strangers, and this promotes good trade and positive feelings.

S

Santa Fe Trade—the area of Santa Fe, and the Santa Fe Trail was claimed by Texas. It was hoped that Texas could tap into that trade that had solid backing in silver, horses, and agriculture. It was hoped that some of the taxes put on goods could be circumvented to help pay the (10 million dollar plus) war debts of Texas. It seems that Santa Fe did not want being obligated to pay taxes to a distant Texas, than Texas felt strained to pay taxes to a distant Mexico City. They fought against this as much as Texas did to Mexican rule. Sam Houston has tried to tap into this trade, as well as Mirabeau Lamar as the presidents of the Texas republic. They failed in this and this is what prompted Texas to be annexed to the Federal States to help make their government more stable with solid backing for their trade dollar. A bad trade dollar kept roads and schools from being built, or taxes raised to pay for the army.

Samson—Deacon Brown, and Belle's son. Samson played with a flint and steel striker (fire starter) and he burned down half the settlement where Andrew and Red Bird lived. For that reason, Deacon and Belle Bathsheba moved to Free City to live.

San Jacinto—The battle that led to Texas' Independence. (April 21, 1836.) Also, the land, or place where the battle was fought. Andrew and Ben fought in this battle with Sam Houston.

Sarah, or Sara: Say-te-Qua's Christian name. (Andrew's Cherokee wife, "Morning Star".) It sounds like the Cherokee word "**sa-re**"—(Ser-REE) "persimmon." A term of endearment, a "pet name" for a young child in some tribes. Sarah loved persimmons, especially green ones. When she was a child she was eating so many green persimmons her mouth stayed puckered for an hour from all the alum that green persimmons contain. She remembered the name that stuck with her until she became a Qualls, and a dream interpreter for the Cherokee.

Seguin, Juan: a great tejano that escaped the Alamo siege to get help before the Mexicans could bring more reinforcements. He later left Texas to live in Mexico when he was accused of being disloyal and a traitor. He was devastated for he had given up all he had fought for to have the new settlers take it all away from him. He had been the first vice-president of Texas during the provisional government when David Burnett was the temporary president. Seguin is a great Texan who needs to be well remembered for his sacrifices to make Texas safe and independent.

siesta: (see-ES-ta) A tradition from Mexico and Latin American countries. During the hot part of the day people took a nap and rested until the afternoon cooled off and work could resume again. General Santa Anna was captured when he was caught with his guard down, with no sentries posted during the Battle of San Jacinto. He was caught later in the day, as he hid among the dead dressed as a private (soldier) hoping to escape in the night to safety. Andrew also saw the Mexican deserter as the captured Santa Anna, dressed in rags to hide who he really was.

Sook, or Sookie—a slang word for cow. So "sook-pied" means it was a "spotted cow."

stand—used as a verb—to make secure—to fight unflinching, unafraid, and bold.

Sugar Hill: Texan Captain Y.B. Yeary of San Jacinto got his land grant and opened a trading post northeast of present day Farmersville, Texas. He was shot and killed trying to break up a fight during a Christmas celebration in 1848. Two brothers in their mid-twenties named Glass were killed by friendly fire, being in the wrong place at the wrong time. Sugar Hill got its name for a time when wagons came from Jefferson with just sugar and flour while the other wagons were delayed by a storm and wagons that were bogged down. So for about a week there was plenty of sugar and flour but no coffee, or other staples until the other wagons arrived. It was a long-standing joke for many years and the name stuck for that trading post. The Sugar Hill area is now a group of fine houses called Willow Brook, outside of Farmersville, Texas.

sweat lodge: A ceremonial lodge used for cleansing rituals.

switch: A long wooden stick, or tree limb used as a tool to reach something.

T

TABOR: Texas Abolitionists Being Organized (for Rights.)
The name comes from the Bible, the Book of Judges, Chapter 4. Also the name of the many abolitionist supporters were called the Knights and Daughters of TABOR. Many Texan churches and **citizens of different races** supported this group as the acquisition of new territories: the question of spreading slavery was always in question. Some say that this group started in England.

tack—goods used for riding a horse: reigns, a rope lasso, a bit, and bridle, saddle, blankets, and such.

tare—an old English word, or term for a weed, or useless undergrowth.

Tejanos: Mexican born citizens of Texas. They were farmers and horsemen that rebelled against high taxation and joined the movement for Texas' Independence. Many of their sons were conscripted against their will for fight the Texans for the Mexican army. Their crops, and horses were taken with out consideration of payment. This book celebrates the action of the Tejanos' fight against a well-trained Mexican army, out numbered, against impossible odds. They joined the Texan settlers as they were all in the same boat, trying to make Texas a good, and safe place to live and make a living by farming. As new settlers came, some tried to make them out as villains, or traitors, as this was false. Texas Independence was achieved because of their fierce opposition to Santa Anna. They are true heroes, often unsung and forgotten in most history books, movies and commentaries.

Tejanos: (second definition) Mexicans that were loyal to the Texas cause. Many of the Tejanos were farmers that struggled in poverty due to paying high taxes to Mexico. Some were poor even though they had bountiful crops. They still suffered in poverty. This was their reason to fight against Mexico. Many of them had lost part of family, and some had lost all their family at Goliad, Zantacas, and related battles of the Alamo fortress. Also, members of the Consultation suffered losses of kin and went against the Mexican government to make a new Texan government.

Tejas: (Te haas') Spanish name for the friendly Caddo Indians. The name comes from the Caddo word "Tey-Sha," or Friend! ("Tey-Shaw! Wha-she-knee Washita." Friend, save us from the enemy." The person hearing it repeats the same words, then it means, "save us from the outsiders.")

It is used as a test used by the Caddo as a "password" to see if strangers were enemies, or friendly traders. The "Crying Greeting" met strangers. This was to throw the strangers into confusion, so it would give time for the Caddo to figure if the stranger was a friendly trader, or a foe. The Tejas were the Yoiuane tribe. (Members of the Xensi warrior society.) Texas got its name from this tribe of Caddo Indians. Natchitoches, and Nacogdoches (Nack-A-Dish, and Nack-A-Doches.) These are two Caddo names that figure in Texas and Louisiana's history.

Telaqua-the new Cherokee capitol after the **Trail of Tears**—July 22, 1840 was the forced removal of the Cherokee from east Texas, to Indian Territory, which is in present day state of eastern Oklahoma. Chief Bowles, and Chief Mush were the principal chiefs if the Cherokee in east Texas. They died in battle protecting the tribe from the Texan army, under president Mirabeau Lamar's command. Telaqua is the focus of Cherokee history, and culture.

Texas Land and Emigration Company: W.S Peters of London, England, came to Louisville, Kentucky to make legal land grants to settle parts of Texas. These land grants were sponsored by
United States President Andrew Jackson, a mentor of Sam Houston. These emigrants to Texas were called **Peters' Colonists**. This is how the Red River settlements came to be settled.

Texas Rangers—a well-trained group of men that acted as a proper militia on the Texan frontier. The idea for a group of men that were para-military that helped capture outlaws, and renegades that preyed on settlements. (This idea of men who acted as a "go-between" of the citizens, and Texan soldiers' was conceived by Stephen F. Austin, and implemented by Sam Houston as president of Texas.). *The Texas Rangers kept the peace to make living here a worthwhile experience. Outlaws were hunted down and expelled, or imprisoned. People came here to start a good place to live where crime and lawlessness was not tolerated for long.

tinja-(TEEN-ya) A covered well, or cistern. A well that was covered by a stone, or a piece of wood to keep the water cool from the sun and clean from debris.

trace—a trail, or pathway. "Trammel's Trace: a pathway going from the Red River through Caddo country to the east Texas settlements.

travois: (Tra-Voys) A dragging device made of green wood so that it will bend. It was pulled behind a horse carrying people, (or a slaughtered animal back to camp.) The horse pulls the "V" shaped wooden posts with the narrow part of the "V" on the horse's neck. Cross members of wood were added to secure the carried item.

Treaty of the Guadalupe-Hidalgo—The peace treaty that was to settle the Mexican War with the United States. The treaty was written by American diplomat Philip Trist. He studies law under Thomas Jefferson. He helped reopen negotiations with Mexico, which made President Polk angry as Polk did not want to negotiate with Mexico at that time. Trist was recalled to come home, but he saw an opportunity to make peace, so he went against Polk's orders.

Treaty of Velasco: the 1836 peace treaty made of Texans to the Mexican government declaring Texas independent, and free from Mexican rule and taxation. The main reason that Texas rebelled from Mexico was over taxation without representation. Santa Anna was sent back to Mexico with the treaty proposal. It was argued by Mexicans that the treaty was not valid since Santa Anna was a prisoner of war, and not free to negotiate a peace treaty.

U
V

varmints—animal, or person that is a pest, or troublesome. Some were four-legged, and some have two legs.

Velasco: Southern Texas port where Santa Anna, Sam Houston, Mecham Hunt, and James
Pickney Henderson made a peace treaty to the Mexican government under Mexican general Santa Anna. Santa Anna later stated that he was a "prisoner of war" so he was not free to make a binding peace treaty.

W

wagoner—a carpenter that makes wagons, the chief mode of transportation, and movement of materials, people, and products in the 19th century.

Washington City-the earlier name of Washington, the District of Columbia.

Washington-on-the Brazos: The Consultation (the infant Texas congress) of delegates met for over a month during the weeks ending March 2, 1836. The representatives of the Texas settlements met in dire cold, and under the stress of losing family in recent attacks made by Mexico. Also, Santa Anna had men out looking to capture them and destroy the Texan Rebellion as an example to others who would rebel against his rule. Washington-on-the-Brazos was also the temporary Texas capitol when Austin was under Mexican siege, and during the "Archive War" when Austin and Houston City were rivals over government documents, and over the rights to be the legal capitol of Texas.

Washitas: (Wah-She-Talls.) Non-Indians. A person that was not born, but "adopted as an American Indian." Also, a non-member of a certain tribe that trades with them. A good ally of the tribe. Andrew, and Ben Bird were considered "Washitas" to the Comanche, Kiowa, and Kick-a-Poo nations.

Waunell: Kiowa name meaning "sweet little one." The mean qualls was named something sweet.

wigwam—A shelter made of wooden poles, and posts, covered with animal skins. A tee-pee like structure used for shelter. A fire pit was dug in the center to make a smudge fire of green leaves, or cedar to keep mosquitoes out. Small stones were put on the floor where the floor would be warm, and weed free. It was a suitable shelter and could be adapted for winter use.

window lights: a slang term for "panes of window glass." Pronounced by some elder Texans as "winder lites." A slang word that was a popular description for "glass panes" in early Texas.

Winter Count: The first day of spring. March 20th, the Vernal Equinox. A birthday: Indian tribes deem that if you survived the terrible winter that you have made it to another Winter Count.

Children born during the winter were held up and given the name that they would be known by. A good life is always a great reason to celebrate.

X

Xensi: (Zen-SEE.) An elite group of Caddo Warriors. They were fierce warriors. Well respected by the Red River tribes. Chief Bintah (Bent Tree) was a notable Xensi member of the Yoiuane Caddo. Some of their leaders were the elder women of the tribe. Qual-Li, or Qualls: A type of name that has the variation of "Qua," or "Quals" represents.)

Y

yard bird—slang word for a chicken, or chickens.

yellow roses: symbolizes death. "The Yellow Rose of Texas" was a song about the plot to defeat of Santa Anna's efforts by a female spy that found out about the troop movements of the Mexican forces which kept the members of the Texas government from being captured and put to death. It was a popular song among the African-American community, and it was picked up, popularized, and sang in popular plays, and in saloons frequented by soldiers.

Yoiuane—(Yo-AINE) It means the "River People." This band of Caddo Indians were called "the Tejas" (friendly) Indians lived along creeks and streams that flow along white rock, (Austin chalk) in north Texas.

Z

Zantacas: The mining town that refused to pay tribute, and higher taxes to Santa Anna, and the Mexican government. Santa Anna made an example of this town since he was in dire straights for tax money to pay his country's high war debts to France. Santa Anna ordered this town utterly destroyed, and the miners killed, to make an example of them to the rest of Texas.

This was the start of the Texan rebellion over paying higher taxes to Mexico. The next was at Anahuac, close to Galveston when unfair taxes were levied. The next rebellions were at Goliad, then at San

Antonio, at the Alamo. Zantacas was one first catalyst for the Texan rebellion and the start of the fight for the Tejanos, and Texans for independence.

Notes:

WHY SHOULD WE REMEMBER OUR HISTORY?

The past is the foundation on which we build our future. That is why it is so important to understand and pass down our history to be understood and treasured by young and old alike. Our successes and failures give us a yardstick in which to measure our society as a whole. For without history there is no sense of direction as a starting point of reference in our lives. Our past is the only thing that we can be certain of in a struggling society.

Many people came to America to have a better life. Most families worked for a landowner many years to barely make ends meet. The same was true of Texas when it was a Mexican state in 1824. Many people in the Federal States were under the heavy burden of taxation. They faced going to a debtor's prisons, which is nothing like the luxurious prisons of today. The debtors were usually charged with high taxes and a large family to support. Judges usually offered the choice of, "going to prison, or going to Texas!" Texas was the lesser of two evils! My family came from Kentucky as Peters' Colonists for the chance to start over again fresh and new. They came to a place called "the Cross Timbers" in the Red River Settlements in 1846. This was the historic "Lonesome Dove" settlement. (The true Lonesome Dove is located in Southlake, Texas.) My paternal grandmother's family was named Torian and they were proud to be here considering the tough circumstances that they came from. Getting a land grant of their own to farm and do as they pleased was a dream come true! My grandfather's family also came to the Dove Branch. My mother's family settled in the Dallas area close to Walnut Hill, and Farmer's Branch. They were named Combs and Latham.

It was the first real organized settlement and a church built as a focal point. In those days most people kept close in their faith and church met every third Saturday of the month. It was also the place that people got to meet and know each other. Many times your spouse was someone that your parents met at church and marriages were sometimes arranged that way. (Especially when people had adjoining farmland, which would double your land grant and water rights.) Sam Houston made a Great Council of the Red River Tribes in 1843. Grapevine (Tah-Wah-Karro Creek or Tawakoni, as some said it, was the location.) There had been an Indian war here for three years. Sam Houston as the new president of Texas, saw that there was a chance for peaceful councils to be made and a chance to resume new settlements that had been halted until there was some resolution between the tribes living here. My grandfather's family was of Choctaw and Cherokee descent, so Sam Houston was someone that they respected well as a leader or "chief" of the Texans.

Many Indian tribes came from the northern Federal States to Texas as a last refuge. These were the Cherokee, the Delaware, the Arapaho, the Kick-A-Poo, and the Alabama and Coushatta nations to name a few. There were plentiful wild horses here so the tribes that lived here were quite fine horse traders and they were quite rich according to Indian standards. A person on foot did not fare well or live long so a good horse held a good value to trade when the dollar in Texas was "discounted" heavily. A discounted trade dollar in Texas was due to several reasons: republic President Mirabeau Lamar's Indian war and the building of the Austin capitol. Also the printing of the "Red Backs" paper money due to huge Mexican War debts made the Texan trade less useful to outsiders. (To people that we owed debts to in the Federal States.) It was President John Tyler's push to make Texas the 28th state in late 1845, did our economic situation change for the better. (After two failed attempts.) We live in a tough time now, but what we have today is paradise compared to what terrible hardships our pioneer ancestors endured.

Joe L. Blevins *After the Republic.*

THE PETERS' COLONY IN TEXAS

What was the Peters' Colony? Why was it important to North Texas? Many of our families came to Texas as Peters'Colonists.

There were a number of reasons this happened: After the 1812 War many soldiers came back home to a troubling situation. Like many times after a war there was high unemployment, a bad economy due to war debts, and a drought covering much of the country. High taxes were levied against farmers whom were the largest proportion of the population. Most families were large in those days; and with a large family to support there were limited opportunities to change professions. What were their options? There were debtors' prisons where the whole family could go to work off their debts, but who could put their family through that ordeal? Judges would offer delinquent taxpayers few choices. They could "Go to jail, or Go to Texas!" Debtor's prisons were full and terrible places.

The frontier of Texas was the lesser of two evils . . .

People would put "GTT" on their cabin doors: "Gone to Texas."

In France they were finding themselves facing a civil war after Napoleon's defeat at Waterloo. England and Germany were also seeing a similar situation in their respective countries. So trying to find a way to ease the burdens of a large population, and ease the threat of a possible civil war was a big agenda item to be considered. Also Texas had its own problems with a struggling economy and trying to man its army and navy. The Texas government was looking for supporters to buy bonds, and sent immigrants to settle Texas. The Texas government wanted diversified settlements that would represent many interest, not just the interest of one country. The Texas trade dollar was discounted terribly because of the Texas Revolution.

The old Mexican EMPRESARIO system offered free land grants of 4,605 acres. The Peters' Colonists system in Texas offered every male 640 if married. 320 acres if a single man over 17 years old. Five or more women could join together to get a "single status" land grant in an effort to attract a husband. If a young man served in the army he would get 350 additional acres for serving 3 years' service as a citizen-soldier to protect the Texas' frontier. They were to put up a good cabin with stout fences. Also within a single settlement was provided to put up a section of land to put up a place of public religious worship. That church was the center of the whole settlement.

For 5 years there was a great effort to avoid opening the Land Office. There was fear that the Texan army might rebel and leave their post, and older Spanish and settlers' land grants were threatened by the newcomers wanting to grab up all the good land. So there was more possible threat from internal strife than from the Mexican army, or Indian problems put together.

In late 1838, Sam Houston had proposed land grants from the French government since the French wished to buy Texan Wheat Bonds. General Sam Houston's Franco-Texian Project was failed in the Texan Congress. It was well known that France not only sponsored the Texans, for independence: France also sold arms, and supported Mexico as an effort to play both sides of the war to profit from the conflict by keeping things stirred up between both countries. (This is why Colonel Stephen F. Austin was in the Mexican prison those 8 weeks, when he was only the Texan diplomat to Mexico.) Many persons hated this and they made it impossible to try to make any type of French proposal.

But then there was fear of persons coming to Texas unregulated, making claims to land that was possibly another's land grant.

The 1841 Peters' Colonists proposal came at a time that some viable proposal was needed. The Texan army would be in turmoil trying to fight the Mexican army, and trying to keep the settlers from fighting each other. So if the government could not support itself then the Texan government had bigger problems.

The original source of the Peters' Colony proposal is not known. It may have been proposed in Texas and the proposal put forth to the U.S. Congress by the American Phineas J. Johnson. Johnson went to Texas a number of times on business but he never moved here.

Since land was the biggest resource in Texas. Most land grants were free, but Government land could be sold for $1.50 per acre and with such a large area to choose from it was considered a bonanza to make millions of dollars in royalties to support a struggling Texan economy. There was a fear in the United (or Federal States) that Texas would **not** be settled by any single particular country, or any political group that would be a threat to them. That was the intent of the law.

These 20 Peters Colonists' petitioners were 11 Englishmen and 9 Americans were from Louisville, Kentucky. The Englishmen were: Daniel S. Carol, Alexander McRea, Roland Gibson, Robert Espie, William Oldmixon, Daniel Spillman, Robert Hume, John Salamon, William Byrne, Henry Richards, and Robert Stringer.

The Americans were: W.S Peters, John Bansamere, William Scott, Phineas J. Johnson, Timothy Cragg, and Samuel Browning. The Americans were prominent businessmen of Jefferson County Kentucky. William Smalling Peters' name was the most prominent of the group of men and since his name headed the list. Since Peters lived in the United States and was born in England; he was thought the best choice to understand the different situations between England and America. Peters' family members held a piano making company in Kentucky, and a music publishing company in Cincinnati that gave his family some financial backing and influence in some political circles. His most notable published songwriter was Stephen Foster of "Oh Susanna," and "Camp Town Races." And others. But since W.S. Peters was in the promotional business and he was shrewd at it, it is respected that he was thought to be able to spot a good deal when he saw it.

Because of the distance between the English petitioners and the Americans, then Samuel Browning son-in-law of W.S. Peters went to Austin to sign the proposal to get the deal going before the interest was lost. Mirabeau Lamar the Second Elected President of Texas signed the proposal and they also signed the names of the others on their behalf of the 20 petitioners.

600 families were to be settled here total. 200 of the 600 families were to be settled here within a year. 400 were to be settled within 2 years. The first petition failed because it was feared that trying to settle 600 families within a colony limits would not be possible to maintain and that there would not be enough unappropriated land in a colony to allow for growth and roads, hunting and timber needs. (It was feared that the area would be settled so quickly the area would suffer from growth pains that could not dealt with in a timely fashion.) Also surveying an area that large required more time than they had planned. So there was quite an undertaking to get all the wheels in motion to make the details work. By July 1842 the third contract was in place was modified to be able to make boundaries extended and a timeline for a full survey was left open as it could be attempted or done. Trying to make an open prairie into a viable settlement is a logistic nightmare. Sam Houston made this extension possible by his interest and concern as the new Texas president.(Since the Texas constitution prohibited Lamar from running two terms in a row as president.) Lamar has made an Indian war with the

Kiowa, and Comanches. Lamar exterminated the Cherokee from the piney woods of east Texas. It was up to Houston to address any Indian problems that would keep new settlements from forming in Texas. Fears and ignorance by the average settler slowed down any new interest in new land grants.

The English transferred their interest of the Peters' Colony to another group of Englishmen, since they were not involved as they should be. One particular Englishman Sherman Converse

Took the reigns of power and control on the English side.

The name of the Peters Colony was now a corporation that was called The Texas Agricultural, and Manufacturing Company. The next events as the company changed hands and faces as the new English "owners" try to negotiate in Texas, and New York as some slick business deals were happening. It would put some modern scam artists to shame. Many of the details were done under the table, as one Sherman Converse, an Englishman, was able to obtain the whole and full ownership of the original Peters Colony contract from the Louisville, Kentucky group, also! This Englishman Converse was a "Slick Willie" promoter that had more promises than potential.

December 3, 1842, Because the new name was not attracting interest and it was losing money and support it returned as the Peters' Colony that it was formally known as. Sherman Converse made undocumented deals in Texas with both houses of Congress on January 20th 1842. Converse was given the power to make land policy that was unthinkable and unbelievable. The desperate situation in Texas called for some drastic measures as the government was about the split at the seams and the trade dollar was discounted 7 to 1 and then 10 to 1! There seemed no choice but to accept whatever carrot was tied to the stick, no matter how rotten it was! It seems that this desperation made common sense go out the window! Lamar's printing of the Red Dollars (paper money) made any choice was better than no choice. So Houston made the choice to leap before he looked. There was not any other choice for him to do!

Converse and D.J Carroll added 10 million additional acres to the contract. They had signed the names of interested parties on their behalf. The distance of 160 miles were added and the eastern and western boundaries. This latest contract made a dispute that lasted for years for so little of the details are actually documented. It did become the permanent basis for the Peters' Colonists. The total contract included over 16,000 Square miles!

January 4th, 1844 Sherman Converse went back to London to try to establish more conservative partners as an effort to give his promotions of Texas land venture a greater credence. Europeans received him more casually than he had hoped for, but he was later received as the lead person and empresario of the venture after Texan diplomats Henry Daingerfield to the Hague, and Ashbel Smith in Paris promoted by their belief in Texas as a worthwhile investment. Still other Texans had reservations such as Secretary of State, Dr.Anson Jones who felt that Sherman Converse was a crook and should be locked up and never should have been kept with such a free reign, as Converse had no reason to be trusted. So it was a matter of whom you ask what should have been done. The newspaper notices that the English had not taken Converse seriously and that the Americans had been duped and taken for a *wild goose chase* in business affairs.

So Charles Mercer made a proclamation that Converse was a scoundrel and that he, Mercer, was taking the reigns of the company. He sent Peters Colony secretary, and auctioneer E. B. ELY to try to save the company. In Texas, Ely and Mercer wrote the government to say that he was the new head of the company, and that Converse and their associates were no longer involved or be trusted. While Ely and Mercer were in Texas, Converse was trying to mend his broken ties with the Kentucky businessmen. He managed to do so being the slick operator he was. Converse was welcomed as the "Prodigal Son" as he tried to make his past indiscretions better. Converse went to Texas to find that all he had done in Kentucky was lost and now void.

It seems that the Americans had met with Sam Houston at Washington on the Brazos where the temporary government was being hosted. (Since Austin and Houston fought over the status of being the capitol of Texas, Washington on the Brazos was the safest place to be holding government because of the "Archive War." So this tells you that Texas was a crazy place to be as far as holding government was concerned.

The Texas government had voted to nullify all the colonization contracts! This would give the Mexican army the opportunity to come back to ravage Texas, and make raids of cattle, people, and horses. The Tejanos suffered the most losing their sons to a cause they did not support.

Sam Houston vetoed the bill and put forth his own bill putting the Englishman Charles Mercer over the Peters' Colony project now called "The Texas Emigration and Land Company." The next day January 30th 1843 congress made a new law prohibiting Sam Houston as president to repeal or make any new laws concerning colonization of Texas. Houston's veto gave Mercer his own colony called the "Mercer Colony" or "The Texas Association," which was the reinstated "Fourth Contract." Converse and his associates lost all their rights. (Mercer, who was an abolitionist and "monolopolist" as he was called.) He eventually lost his colony and claims to land there since he had not settled 250 colonists (families) by the contracted date. There were 197 families settled, and 184 single men. So not all families that had promised had moved here, as they should have because of fears of retaliation of the Mexican army, and uneasiness over peace treaties with some Indian tribes.

(The author's family moved here at this time, to the Dove settlement, at the Cross Timbers of the Trinity River, on Dove Creek, close to Grapevine, Texas.)

October 15th 1844.

The Texas Emigration, and Land Company was reformed by the company with new Louisville businessmen in tow. This is the time and place that my family came to Texas, (once all the dust settled.) They had planned to come sooner, but the turmoil and the scandal keep them from investing their time and money in the venture. Willis Stewart was the main person over the new venture along with W.S. Peters, and W.C. Peters, son of W.S. Peters.

A great many members of the earlier contracts had taken their lumps on the head and they had "woke up" as far as seeing their earlier mistakes. So they were now valued members again in the remake of the old business venture. As always there was bickering with in the ranks but it managed to stay afloat as a business venture. Some settlers came here and could not stand the hardships in Texas, and returned. I find that many persons missed their family that had stayed behind and that was the biggest concern for most that returned. Also coming here during the winter corn was especially high to try to buy and it was the most used staple food. In 1843 was a record wheat crop in Texas so that drew the farming interest here to raise some cabins and make their fortune here on their own land.

The author Joe L. Blevins heard many stories about these days from both his grandparents that were part of the Lonesome Dove settlement in the cross Timbers of the Trinity River. A great place to live and farm. His early life was filled with these great stories and they became the seeds for these books!

The story just gets more twisted as there are land grants in the middle of Comanche lands where no white person could live without being short sighted as having a future there. So this intrusion into their lands to survey brought war parties in the regular settlements looking for revenge. This is what happened at Honey Creek here in McKinney on Christmas Day, 1842. Also another attack on Dr. Ben Calder in February 1843 as he rode from

McKinney to Ft. Inglish. (Dr. Calder had chopped down a bee tree that the local tribes of Kiowa's had thought the tree to be a sacred thing.) And the Muncey Family along Spring Creek on what is Highway 5 in Plano, Texas.

In April 1843 Sam Houston made a "Great Council" of the Red River Tribes so that unmolested settlements could be made in North Texas. So there are many different stories that come into play as we speak of the Peters Colonists. This area of North Texas, Collin, Dallas, Denton, and Grayson counties were formed in 1846, the same year that Texas was the 28th state. At that time the colony was just in name only. Many had experienced difficulties in getting claims resolved, and few had proper deeds to attest to ownership. A year or so of controversy rocked different elements of the settlements as some local governments tried to tax properties that they had no right to without a proper survey of the boundaries. Those that lived on the boundaries were being taxed with out know if they were actually a part of the area being taxed. They had no deeds to prove either way, so they were threatened to lose their lands that they had worked into a livable area of cabins and small farming communities. This was in Dallas area.

In May 1847 an Englishman named **Henry O. Hedgecoxe** was made the agent over the Peters Colonies and he kept surveyors from taken land that was already in dispute. But his arrogant attitude, British accent, and his less than tactful ways rubbed many people the wrong way, especially prominent citizens that were in error living on even numbered tracts that belonged to the government, and that they would have to move off land that had been developed by rivers. Others were issued half rights of 320 acres and so many would loose half of their land rights to another landowner. This British agent made many enemies as he sent out letters saying that the earlier Peters Colony contracts had voided their land interest for the most parts. This conflict continued for about 7 years. In the end Mr. Hedgecoxe found himself hiding in a cornfield while many settlers were looking for him to give him a "neck tie party." Not a place to be honored in any *stretch* of the imagination. He went to an extreme to do his job. He rubbed people the wrong way for too long. It happens that way sometimes when you are dealing with so many people from so many different places, with different cultures where what is appropriate protocol one place, is not setting well in another place. Many people were just hungry for land of their own, and they feared being left out in the rush to settle the frontier. The army feared all the land being grabbed up, and there was a fear that the Texan army might leave its post to grab up their land, before "squatters" took up their choice land. (So the land office in Austin was many times closed by Sam Houston to avoid some battles at the new state capitol.)

Mr. Hedgecoxe left Texas for "health reasons," for he had "wore out his welcome." He did help organize the colonies, but his motivation was to buy back properties with past due taxes as a hope to recoup on the future sales at some point when land values and demand for land increased. A scarecrow was found in a distant corn field wearing Hedgecoxe's top hat.

In conclusion:

The Peters' Colonists was a good idea that was handled badly over many failed contracts. In spite of the troubles it brought over 10,000 settlers to 17 counties of North Texas.

The Peters' Colony was the largest Empresario colonization that was bigger than the Texan and Mexican empresario attempts combined. The Peters' Colony and Texas Immigration and Land Company's efforts between 1841-1848 brought people coming to Texas for the next twenty years following the first contracts. It brought widely diversified groups of farmers, tradesmen, landowners, merchants, and artisans. This balance of different persons is what has made Texas great, for our differences are what make us strong, as a state, and a country.

Joe L. Blevins *After The Republic* © 2008

THE CADDO NATION IN TEXAS

The Caddo tribe extends from the Red River area to east Texas, Arkansas, and Louisiana. This tribe was descended from the Mississippian mound builder cultures from prehistoric times.

This culture was quite large and extensive forming many branches. In east Texas was the Timber Hill, close to Jefferson, the Honey Grove that lived along the Sulphur River close to La Donia. The most notable groups were the Yoiuane, which means the "River People." They lived along the spring-fed creeks and rivers in this area of north Texas. One group was located in an area now called Richardson. (Where Tejas Trail and Spring Valley cross is now called McKamy Springs.) The Yoiuane (Yo-I-Anne) were called the Tejas (pronounced Tey-HAAS) by the Spaniards who took their friendly greeting of "friend," or "Tey Sha" to be their name. Texas got its name from this tribe of Native Americans. They befriended La Salle in his travels through early Texas. The Caddo had a specified group of warriors called the Xensi (Zen-SEE) that were the fierce warriors whose only job was to make weapons and protect the camp. They lived in permanent camps and they did not travel to different camps like some tribes did as the seasons changed. The hunters would go out in large groups and make a great hunt and bring it back to camp. The Caddo fought the Cherokee over the trade up and down the East Fork of the Trinity in 1803-1807. The Caddo learned of the powerful use of the bow from the Cherokee during this war. They did not have use of the bow until historical times. They used an alt-latal, or spear throwers, a stick that was used to throw over handed a feathered arrow as large as a spear to kill a deer or buffalo. Having that ability to hunt better meant that the tribe ate better and that they enjoyed better health because of that. "Being hungry improves your aim," I have been told by my paternal grandfather. There is great truth to that.

The Caddo would meet strangers with a "Crying Greeting" as a ploy to see if they were friendly traders, or foes. The whole tribe men, women, and children would cry out in a loud voice, while the warriors would circle about to defend the camp in case of trouble. There was a chief, but the spokes person was an elder woman called a Qual-Li. She would say, "Tey Sha, wha-she-knee, Wha-she-ta?" Which means "friend, save us from the enemy?" A smart trader would make the "friendly signs" by pointing his right hand and index finger in front of his face and keep careful eye contact. The visitor would repeat these same words carefully, and then it would mean, "Friend save us from the outsiders!" The Qual-Li, or "Qualls" were usually a revered elder woman who was mean, and fierce looking by the way she dressed and acted. She was the only person who could question the chief's orders and she was the one who supervised the planting, the hunting and building projects. Some men were designated hunters, some were farmers, and some were meant to tend to the building programs that the Qualls dictated. This included a fire temple where a fire burned continuously night and day. To let the fire go out in the fire temple was disastrous. To let the fire temple burn down was a worse fate. The Caddo lived in dome shaped homes that were built from a circle of cedars about 30 feet in diameter. The cedars were toped off and the trunk was cut around the base to keep the trees from coming back out. Additional saplings were added to make a durable wigwam that would fare well in bad weather. Reed mats and animal skins were used as covering to keep the rain out. The fire pit was in the center of the home for cooking and green cedar was burned to keep mosquitoes out. Mud was used in some cases to make a good and durable home that would provide a home that would last for many years. Little river stones covered the floor of their homes to keep the weeds out and make the floor warm by the fire in the winter months. The Caddo also staked and bent young oak trees to make them point towards good water sources and campsites. Bent trees can be seen many places in Texas along the East Fork of the Trinity River.

The Caddo had cornfields that went for miles, called milpas. They planted yellow and blue corn, which was quite hearty and it resisted disease and drought better. Sam Houston befriended a Yoiuane chief called Bintah ("Bent Tree.") Chief Bintah was also a member of the Xensi warrior society so his approval was important to get the Caddo, and the Comanche to join the 1843 Great Council. Some settlers in that area had come and helped themselves to the Caddo's corn and gave them nothing in return. The Caddo came and took all the area settlers' horses for payment for all the corn that they took.

Sam Houston feared that trouble between the settlers over that incident might alienate the Caddo, or their Qualls from allowing them to participate in the Great Council which was set to unite all the Red River Tribes. This allowed continued settlement in north and east Texas up to the Red River.

The Caddo Nation © 2008. Joe L. Blevins.

Notes :

MEDICINE MEN AND GOOD MEDICINE

Modern medicine could learn a few things from Native American medicine. Many of the medicines that we now use had their origin as plant extracts and poultices. Poultices are applied as an external method of drawing the poison, or foreign material out of a difficult wound. Here I will speak of a limited group of plants native to Texas, (and the southern states) that were used as medicine and useful remedies for serious and life threatening ailments. (I in no way encourage the readers to use some of these plants, for the exact potency and use was done by someone that had generations of instruction and advice on proper dosage.) The potency of plant extracts was well understood and the shaman (or medicine men) well understood these things from a lifetime of instruction. One great shaman that once lived here in this area was a Cherokee man named Red Bird. He was also a sign-talker that spoke several languages. He used sign language so well that he was able to help negotiate the 1843 Great Council between nine different tribes. (The Red Bird Treaty.) An area south of Dallas was named to honor him for his greatness and commitment to peace. Unfortunately over time he has been forgotten, and his name lost and his methods lost to modern thinking and "modern" ways. Unfortunately most of our ailments have endured over time and these great people's wisdom has been forgotten. A shaman named San-See trained Red Bird. He was also a great healer and an elder in the Cherokee nation. He lived to be over one hundred and eight years old, so he knew something unique in wisdom to prolong his life and the lives of others. These great people understood all about suffering and healing.

This is a short list of some of the plants and their use for healing.

Modern medicine could benefit from some of these remedies. Used properly there would be "new cures" for our ills:

1.) Dewberries, mulberries, and black berries were used as preservatives mixed with chopped meat to make pemmican. The citric acid from the berries did not allow bacteria to form readily in the summer heat. It also gave meat a good taste and was good for the diet and digestion.

2.) Sarsaparilla was a vine that grows wild. It was boiled and cooled for a healing drink for bad stomachs, and help with digestion. Root beers were made from various roots and kept in gourds for storage. Roots from the cattail reeds were used also.

3.) Primrose was boiled as a tea and used as a laxative since it is poisonous, much like sienna; it purges the body of poisons.

4.) Foxglove was a plant used for heart attacks. It has digitalis, which would restart an ailing heart, and give relief from the terrible pain associated with strokes.

5.) Dill weed was used for colic's and crying babies, for a tribe could not stand to have an unhappy child that might give away their hiding place. Sound carries for miles across the prairies.

6.) Bull nettle was dried and then boiled to make a great antiseptic which rivals anything that can be found in modern stores. Blevins' paternal grandmother had this remedy that she used often. Green bull nettle was brushed over the arms and legs of warriors to test their bravery and push them past the pain of battle. Dried, then boiled, and cooled, this makes a soothing antiseptic solution for wounds, cuts, and insect bites.

7.) Garlic's and onions were used for fever and cold ailments.

8.) Sage was burned in bundles to promote healing. The original form of aromatherapy, for certain. Sage's scent promotes a calming and restful sleep for the suffering.

9.) Five Fingers, a stout vine was cut and saved much like bull nettle. This was used for small pox when it broke out in this area after the Civil War. Close to Fort Buckner lived Kiowa chief Spotted Tail. He used this to help his tribe, refusing it for himself since the grasshoppers had come and eaten most of the vines in the area that year. He died since he did not use this cure.

Pieces of rawhide were soaked in a boiled solution of Five Fingers and then placed on the person affected with small pox to help with the infection and fever that followed. This is one cure that would be good to investigate for some possible future need.

10.) Puffball mushrooms (blanco kondos) were applied to knife and gunshot wounds to stop bleeding and allow healing. Spider webs were also used in this manner to help healing begin.

11.) Mesquite leaves were made into a tea for broken bones, and tooth pain, and for when women gave birth. The sap of the tree was used for chewing gum, and many had few cavities due to it.

12.) Tree bark from the Willow tree was used for aches and pains and it is the now the main active ingredient in aspirin.

13.) Poke Sallet (Pol-Kay—Salid, "Big Root-Poison.") This was picked in early spring to be used as a "tonic" to purge the body of poisons that cause cancer and illness. This is an extremely toxic plant that was boiled two times, (sometimes three times) and the water poured off and then served with a few potatoes and onions to hide the terrible taste. It worked very well, and after July it could not be picked at all when red lines appear on the stalk. The stalk was then cut back for next year for it is an annual plant. The red berries were used for war paint, and decoration. Modern winemakers used the red berries to make the wine red colored and more appealing to the eyes. The 3-foot long roots of this plant was used to make modern medicine.

During the American Civil War the Gulf Coast was blockaded by ships of the Union army. This caused many apothecaries to use native plants to compound into the much-needed drugs for surgery, and to end suffering, and malaise. Some of these cures might be helpful for a future time when we find ourselves short of a smallpox cure, to stop a terrible plague, or whatever the case might be.

14.) Honey was put on wounds to help seal them up and keep out dirt. It also has an antibiotic action that prevents infection.

15.) Spider webs were rolled up and pushed into wounds to stop bleeding and terrible wounds.

16.) Skunk oil was used to put on a person suffering from a cold, influenza, and pneumonia. It was so strong smelling that it opened up the lungs, and sinuses. It kept away anybody else for miles.

17.) Milkweed sap was used for pain such as arthritis pain, back, leg, and arm pain.

These things were taught to the author, Joe L. Blevins, by his paternal grandfather, Lesley Green Blevins. He was born in 1889. He was Choctaw in heritage, and he grew up in (Waurika) Indian Territory. *Indian Territory became the state of Oklahoma in 1907.*

This article "Medicine men and Good Medicine,"
© 2008 Joe L. Blevins.

NOTES:

ACKNOWLEDGEMENTS

1. THE LONESOME DOVE CHURCH.
   2380 LONESOME DOVE ROAD,
   SOUTHLAKE, TX 76092.

   Dr. COY QUESENBURY,
   and the LONESOME DOVE CHURCH.

2. The HEARD NATURAL SCIENCE MUSEUM,
   AND WILDLIFE SANCTUARY, INCORPORATED.
   ONE NATURE PLACE,
   McKINNEY, TX 75069

   MICHELE DUDAS, LEAD NATURALIST.

3. The UNIVERSITY OF OKLAHOMA,
   630 PARRINGTON OVAL, Room 452,
   NORMAN, OK 73019.

   Dr. DONALD DEWITT,
   CURATOR OF HISTORICAL ARCHIVES.

4. THE BLEVINS' SIGNATURE GALLERY—
   FEATURING THOMAS KINKADE.
   102 McKINNEY STREET,
   FARMERSVILLE, TX 75442.
   "From Placerville to Farmersville."

   ROY JOE AND HELEN BLEVINS, Joe's Dad and Mom.

5. THE BOY SCOUTS OF AMERICA,
   1325 WALNUT HILL LANE,
   IRVING, TX 75015

   Mr. MILTON H. WARD,
   PRESIDENT OF THE BOY SCOUTS OF AMERICA.

   The Boy Scouts of America are mentioned in the introduction of this book. Joe participated at the Heard Museum with Boy and Girl "Scout Days" as part of the museum's "Life in a Tee-Pee" out reach program. For three years we held programs to benefit North Texas Scouting for both boys and girls. One thing that Joe learned is that our young people have an interest in our history by the wonderful questions they would ask him. They want to learn from the past, so they can build a better future.
   These were the seeds for *After the Republic*. The BOY, and GIRL SCOUTS OF AMERICA continue to build children in their character, by giving them goals for the future. Opportunities for growth to make them capable adults. It helped Joe grow as a person. It continues to help young people with their great efforts. Our country needs more organizations such as this one.

6. THE SAM HOUSTON MUSEUM,
   Box 2057, SHSU, Huntsville, Texas 77341.

   DIRECTOR, DR. PATRICK B. NOLAN.
   A GREAT MUSEUM THAT HONORS GENERAL SAM HOUSTON.

7. PAMELA BLEVINS, Joe's wife.
   Thanks for putting up with him these past 18 years!

Made in the USA
Lexington, KY
15 February 2010